Václav Havel

T0345557

Titles in the series Critical Lives present the work of leading cultural figures of the modern period. Each book explores the life of the artist, writer, philosopher or architect in question and relates it to their major works.

In the same series

Václav Havel

Kieran Williams

REAKTION BOOKS

In memory of Professor Charles E. Townsend

Published by Reaktion Books Ltd
Unit 32, Waterside
44–48 Wharf Road
London N1 7UX, UK
www.reaktionbooks.co.uk

First published 2016
Copyright © Kieran Williams 2016

All rights reserved
No part of this publication may be reproduced, stored in a retrieval system,
or transmitted, in any form or by any means, electronic, mechanical,
photocopying, recording or otherwise, without the prior permission
of the publishers

Printed and bound in Great Britain by Bell & Bain, Glasgow

A catalogue record for this book is available from the British Library

ISBN 978 1 78023 665 0

PERMISSIONS
'Kontruktivní satira' © Václav Havel – heir c/o DILIA, 2016
'Vazby' © Václav Havel – heir c/o DILIA, 2016
Graph 1 from Commentary on *Eduard* © Václav Havel – heir c/o DILIA, 2016

Contents

Note on the Text

Citations from Havel's works are given in the body of the text by reference to the volumes of his collected works in Czech (*Spisy*), all published in Prague by Torst in 1999, except for volume 8, which appeared in 2007. All translations from these texts are my own, and I thank Dagmar Havlová-Veškrnová and Alena Jakoubková at DILIA for permission to quote from Havel's work.

S1 *Spisy 1: Básně. Antikódy* [Poems; Anti-codes]
S2 *Spisy 2: Hry* [Plays]
S3 *Spisy 3: Eseje a jiné texty z let 1953–1969* [Essays and other texts from 1953–1969]
S4 *Spisy 4: Eseje a jiné texty z let 1970–1989. Dálkový výslech* [Essays and other texts from 1970–1989. Questioning from Afar]
S5 *Spisy 5: Dopisy Olze* [Letters to Olga]
S6 *Spisy 6: Projevy z let 1990–1992. Letní přemítání* [Speeches from 1990–1992. Summer Meditations]
S7 *Spisy 7: Projevy a jiné texty z let 1992–1999* [Speeches and other texts from 1992–1999]
S8 *Spisy 8: Projevy a jiné texty 1999–2006. Prosím stručně. Odcházení* [Speeches and other texts 1999–2006. Please Be Brief. Leaving]

Introduction

Biography was a problem for Václav Havel. In childhood, his wealthy family background embarrassed him before poorer classmates; in adolescence, after the Communist Party seized power in Czechoslovakia, it blocked him from the education and profession he would have pursued. In his twenties, as a famous playwright, he started to tell the story of his life to satisfy a curious public, but he did so reluctantly, fearing that once a writer begins to regard himself as worthy of special attention he loses sight of the world in its true proportions. In middle age, as a blacklisted dissident, leader of the revolution that ousted the Communist Party in 1989 and president of his country, he had to retell that life story often and at length, because it was the source of his authority, and do so defensively, because enemies and critics were coming up with less flattering versions. In his maturity, his legendary past became an impediment to communication, for it overshadowed the present-day warning of planetary disaster he wanted audiences at home and abroad to hear.

Biography is also prone to a still bigger problem that vexed Havel: that something easily, viscerally felt might not lend itself to expression in words. A life has a structure, purpose and rhythm, but he compared his attempts to say what they might be to a scene in Eugène Ionesco's absurdist play *The Chairs*: an old man and woman hire an orator to announce their great discovery, whereupon he produces only the guttural moans of a deaf mute. Havel, however, did not see this difficulty as grounds for resignation. The meaning of a person's experience may be ultimately ineffable, but miraculously, language is able to at least circle around and grasp something of it in abbreviated, exaggerated terms.

How a biographer chooses to abbreviate and accentuate (if not exaggerate) is all the more daunting when the subject is Havel himself, who lived 75 eventful years and wrote in diverse genres: poetry, plays, essays, prison letters, speeches and memoirs.[1] This book will present Havel as a poet who stopped writing poetry at an early age but never lost the poet's disposition as someone who dissents and disturbs. To write poetry is to place a stumbling block before readers, to force them to fight with language and step out of everyday discourse and routine.[2] Havel continued that poetic subversion in his essays, which used metaphors, neologisms and demanding syntax to defamiliarize the obvious, while his plays aimed to make spectators laugh quietly throughout but leave the theatre existentially shaken. The very titles of his plays, often just one word, pulse unnervingly with nuances that even the best translator would struggle to render.

Poetry is all the more subversive in periods of domination by speakers of another language and of undemocratic government, when it can become a substitute for political action. This was the case for much of modern Czech history, such that 'every Czech poetic work, simply by being written in Czech, had a tendency, a tendency to covert revolt.'[3] A poet irritates because of a compulsion to tell the truth, which to Havel was not reducible to imparting correct information – especially not in the guise of quantitative, empirical science practised by white-coated experts. Following Josef Šafařík, the philosopher who most influenced Havel in his poetic phase and beyond, he accepted as truth any statement of belief for which a person is willing to vouch and stake a personal guarantee.[4] In extreme circumstances, that avouching may take the form of accepting death, as Socrates and Jesus did,

Havel at home in a Czech meadow, 1975.

or it could mean risking one's freedom or reputation, as Havel
said Thomas Jefferson and the first Czechoslovak president,
Tomáš Masaryk, did at times in their careers. So important was
this conception of truth to Havel that when he was inaugurated
as president of the Czech Republic in 1993, he topped his list
of values with 'faith in a truth for which it is necessary to vouch
personally' (s7, 40).

Havel freely admitted to being a man of contradictions; at times
he described himself as an artist who would cause trouble no matter
where he lived, at others as an idealist who yearned for a world
inhabited by a 'whole, harmonious humanity, unfragmented,
unalienated from itself and uncommercialized' (s3, 264).[5] He was
no utopian but he was a poet in search of an authentic sense of
home (*domov*).[6] Using terms acquired from Jan Patočka, another
Czech philosopher he read as a teenager, Havel built his meaning
of home out of three horizons: the immediate surroundings into
which a person is thrown; the 'concrete existential horizon' beyond
it (family, friends, community), which acts as life's hidden perimeter,

inspiration for civic courage and font of solidarity; and the 'absolute horizon' that is the origin of a person's values and purpose. Home is a spiritual, emotional experience of placement in the natural world, surpassing reason with its warmth and 'fragrance of roots' (s6, 55). Although Havel was never a writer of pastoral poetry or narrative fiction, his essays, speeches and prison letters are punctuated by vivid glimpses of dwelling on an organic, humane scale, in 'avouched rootedness in the *genius loci*' (s4, 418), but also of belching smokestacks, industrial farming and anonymous housing estates devoid of history or mystery. He used his native city, Prague, as a dual symbol of all that is wrong with modern life and of the spirit of resistance to those ills. Such images were residues of the pantheism of his poetic phase, and he continued to think of nature as a mysterious order that sends signals to anyone attuned to receive them. This order is so finely interconnected that the slightest shift can have far-reaching, even revolutionary, consequences, especially if it originates in a hotspot (*ohnisko*) of conspiratorially creative activity, such as an experimental theatre or underground journal. These cosmic assumptions sustained Havel through the 1970s and '80s, when Czechoslovakia's tiny dissident community seemed to be toiling in vain against one of the most rigid regimes in the Soviet bloc.

In a world properly organized as home, men and women could be true to themselves, would not have to dissemble or worry that a friend was actually an informer, impostor or usurper. In short, home would be a world of firm identities rooted in responsibility, another form of personal guarantee. To be responsible in one's identity is to be the same person in public as in private and across time, vouching today for one's yesterday (s5, 548). Havel's plays depict a grotesque land without home, responsible identities or personal avouching, a world of deception and self-deception, often centred on a male anti-hero who, while not a self-portrait, is drawn from Havel's experience.[7] He wanted his plays to be received neither as satires of life in his country under Communist rule, nor as pessimistic pronouncements of an inescapable human condition; they appeal to us to rely on our own ability to avouch truths and not expect Havel, or anyone else, to provide easy answers or solve all problems.[8]

As president, Havel reconceptualized home as a set of concentric rings encircling the individual, radiating outward from family, friends, residence and workplace to embrace the broader culture and language in which we feel most at ease, all the way to a continental, civilizational or planetary affinity. It could comfortably accommodate national belonging, and Czechness was at the heart of Havel's sense of home.[9] He never actually led an ordinary Czech's life – his was either more comfortable than what was typical, owing to his parents' wealth, his success as a playwright and the trappings of presidential office, or more arduous, owing to decades of political discrimination and persecution.[10] He was a passionate traveller and always open to foreign ideas and examples, but he was not allowed to go abroad for fifty of his 75 years. A self-described 'linguistic anti-talent', he was continually learning English and German but mastered neither, and thus never became a truly cosmopolitan artist in the manner of Vladimir Nabokov, Joseph Conrad or Milan Kundera.

Kundera, like Havel, was Czech, and like Havel started as a poet, but was born seven years earlier, in 1929. Although that difference might seem trivial, Czech literary generations could be separated by only ten or fifteen years,[11] and my account will emphasize the fact that Havel's early poetic rivalry with writers of Kundera's age continued to influence his work for decades, long after many of them had switched to writing plays or prose. (By contrast, Havel got along very well with the preceding biological generation, born between 1900 and 1915.) Havel's rivals were just older enough to have had very different formative experiences. They came of age as the Communists took power in 1948 and many, including Kundera, had been ardent Stalinists. After Stalin's death in 1953, they were forced to start again, reactively and self-critically.[12] They were no longer toadies, and in some instances so overcompensated for their youthful fanaticism that they ran into trouble with the censors. They failed to impress Havel, however, because (with exceptions, such as Kundera) they traded socialist realism for a non-threatening 'aesthetic of banality', 'a genial petty-bourgeois morality; the sentimental philosophy of neighbourly humanity; the joviality of the kitchen' (s4, 86–7), like the nineteenth-century Biedermeier style against which Czech poets had once rebelled.[13]

As the following chapters will show, Havel's rivalry fixed at times on different members of this slightly older set of writers, but by the 1970s it was primarily on Jaroslav Dietl (born, like Kundera, in 1929). Dietl wrote plays but was more at home with television (the medium Havel hated most) and strove to match the mass appeal of cinema (the medium Havel wanted most to break into) by dispensing with theatre's psychological 'half-tones and quarter-tones', subtexts and pregnant silences.[14] A pioneer of the multi-episode serial, Dietl took the family sagas of Balzac, Dumas, Galsworthy and Thomas Mann and set them in the farmhouses, offices and hospital wards of the socialist present.[15] He was tremendously successful because he did not whitewash life under the Communist Party, but neither did he threaten it, nor did he push viewers to search their souls. Unlike the plays Havel wanted to write, which would take the author and audience on a journey into the unknown, a Dietl work operated in and reinforced the world of familiar appearances. Sitting in prison in the early 1980s while the prolific Dietl had a popular new show on television almost every month, Havel tried to comfort himself with the thought that an edgy play seen in a fringe, *ohnisko* theatre by a few people might have a bigger impact on the mysterious workings of the universe.

Some of Havel's antipathy could be put down to jealousy and resentment: the older writers always had privileged access to print, stage and screen, and even though Havel would become internationally acclaimed, it was Dietl who had the greater effect on how Czechs told stories to and about themselves. And like many artistic rivalries, that between Havel and writers born in the 1920s stemmed from having a certain amount in common: Havel's harmonious home could, with a dollop of schmaltz, become the cosy nest of a Dietl soap opera. What ultimately kept the two apart was the older writers' *polovičatost*, as Havel called it: a half-heartedness or 'halfway-ness' that restrained them from pushing their art into truly, offensively poetic forms. The 'stark picture of halfway-ness'[16] that one reviewer found in Havel's third major play, about an irresponsible intellectual born in 1928, represents the trepidation that Havel would oppose whenever he encountered it in art, politics or himself.

1

'Every Soul is a Certain Architecture' (1936–52)

> Every soul is a certain architecture,
> and while none knows where it will be a moment from now,
> somewhere in its cellar it has the plans stashed away
> by which it grows.
>
> Václav Havel, 'Friendship' (s1, 170)

Havel chose well when, at age twenty, he used the metaphors of architecture and blueprints to describe the process by which a personality, or at least his own, unfolds. He was born on 5 October 1936 into a family that looked at the world in terms of design, building and landscape. Although he at times rebelled against the 'spirit of the family'[1] that his younger brother Ivan (born in 1938) would more faithfully embody, it left its mark on him in three ways.

The first was that the Havels prized organic, harmonious integration into an environment that they helped to create by mixing national and international values, styles and ideas. The family had a history of enterprise in Prague, primarily as millers and merchants, and a custom of naming the firstborn son after the Czech patron saint Václav (Wenceslas). Havel's grandfather Vácslav (1861–1921) started a building firm in 1887, specializing in public works such as drainage and paving. His marriage in 1891 gave him access to capital that enabled him to deal in rural tracts, which in turn enabled him to build apartment blocks on lots in central Prague made available by the demolition of the Jewish

Josefov district and the development of the banks of the river Vltava.[2] Vácslav's business success was due not only to acumen but to connections, especially with the Czech-speaking political parties that were changing the look of the city and with the talented architects and designers he was able to recruit.

In their appearance, Vácslav Havel's buildings expressed the family's national pride and its openness to foreign inspiration. His neo-Renaissance and neo-Baroque edifices of the 1890s, adorned with busts of national heroes, reflected the appetite of the confident Czech middle class for reminders of Prague's earlier glory. After 1900, the impact of the Vienna Secession and Art Nouveau began to be felt, with a turn to plainer facades, wrought-iron balconies and bas-reliefs connoting springtime and rebirth.[3] Old and new melded in the block Vácslav commissioned in 1905 for his own family's use, number 78 on an embankment named after the nation-building historian František Palacký. Its continuous vertical bay windows and string courses were reminiscent of the local past, while the ornamentation – female faces surrounded by twisting floral patterns, insect patterns in the balcony metalwork – lent a natural, transnational touch. One expert sums it up as a textbook central European hybrid, a 'historicist building in modernist dress'.[4]

Vácslav Havel picked up ideas while taking his family on frequent visits abroad – their home on the embankment was fittingly topped with a large globe – which also fuelled his patriotic wish to lift Prague to the level of a major metropolis.[5] To that end he sold off almost all of his assets to raise capital for the Lucerna (Lantern), an innovative three-storey complex comprising a cinema, bar, restaurant, shopping arcades, offices, apartments and a concert hall on Vodičkova Street, off Wenceslas Square. Completed in 1920, it was envisioned by Vácslav as the principal family concern, which the next generation of Havels could manage.

His sons, however, had somewhat different plans. Havel's father, Václav Maria (V. M.), born in 1897, wanted both to see Lucerna

The Havel family's apartments at Palacký (now Rašín) Embankment 78.

flourish and to make his own mark on Prague. As the capital of the new Czechoslovak republic established in 1918, the city urgently needed more housing, so its authorities relaxed codes and taxes to encourage construction; the result, to V. M.'s horror, was 'unorganic' sprawl.[6] For a solution he looked not to Europe but to the United States. While on a grand tour there in 1923–4, V. M. had been struck by Joseph Leonard's Ingleside Terraces in San Francisco, an urban 'residence park' of spacious Arts and Crafts bungalows based on the nineteenth-century British 'villa park'.[7] Back in Prague, he imagined an enclave of family homes on 54 hectares of a bluff overlooking the left bank of the Vltava, an area he named Barrandov in honour of a French engineer who had explored its trilobite fossils. V. M. wanted houses that would evoke the haciendas of California while avoiding the homogeneity he disliked in American society, so he encouraged prospective buyers to commission unique blueprints, subject to approval by the architect Max Urban. Seven were designed in the 1930s by Vladimír Grégr, who softened the austere horizontal lines of his functionalist architecture with materials and flourishes that mirrored the natural surroundings and reflected his own travels in the American West. While to purists the compromises smacked of commercial pandering, Barrandov offered a comforting 'domesticity, cheerfulness and safety' at a time of crisis and impending war.[8] This vision of harmonious, integrated dwelling lodged in the family consciousness, arising again six decades later when Havel was asked what he would build if he were an architect rather than president:

> I would try to come up with some not-too-expensive family homes, which could make up a sort of suburban village. I would look for something that could replace those ugly housing estates [from the Communist era]. No villas for big rich people, just pleasant housing for one or two families surrounded by greenery.[9]

The Barrandov villa designed by Vladimír Grégr for Havel's uncle, Miloš.

V. M. envisioned Barrandov as a self-contained community within easy reach of the city centre 7 kilometres away. To add to its appeal, he commissioned Urban to design a restaurant on the model of Cliff House, perched above the Pacific Ocean in San Francisco. Swamped by 50,000 visitors when it opened in 1929 to coincide with the millennium of St Václav's death, Barrandov Terraces fast became one of the city's most popular spots, routinely serving 3,000 people on summer Sundays. Political, artistic and business elites frequented its French restaurant and late-night Trilobite Bar, with the president Tomáš Masaryk occasionally lunching there.

While the Havel men had a long association with Prague, the country roots of their spouses extended the family's sense of home. In 1908, to help his wife recuperate from a heart attack, Vácslav built Havlov, a lodge in a remote wooded area of the Moravian highlands near her birthplace. Featuring ten bedrooms, a tennis court and swimming pool, it was a place of recreation, relaxation and, during the Second World War, refuge: V. M.'s wife, Božena, and their young sons stayed there until 1947, because the Prague apartment had been badly damaged in an American bomber raid. Havel occupied the seventh bedroom, which one poetic visitor recalled as smelling of dahlias, green apples and high summer.[10]

Havel's mother made her own large contribution to the pursuit of a pleasing, harmonious environment. Born in 1913, Božena had spent much of her youth in Vienna, where her father was the Czechoslovak ambassador; on returning to Prague in 1932 she studied painting and art history, and later designed some of the decor of restaurants at the Lucerna and Barrandov Terraces. In the absence of visually stimulating lesson books for her children during and after the Second World War, she created her own, paying special attention to astronomy because, as Ivan remembered, 'at Havlov there was clean air and few lights, at night we looked up into a sky crammed with stars.'[11] Božena is remembered as being vibrant and sunny, but as the Anglophile

V. M. and Božena Havel, 1935.

daughter of a diplomat she was also very concerned with etiquette and easily unsettled by any quarrel or faux pas – a trait Havel at times admitted to sharing (s5, 145, 147, 316, 365).[12] The lovingly protective home she created could easily become a 'somewhat stifling environment' in which difficult subjects were avoided and secrets kept (such as the fact that V. M. had had a wife before her).[13] Later, Božena would play the hospitable hostess to the adolescent Havel's bohemian friends but not conceal her fear that her older son was going down the wrong path, unlike her younger, who in the 1960s would be trained in the new field of computer science and study at an American university. The twenty-year-old Havel was probably drawing on real conversations when the narrator of his poem 'Loafing About' (1956) reports:

> Mother tells me: When you were a child,
> you were completely different. Forthright, kind,

Hugo Vavrečka with Ivan and Václav Havel, 1941.

Ivan, Božena and Václav Havel, 1943.

not like today. It's a shame that you cannot be
still a child . . .
(s1, 144)

One last example of the family's attraction to harmony was
the decision of Božena's father, Hugo Vavrečka, to swap his
diplomatic career for a top job at the headquarters of the Baťa
shoeworks in Zlín, a company town modelled on American
ideas of welfare capitalism.[14] Baťa's heavily paternalistic culture
of standardization finds reflection in one of Havel's earliest
surviving texts, a fantasy probably written in 1946 but imagining
his life on 4 January 2000: after achieving international acclaim
as a professor and explorer of the Arctic, he would use his
wealth to finance his 'goodness factory' (*Dobrovka*), a complex
of ten great and 100 smaller halls, with 88,000 workers,
1,000 machinists, 100 engineers, fifteen directors and two
executives, with branches in all towns that had a Baťa store.[15]

The second formative element of the Havel household was its commitment to the moral improvement and better governance of society. One approach involved forms of spirituality outside the Catholic Church, which had dominated Bohemian culture since the Counter-Reformation. Grandfather Vácslav, on his own account, had never been religious but sensed an underlying purpose and guiding intelligence in the world. Like many of his class at the end of the nineteenth century, he felt drawn to occult inquiry. Under the influence of Anna Pammrová, his nearest neighbour at Havlov and a devotee of Mazdaznan (a California movement combining vegetarianism, yogic breathing and Zoroastrianism), Vácslav delved into theosophy and hosted séances during the First World War.[16] His account of these interests, published under a pseudonym, presented his endeavours as a kind of scientific research through which he had uncovered a progression of souls reincarnating towards higher planes, each an atom in a grand harmonious spirit (Vácslav chose 'Atom' as his nom de plume). It was a universe animated not by a traditional God but by the twin forces of 'love' and 'forbearance' – two words he had engraved into a crystal paperweight on his desk.[17] Vácslav's explorations were preserved in the family's memory and are echoed in his grandson Václav's early pantheism, his later spirituality and his view of the artist as a medium through whom Truth expresses itself.

V. M. identified more decisively as a Christian, but left the Catholic fold as a youth, seeing the Church as too compromised by association with Habsburg rule. The seminal moment for him occurred in March 1920, when, at the age of 22, he heard President Masaryk appeal for the formation of a 'public mafia' to reshape culture and morals, in part through non-established, sincerely professed religion.[18] (Decades later, as president, Havel likewise invited fellow writers to act as a 'conspiratorial mafia' to improve political life [s, 318].) The notion of a moral brigade akin to the *Maffie* (the wartime network that had agitated for

Czech sovereignty) so electrified V. M. that he threw himself into the organization of an ecumenical student 'renewal movement'. He promoted a rugged, abstemious improvement of the self that led by example, starting with a hall of residence constructed and financed by students tired of waiting for places in university hostels. There soon followed affiliation with the World Student Christian Federation and the creation of a Czechoslovak YMCA in 1921, with American-style summer camps. In 1925, on the initiative of President Masaryk's son Jan (who was American on his mother's side), came the formation of a Prague Rotary Club, in which V. M. represented the real-estate sector (and chaired its meetings in 1937).

Less public but involving many of the same people was Freemasonry, into which V. M. was initiated in 1923. Four years later, a group involving V. M. set up its own lodge, named in honour of Bernard Bolzano, a Leibnizian philosopher of harmonious natural balance whose ethical maxim was 'Always choose from among the actions possible to you those which, when all the consequences are weighed, will best promote the good of the whole, no matter in which parts.'[19] The Bolzano lodge, of which V. M. was the leader by the mid-1930s, enjoyed a reputation for a progressive, Anglo-American realism that took seriously the Masonic belief in unchanging, universal ethical rules, embedded in humanity by an unnameable creative force.[20]

Politics was seen as another avenue to the improvement of public morals, and Vácslav and V. M. came easily into contact with legislators and party leaders through their entrepreneurial and cultural activities. Vácslav had a long-standing affiliation with the tendency that became the National Democratic Party in 1919 through the merging of five parties catering to the urban, patriotic middle class. V. M. was less partisan; he was a National Democrat until 1935 but at home only in the most centrist faction, and was more positively inclined to President Masaryk, with whom the party had tense relations.[21]

By the early 1930s, the peoples of Czechoslovakia were broadly dissatisfied with their politics. Governments fell regularly but were reconstituted from a cartel of dominant parties, creating the semblance of a conflict-management mechanism. Below the surface, however, the republic was failing to achieve the social integration necessary to its survival: Czechs dominated the parties and bureaucracy, to the growing displeasure of the country's two million Slovaks and the even more numerous German minority.[22] The entrenched parties divided the spoils, and constitutional liberties were eroded by emergency legislation after the assassination of finance minister Alois Rašín, a National Democrat, Mason and friend of Václav Havel, in 1923. The only counterweight to the party cartel was the president's office in Prague Castle, which used its ample funds to operate intelligence networks and buy the services of journalists.[23] This system was in plain view of V. M., who admittedly benefited from it; the global Depression struck just after the Barrandov Terraces opened and V. M. was able to win relief from payment of taxes and debts through friends he had in key places (the National Democrats had a grip on the Ministry for Industry, Business and Trade).[24] However, he feared for democracy's viability at a time when fascism was gaining followers in neighbouring countries and a Stalinized Communist Party was legally very active in Czechoslovakia, winning between 10 and 13 per cent of the vote. What was lacking was a loyal opposition, working over time towards democracy of a different quality.

V. M. was no theorist, but his preference for functionalist architects such as Max Urban and Vladimír Grégr revealed much about his intuitive sense of the 'good society'. Urban had caused a small sensation in 1919 with a 75-page plan, exhibited at the Lucerna, for an Ideal Greater Prague. It proposed that much of the historic centre be razed and the city segmented into sections with specific purposes – government, business, recreation, edification and a dock for airships on Petřín Hill. Critics such as the writer Karel Čapek were horrified by the proposal's radicalism and its relegation of housing to the city's margins, which would force residents into long commutes.[25] Having built Barrandov in the spirit of Urban's scheme, V. M. sought a comparable functional reorganization of society that would be less dependent on dedicated locations. In 1932 he found what he was looking for in the writings of Josef Ludvík Fischer.

Fischer was a polymath; like President Masaryk he was equally at ease with philosophy, sociology and psychology as well as all major European languages. Prolific and prolix, Fischer progressed from an early sympathy for Bergsonian vitalism, American pragmatism and Marxism to arrive at his own philosophy of a 'composite order' that would be centred on individuals but would not neglect their social integration.[26] He took as his starting point the fact that interwar democracy and capitalism were based not on laissez-faire competition but on collusion and corporatism. Along with these came a culture of quantification, standardization and division of labour rooted in a view of the cosmos that was mechanistic, 'dehumanizing, automatizing and asocial'. Instead, Fischer wanted a qualitative, 'humanized world' organized into highly decentralized units – in essence modern-day guilds, responsible for tasks, firms and services and subject to locally accountable bodies.[27]

To avoid charges of utopianism or affinity for Soviet 'state capitalism', Fischer sketched his composite state with only a minimum of practical detail but in full 'faith' that it would result in workers' 'vibrant and joyous awareness of co-responsibility for their "own" social "home" and enable each person to create as many such "homes" for himself as possible'.[28] Always thinking globally as well as locally, Fischer offered his composite state as a way by which the continent, perhaps organized as the 'United European States', could regain the lead it was losing to America and Asia.[29]

V. M. combined Fischer's ideas and the architecture of Urban and Grégr in a speech to the Bolzano Masonic lodge in March 1933. Just as functionalism pared away ornamentation and

Josef Ludvík Fischer.

configured buildings around the needs of their occupants, so
V. M. wanted the political system to strip away bureaucratic
dead weight and facilitate initiative. Just as functionalism used
horizontal lines to embed a building on terra firma, so the polity
had to be a democracy of quality and equality. The era of atomized

liberalism was passing, and a new one of socially conscious, rooted individuals had to follow. The new economy would replicate on the national scale what the Baťa shoeworks were doing to meet workers' essential needs, remove grounds for class conflict and enable each person to do his part responsibly. (Responsibility had always been a keyword in V. M.'s discourse.) Small nations would be strong and secure in their identities, while cooperating through no less strong and secure international organizations.[30]

The sentiments V. M. expressed to his fellow Masons were publicized in the manifesto of a circle of around forty associates (including Fischer, who helped draft it) that he was convening at the Terraces and Havlov.[31] The 'Barrandov Group', however, was short-lived, and its impact negligible. President Masaryk resigned in 1935, two years before his death, and his long-time ally and fellow sociologist Edvard Beneš succeeded him. The unresolved grievances of the republic's nationalities were exploited and exacerbated by Adolf Hitler to provoke a showdown in September 1938 when he demanded that Czechoslovakia cede its more heavily German-speaking borderlands to the Third Reich. A conference in Munich involving British, French and Italian leaders found in Hitler's favour. President Beneš, who was not invited, had mobilized his country's defences, backed by a large armaments industry. But with no allies and every likelihood of eventual defeat following wanton destruction, Beneš yielded the borderlands. Among the government ministers who had to explain this decision to the public was Havel's maternal grandfather Hugo, who had just been appointed with a special portfolio to refute German propaganda because of his success in organizing a Czechoslovak exhibition at the upcoming New York World's Fair. Once it was clear that the great powers had abandoned them, Hugo told the country,

> it was not lack of courage which has brought us to this
> decision, which is grieving us all inwardly . . . We shall

Miloš and V. M. Havel, 1903.

now be quite alone, we shall be strong, and it will depend
on you, whether out of the darkness which enshrouds us
for a time the rays of a new dawn will shine upon us.[32]

While most of the political elite accepted the Munich Agreement,
National Democrats and intellectuals such as Fischer wanted
to call Hitler's bluff, to see whether or not he would attack if
Czechoslovakia resisted.[33] Something of their attitude rubbed
off on Havel. Although an advocate of peace whenever possible,
as an adult he was no pacifist, would oppose any deal that smacked
of 'appeasement' (he often used the English word) and liked to point
out that by responding to Beneš's aborted mobilization the people of
Czechoslovakia had shown a willingness to fight for democracy and
territory (s7, 125). He often derided Beneš's brand of 'realism', which
failed again in February 1948 when the Communists were intent
on seizing power – a situation Havel re-enacted in the opening
scene of his second major play, *The Memorandum* (1965), as a

Ivan and Václav Havel, early 1940s.

confrontation between a Beneš-like office director, Gross, and his
upstart deputy, Baláš.[34] As president in the 1990s, Havel softened his
view somewhat to one of pity for a physically frail man twice forced
to choose between the cost in human life of defiance and the moral
harm of capitulation. But Havel still implied that, put in Beneš's
position, he would have acted differently (s7, 247–52, 467–9).

   The third formative element in the family story consists
of a cautionary tale involving V. M.'s younger brother, Miloš,
during and after the war that Munich failed to prevent. Miloš
Havel had, like V. M., been groomed to manage their father's
Lucerna company, but Miloš was drawn strongly to its association
with the new film industry. A cinema had been one of the first
sections of the Lucerna to open to the public (in 1909) and one
of its most lucrative. Vácslav had also acquired a film company
in 1912, which he entrusted to the very young Miloš six years
later. After the war, Miloš capitalized on the mania for all things
American by becoming a distributor of Hollywood movies,

and in 1931 followed his brother to Barrandov, for which Urban designed the then largest film studios in central Europe.[35]

The relative success of Miloš's film enterprise (like his brother, he needed occasional bail-outs and reprieves) became problematic after the German occupation of the Czech-speaking lands in March 1939, as the Nazis wanted to put the state-of-the-art Barrandov to their propaganda purposes. What followed was a dance of intrigue and bargaining that Miloš's biographer needed more than a hundred pages to do justice to; the gist was that rather than keep his hands clean by turning over the studios entirely to the Nazis and walking away, Miloš negotiated a residual stake that allowed him to produce more than fifty films in Czech during the war, some of them even promoting Czech patriotic themes. Given the Nazis' ultimate intention of eliminating Czech identity through assimilation and expulsion, Miloš felt – as a National Democrat who had briefly flirted with an anti-German strand of Czech fascism in the mid-1920s – a responsibility to the nation and to his employees to stay involved and preserve a facet of Czech culture. He saved dozens of scriptwriters, directors and other staff from being pressed into hard labour, but threw all-night parties at the Lucerna to keep his German contacts happy; some were even invited to the lodge at Havlov.[36]

In the wave of retribution that engulfed Czechoslovakia after the war, Miloš repeatedly had to justify his apparent collaboration. With many witnesses testifying in his defence, Miloš was acquitted of the charges, but his career in the now nationalized film industry was over. Denied permission to accept invitations to work in Egypt or Israel, Miloš tried to escape to Austria in 1949; he made it over the border but fell into the hands of Soviet officers, who sent him back, and he was imprisoned for two years. He tried again to escape in 1952 and this time succeeded. Miloš settled into exile in West Germany, but failed to thrive; like his father and brother, he had depended on friends and political connections to prosper in

Prague – circumstances he could not replicate in a foreign setting. After Miloš's death in February 1968, his brother and his nephew Václav were allowed to travel to Munich to collect his ashes; when they opened his safe, they found only a solitary cufflink.[37]

The immediate lesson of Miloš's fate, of which Havel would have been aware from an early age, was that emigration was not an easy option, no matter how bad conditions at home had become. Equally important, it was folly to think that good people can always outsmart bad and stay above reproach if their intention is noble, although Havel did not fully grasp this lesson until he had experienced captivity himself in the 1970s. And it was not just that Miloš had made the mistake of being seen to enjoy himself in the wrong company while the rest of the country suffered. Both V. M and

The Barrandov Terraces under German occupation, 1942.

Havel's grandfather Hugo had tried to be more careful in their business during the war, neither socializing too readily with German officials nor joining the resistance as the architect Grégr had done (for which he paid with his life in 1943). After the war, however, they too had to fight to clear their names, and V. M. lost Lucerna and Barrandov Terraces to state control (which admittedly relieved him of considerable debt: during the war, the Terraces had suffered damage both to its facilities and reputation, owing to its popularity with drunken German soldiers and their Czech girlfriends). Hugo, who had returned to his high position at Bat'a, was less able to avoid embarrassing contact: family albums contain photos of him escorting Jozef Tiso, the leader of the Slovak far-right puppet state, on a factory tour. Hugo was sentenced in 1948 to three years in prison; in poor health, he was allowed to live out his remaining days on the fourth floor of number 78.[38]

After a childhood at Havlov relatively sheltered from the war, Havel was initially spared the full extent of his family's distress. His parents had planned to send him abroad for his secondary education, in the hope he might ultimately study at a prestigious university such as Harvard, so to prepare he attended a small English-style boarding school in Poděbrady, 50 kilometres east of Prague. The school was very unusual for Czechoslovakia; it had been set up as a facility for boys whose parents had been executed by the Germans or were abroad in diplomatic service of the restored republic. Its founders persuaded the ministry of education to fund the school and name it after the fifteenth-century warrior-king Jiří (George) of Kunštát and Poděbrady, in whose castle it would be housed. Havel arrived there in autumn 1947, and after years of indulgence by family and nannies quickly had to adapt to the school's spartan regimen. In its emphasis on teamwork and discipline, King George's tried to preserve the ethos of the interwar Scouting movement while taking into account the Communists' post-war dominance. Havel dutifully wore the blue shirt of the new Soviet-style Czechoslovak Youth Union, but after Miloš's attempted defection and his father's detention for three months in 1949, he was told to leave the school in his third year.[39]

Now, fourteen years old and living fully in Prague for the first time since infancy, Havel could no longer be shielded from his family's troubles. The cost of repairing the damaged apartments had forced V. M. to shoulder new loans and abandon his dream of building the villa at Barrandov that Grégr had designed for him while awaiting execution. Božena had to sell family silver, let go the cook, gardener and driver, and eventually take work as a guide in the Old Town's Gothic city hall. Having already been ordered to relinquish floors of the home on the embankment, the Havels were in danger of being evicted entirely in the course of Operation B, a push by the Communist authorities in 1952 to drive thousands of wealthy families out of the major cities. The Havels would have had to relocate to Albrechtice, a borderland village 120 kilometres northeast of Prague that had been emptied by the expulsion of Czechoslovakia's Germans after the war, but V. M. was able to win permission to live at Havlov instead. On arriving at the lodge in October, the family found that the police had sealed it off after Miloš's successful escape, in the belief that it belonged to him. This error allowed the Havels to return to number 78 on the embankment, which was now named after Karl Marx's partner Friedrich Engels; owing to the recent deaths of Božena's parents, the whole family could squeeze into the flat on the fourth floor.[40]

The education that Havel received under these circumstances was accordingly irregular. While a child at Havlov, Havel had flourished in the arts and sciences alike; his mother and grandfather Hugo guided him towards the latter, yet their own handiwork interested him in the former. Božena's vivid, didactic paintings focused on recent advances in technology and understanding of the universe but acknowledged that 'we can still only guess at the meaning of our lives.'[41] Hugo, a trained electrical engineer, had published a

Sherlock Holmes novel and worked as a correspondent and editor at the newspaper *Lidové noviny* (The People's News). Havel later claimed that at the age of nine he could easily imagine himself becoming 'either a scientist, or a politician, or a journalist'.[42] As a teenager he rejected a friend's narrow preference for politics and economics to the exclusion of the natural sciences, underscoring 'the importance of an all-sided perspective, the importance of striving for knowledge *from all* fields and sciences'.[43] And in middle age, he thanked an émigré scientist for articles on nuclear energy because

> I terribly enjoy reading specialized articles and it does not bother me at all that I don't understand half the things in them; it is even precisely because it is beyond the horizon of my under-standing that it attracts me in some strange way, as a person who is always excited by everything with a whiff of mystery.[44]

But under Communist rule in the early 1950s, class origins would determine who could enter which fields, and the arts were the most sensitive. Havel was informed after leaving the local primary school in 1951 that he could not follow the track that would lead to a university degree in a subject such as philosophy, history or literature, or a profession such as journalism. He was directed to take up a trade, and was steered towards carpentry. He was, however, prone to dizzy spells, and was instead allowed to train as a technician at the Chemical-Technological University's Institute for Organic Chemistry – its director had been a colleague of Božena's brother (who, like Miloš, had emigrated).[45] Havel summarized his duties there in a poem in 1955:

> My work is not at all hard or responsible,
> But it is one-third of my life,
> Which every day I throw overboard.[46]

Havel's secondary schooling was reduced to classes on weekday evenings at an institute for working-class youths in full-time jobs, supplemented by his voracious reading and tutorials with the philosopher his father had recruited into the Barrandov Group twenty years earlier, Josef Ludvík Fischer. In the intervening time, Fischer had spent the war abroad, mostly in Holland, and on returning he had been made rector of a new university in Olomouc. Like Miloš Havel with the Nazis, Fischer thought he could outwit the Communists, formally joining their ranks in order to be left alone to run the university on his terms as a bastion of free inquiry. The strategy failed: he was demoted in 1949 and had one of the nervous breakdowns to which he was prone.[47] Barred from teaching between 1952 and 1957, he may have found some relief in coming to Prague and instructing the young Havel 'rather intensively' at the family flat or the nearby Café Slavia (s4, 717; s6, 161–2). In addition to assigning his own works, which Havel had read by early 1954,[48] Fischer pushed the boy to read Wilhelm Windelband, whose *History of Philosophy* (1893) had also been a primer for Samuel Beckett, a playwright Havel would soon come to admire.[49] Windelband had headed the faction of German neo-Kantians primarily concerned with preserving a distinction between the natural sciences and philosophy as a 'science of values (logical, aesthetic and ethical)', so that the latter not be reduced to a branch of the former.[50]

The desire to take science off the pedestal on which it had been placed by modernity (and the Communists in particular) was fuelled by another philosopher in the family's orbit, Josef Šafařík. Not an academic like Fischer, Šafařík had been a hydrological engineer until an injury allowed him to take early retirement and retreat into his study. In 1948 his *Seven Letters to Melin* was published and sold around 5,000 copies before it was withdrawn in the aftermath of the Communist takeover.[51] It attracted an underground following, with Havel's grandfather Hugo so impressed by it that he invited the author to the family flat. When he was old enough, Havel read it too, claiming later that in his youth 'my personal philosophical Bible was *Seven Letters to Melin*' (s4, 717). If anything, Havel was guilty of understatement: the book's impact on him was lifelong.

Not a treatise but a fictionalized meditation on an artist's suicide, *Seven Letters* confronted humanity's enduring need for truth and salvation, which it will not find in traditional religion, theosophic spiritualism or the sciences in which the author had been employed. Šafařík viewed Nazi racialism and the war crimes then on trial as the fanatical but logical climax of modern Europe's culture of depersonalized science and reliance on socially generated standards of right and wrong, which had produced a society of pliant spectators only too willing to follow orders.[52] Since the moral 'scaffolding' and 'balustrades' that modern man constructed had clearly failed, Šafařík advocated a radical individualism of active participants following the voice of conscience, 'of one's own accord, at one's own risk, on one's own responsibility'.[53]

To guard against charges of unbridled relativism, Šafařík rephrased the Pontius Pilate question 'What is truth?' into, 'For what can I vouch, for what do I vouch?'[54] He confidently predicted that 'life will choose for us those whose voices are worthy to be heard', the 'strong and uncompromising avouchers' whose consciences would guide them through a 'test of viability'.[55] Such persons would be willing to sacrifice their comfort and even their lives as the 'personal guarantee, the certification of truth by life and death'; 'maximum avouchers', such as Socrates, Jesus, Giordano Bruno and the priest Jan Hus (*c.* 1369–1415), had done so in order to put the 'stamp of certainty' on their teachings.[56] Martyrdom in itself did not make a person's pronouncements objectively correct; truth for Šafařík was 'vertical' – within a person – not 'horizontal' as a dictate binding on others. A martyr might appeal for others to follow his truth, but would do better to challenge them to follow his example and arrive at their own truth. The salvation for which people hanker would come from this

Josef Šafařík.

personally avouched truth and its attendant morality, not from a church or other institution, which Šafařík said (citing William James) only want you to 'surrender your own responsibility'.[57]

Šafařík likened his ideal participant in life, avouching his own truth, to Nietzsche's tightrope walker, a person who must keep moving above the abyss, living in the here and the now, relying on a balance and resolve that comes entirely from within. There was no better example of such a person than the artist, who, like nature itself, resisted the discipline of man-made laws of regularity and morality and danced without a safety net.[58] Despite having something of a scientist's disposition, despite encouragement from his mother and Hugo to follow it, and despite (or because of) the authorities' determination to sideline him into a practical vocation, Havel in adolescence resolved to be in some way a participating, avouching artist. He then had to work out which art form would suit him best, and seek role models.

2

Poetry's False Start (1952–7)

At first, Havel was a poet. In the history of Czech literature and national survival, poetry had long enjoyed pride of place and offered many styles a beginner could imitate. There was an equally broad spectrum of poetic personalities, from eccentric outcasts to the very sociable and highly politicized. Elder Havels had associated with two very different exemplars, Otokar Březina and Vítězslav Nezval, both of them among the most acclaimed of modern Czech poets. Březina was a mutual acquaintance of the Havlov neighbour, Anna Pammrová, who had converted grandfather Vácslav to theosophy and the occult. Nezval was one of Miloš Havel's many literary friends and had been a guest at Havlov. Miloš protected him from wartime persecution for his active Communist sympathies, and Nezval in turn intervened several times on Miloš's behalf after the war.[1]

The adolescent Havel, however, was finding his own way to poetry, which he began to compose in late 1952 or early 1953, and in two essays he respectfully rejected the tastes of the earlier generations. Březina was a symbolist virtuoso but Havel found him too remote, loving all humanity but not experiencing tangible, bodily love; the poet, Havel stated, has to come down from his tower, smell the earth and physically embrace the people on it (s3, 27). In private he was even more scathing, denouncing the friendship between Březina and Pammrová as the cold encounter of two 'impotents' who did not truly know each other.[2] (One of

Havel's early, untitled poems alludes to this predicament as 'the worst thing' [s1, 25].) Nezval was more to Havel's liking for his enchantment by modern life and eruptions of love for a world he wished to see made more harmonious. But to Havel, as to his teacher Fischer, Nezval was guilty of a childish attraction to the exotic and the frivolous, to the world of circuses and pantomimes, to Surrealism, the subconscious and free association, resulting in a disordered 'superficialization of poetry' (s3, 208–10).[3]

What Havel did like in the poetry of Březina and especially of Nezval he found more abundantly in other poets, to whom he was exposed not by his family but – and this may have been a mini-rebellion against his parents – by a regime-sanctioned source: *Thirty Years of Struggles for Czech Socialist Poetry*, a 1950 lecture by Ladislav Štoll, the Stalinist gatekeeper of literature, which was reprinted as a booklet for schoolchildren (s4, 460). Among the poets praised in it was the long-dead Jiří Wolker, who had come – like Havel – from a comfortable middle-class family but, on Štoll's account, was able to belong to 'the human element, to the enormous, immortal collective of labour' and participate 'in the collective historic work of deeper truth and humanity'.[4] Wolker's socialism flowed from a prior adherence to Unanimism, an optimistic French poetic movement celebrating the organic power of crowds and the city, which was thought to be able to draw a participant into an almost religious experience.[5] After his early death from tuberculosis in 1924, Wolker became the subject of a sentimental cult, fuelled in part by his legendary friendship with a fellow poet, Konstantin Biebl.

The appeal of a markedly inferior writer such as Wolker to the adolescent Havel speaks volumes about his wish not to settle into the identity of a marginalized loner, no matter how fruitful it might have proved artistically. As he told another young poet in March 1953,

I think it is a bit aesthete-ish to reject today's world with all its good and bad people just because it does not suit the longings, needs and feelings of the poet, that it does not understand or fulfil them. That never happened to any great poet, and nevertheless great poets loved, they loved even those people who by their dry reason and material interests did not suit them and did not understand them.[6]

By nature Havel was outgoing, rooted in a strong sense of self but needing others to spur him to work and then react to what he produced. Although the following is a prison psychologist's evaluation of a middle-aged Havel under great stress, it captures something essential about him:

An extrovertly-oriented personality with a high reasoning capacity, socially adroit, worldly, liberal, free-thought [sic], radicalism [sic], likes to decide independently, self-sufficient. Inclination to intellectual interests, an imaginative interior life and expression, seeks attention, ambitious, perhaps insecure, cunning. Also detected [are] scepticism, refusal to conform, worriedness, 'anxious uncertainty', mild stuffiness, irritability. He is sensitive to the approval or disapproval of others, he lets himself be overtaken by moods, emotionally is rather detached but dependent. Nervously unsettled, choosy artistic taste.[7]

Havel's desire to fit in was not just a reaction to the family's troubles with the Communist authorities. Owing to the destruction or Germanization of the Czech nobility after the seventeenth century, Czech-speaking society had long tended towards egalitarianism. Havel later recalled already feeling estranged from his peers as the child of an affluent family at Havlov during the war, when he attended the local primary school and

'for a time in our class it was all the rage to swat my fat thighs'
(s5, 289). He referred to this condition in a poem in 1956:

> In the village I was always a stranger.
> Behind me usually a shadow: the gentleman's son.
> I did not understand heaps of things that commonly
> would be demanded of a boy there.
> That's all someplace else already
> But nothing passes without a trace.
> ('Friendship', s1, 170)

The gentleman of the poem, V. M., had likewise been discomfited
by his father's success, and like many National Democrats developed
a compensatory receptiveness to socialism if it worked for the whole
country's benefit and eschewed class warfare. The embarrassment
of privilege might also explain V. M.'s first, short-lived marriage
to a woman renowned as a 'salon Communist'.[8] Havel described
himself as a socialist by temperament into the 1970s, but he knew
that doing so did not make him an ordinary Czech: 'I understand
the desire to become accepted by the world, to gain the natural
sense of belonging, and at the same time I am aware that this goal
is forever beyond one's reach.'[9]

With hindsight, Havel would be grateful for this social
awkwardness, as it deflected him from a less fraught but also less
significant life: without the Communist takeover he would have
gone to university and become a 'cross between an educated man
– far more educated that I am now – and a member of the [gilded
youth]. I doubt, however, that I would have become a writer.'[10]
Much later, when president, he reflected that it was the feeling
of being disinherited and not belonging that was the 'hidden
motor' of all his striving (s6, 123).

In the early 1950s, Havel converted his family's social unease
and its propensity for scientific analysis and journalistic observation

into a literary method, upon discovering Viktor Shklovsky's theory of literature as *ostranenie* (estrangement or defamiliarization), the disruption of everyday 'automatism'.[11] Havel later summarized this method as a

> perspective that rids phenomena of the accretions of conventional perception, dislodges them from customary and automatized interpretative contexts and tries to see them . . . 'without glasses' . . . Expose them as absurd. And thus open up inquiry into their true meaning (s5, 184; also 284–5).

Shklovsky had observed that in the hands of a social critic such as Leo Tolstoy, estrangement was an especially powerful tool for sensitizing readers to practices he disliked, whether they be the pretensions of a night at the opera or religious rites and dogmas (s3, 594).

Several of Havel's earliest writings already show him applying the technique of estrangement. One of the first poems in his collected works, 'Once on a Bench in the Chotek Gardens' (1954), deconstructs a young woman as if she were 'a component of the inventory/ of a laboratory next door', itemizing her body parts as implements or devices. The poem concludes with the speaker breaking through the woman's robotic veneer to discover the stormy emotional underworld of a poet and artist (s1, 12). A prose poem from the same year, 'The Apartment on the Embankment', describes skaters on the frozen Vltava seen from the great height of the family apartment as 'half-philosophers and half-ants', like figures in a Pieter Bruegel painting. Still another poem defended artistic distance as a necessary madness, 'so that [a poet] be pretty strange and removed from all people/ because only then does he truly understand what love is' (s1, 41).

The search for connections led Havel to form his first collaborative circle, starting with night-class students from families that had suffered under the Communists. They had fallen into walking home together from their school in Štěpánská Street, not far from the Lucerna, and meeting on weekends at the Café Slavia or strolling around Prague's picturesque Malá Strana quarter (on the left bank, below the castle). In October 1952, around the time of Havel's sixteenth birthday, they formalized their exchanges as a discussion group, with eight founders gathering at the Havel flat. Over the next two years they added and dropped members, hand-printed nine collections of poetry and essays, and held an idyllic symposium at Havlov in August 1954 (the family was finally forced to surrender the property four years later). Since they were mostly born in the same year, they called themselves the Thirty-sixers, but otherwise ranged widely in tastes and philosophies.[12]

In spring 1953, Havel and Radim Kopecký, the son of a diplomat the Communists had imprisoned for life, tried to unify the group through a potential common philosophy, optimalism. Optimalism's core had been defined by Havel in December 1952 as 'an optimistic attitude to life, a life full of active work, not lacking romanticism, a sort of youthful confident progressiveness, but never a rash and

Skaters on the frozen Vltava, below the plinth for the colossal statue of Stalin then under construction, January 1954.

unthinking playing at radicalism'.[13] Kopecký's variant was a muddled mix of Buddhism, Darwinism and economic utilitarianism, in which individuals in unfettered, selfish competition would bring about a steady improvement in material conditions for all. Havel's optimalism was humanist and couched in the keywords of his family's discourse, especially of his father, the sociotropic entrepreneur, and of Josef Ludvík Fischer.[14] Havel started from the assumption that any person strives for felicity on the basis of conscious will and unconscious drives, of which love is among the most powerful. From that premise Havel deduced that it is possible for individuals to seek personal happiness and a general good at the same time, as long as they realize that it is rational to follow their social emotions. The aim to only maximize coldly calculated utility, Havel feared, would paradoxically lead to egoism and less happiness.

The result of these postulates was an altruism that did not require divine commandments or belief in an immortal soul as reasons to treat one another well (as Kopecký argued, following Masaryk), or the suppression of the individual that Marxist levelling entailed. As practical applications Havel cited cooperatives or joint-stock companies in which only employees hold shares, giving each worker an equal interest in the firm's success.[15] He told Kopecký in a separate letter,

> Being a dialectician, I see the path in a merger of the two extremes – monopoly capitalism and Marxist communism – and creation of a new socialism, which would have the good aspects of both. And I must say that exactly such an order is slowly being born in the USA . . . It will be neither pure individualism nor collectivism, but a dialectically arising, better (by a leap) individualism with a collective conscience.[16]

In March 1953, just weeks after the deaths of Stalin and his Czechoslovak counterpart Klement Gottwald, Havel told Kopecký that he hoped to write a 'Humanist Party Programme' espousing an 'individualistic socialism' that met the essential material needs of humans as equals while 'sacred freedom' reigned in culture and ideas.[17]

Optimalism anticipated much of Havel's later social philosophy but failed to glue the Thirty-sixers together. Havel pressed the circle's precocious, headstrong personalities to carry their weight and follow a structured, productive routine; he had observed such organizational skills in his parents and would put his own to use many times in the coming decades. Despite his efforts, the group continued to fracture, and Jiří Paukert, a poet in Brno who had been drawn into correspondence with the Thirty-sixers, became Havel's main partner. Paukert's tastes and ideas were in most regards the opposite of Havel's – he was a Catholic, monarchist homosexual preferring a less demotic poetry (a collection of his poems from 1953 is appropriately titled *A Handsome Knight on a High Crag*[18]). But with Paukert Havel experienced a sincere, mutually respectful friendship, like that between Wolker and Biebl, in refutation of Kopecký's cynical view that only 'acquisitive and selfish reasons' lie behind human dealings.[19] Paukert also sensed that he was filling the gap left by Havel's recently deceased grandfather Hugo, who had so often pushed Havel into new subjects and syntheses.[20]

Havel's growth just in the course of 1953 can be seen in the evolution of his thinking from the outline of optimalism to his essay 'The Hamlet Question', written at the end of the year. Perhaps because many of the poets he admired had taken their own lives, or because of the subject of Šafařík's *Seven Letters*, Havel felt compelled to address the morality of suicide. Weaving along a path between materialist, existentialist and conventionally religious opinions, Havel condemned suicide, but not because life was a gift from God. Instead, he wrote that to take one's life would be to sever one's connection to a universe of which each person was a small but essential fragment. It was a view reminiscent of his grandfather

Vácslav's occult atomism, but also the result of his tutorials with Fischer and engagement with Bergson, Sartre and Masaryk, and Hegel's lectures.[21] Hegelianism in particular impressed the teenaged Havel as an alternative to Marxism that might be tolerated in the circumstances of the time. Havel was trying to work out a 'Platonic-Aristotelian-Spinozan-Hegelian' pantheism, in which Nature (the Absolute in place of God) unified matter with spirit and endowed people with reason, the will to life and sociability. Following Fischer in seeing existence as constant flux, Havel combined Hegelian dialectics with the ideas of Pitirim Sorokin, a Russian émigré sociologist at Harvard. To Sorokin, human history worked through ethical cycles, from ideational (religious) to idealistic (blending religion with an ennobled view of humanity) to sensate (empirical, utilitarian and permissive). Morally conservative, Sorokin denounced the 'sensate age' that had prevailed since the sixteenth century and that had forgotten that 'man is not only an organism but is also a bearer of absolute value.'[22] Writing in 1942, he was convinced that the misery of world war and economic depression augured the transition to the next 'ideational' phase. This prediction appealed to Havel, who felt in the months after Stalin's death that the world was verging on an 'epoch of new faith' (s3, 45).

Havel readily acknowledged that his reasoning was open to attack, and Paukert soon savaged it in one of the Thirty-sixer collections. The fundamental weakness lay in the tension between Spinoza's pantheism, which lent itself to a static, constant view of the universe, and the dynamic Hegelian theory of history as 'a process, becoming, and development'.[23] Havel never would tie up the loose ends of his philosophy, but neither did he replace it with anything more systematic or consistent.

The movement in his prose was matched by new endeavours in poetry which, to Paukert's satisfaction, was moving beyond the 'flatness and colourlessness' of Havel's earliest efforts.[24] The poetry that resulted, from 1954 to 1956, is difficult to characterize because Havel was constantly trying new approaches, but a few attributes were constant. He sometimes played with assonance but rarely followed a metre or rhyme scheme, a choice he defended in two poems as reflecting his disposition: 'my soul also does not rhyme, but grates with a thousand contradictions' (s1, 48), and 'I am fat and would not be able to squeeze into the tight embrace of [regular forms'] slim fingers' (s1, 55). Less glibly, he told Paukert that he wanted to keep his imagery spare and concrete, and he equated formal verse with excessive description (s1, 373). Accordingly, the everyday people of his poems who go about their business in Prague's squares, trams, pubs and parks tend to be faceless and nameless.

Havel's poems referred directly to the period in which he was writing, in a desire to be 'a crater of my time./ Let everything that most deeply seethes within it gush to the surface through me' (s1, 78). Doing so gave some of his poems a tacit political dimension, simply by recording grim realities of life under the Communists – all-night queues to buy meat, mandatory appearances at rallies, a teacher mocking a child for believing in God – and then disrupting them with humanizing elements such as a goggle-eyed woman walking against the throng while carrying a Christmas tree (s1, 62).[25] The poet states his priorities with restrained indignation, after a day of reading clever, admirable books about socialism:

> But when I then went home on the tram
> with a head full of knowledge,
> I realized
> that all these great thoughts
> about a more perfect order on Earth
> are laughable paper constructions,
> if it is not a matter of course for their proclaimers
> to give up their seats on the tram to an elderly lady
> or that they help a granny

whose apples have spilled on the pavement
to gather them up.
('In the Library I Read', s1, 67)

Havel's tone – in keeping with his optimism and expectation
of a new ideational age – was upbeat, often self-deprecating,
sometimes ironic or sarcastic but never bitter or lovelorn.[26] He
had no patience for songs of spleen and despair, which struck
him as phoney imitations of French existentialism (s3, 29–32). He
tended to avoid the psychological big three (childhood, mother,
mortality) that had preoccupied the interwar Czech poets; when
Paukert sent him a poem on the subject of death, Havel advised
him to be more of a lad and not dwell on such things.[27]

Havel never wrote a poem of epic length; in his collected works,
most poems take up only one or two pages. But he did group
them into batches with an implicit theme, as he later would his
prison letters and presidential speeches. This theme was almost
always the challenge of being a poet, pulled by the competing
poles of alienation and solidarity. The first collection, which has
not survived, was composed in autumn 1953 and apparently
celebrated love, friendship and the 'supra-personal bond of union
between people in a gang, in a collective', akin to that shared by
idealized soldiers. Havel had not yet done his military service,
which would disabuse him of any illusions about comrades in
uniform, and he was fond of the Soviet poet Vladimir Mayakovsky,
a 'soldier of verse' who used the language of 'military command'.
He tentatively titled this collection *Battalion in Plainclothes*,
then settled on the more Wolkerish *Heart in Plainclothes*.[28]

The first surviving cycle, *Tremors*, from 1954, is largely an
outpouring of insecurity about his ability to be not just a poet but
a great poet. He wondered whether he would find his own path
'or just end up in a blind marshy pool', discovering, like a vine
growing up the wall of a tower, that the sky is still infinitely far

above (s1, 51, 52). He sensed that his friends were laughing at him for staying up all night toiling over some verses and fantasized about succeeding as a poet but then burning all his work (s1, 54, 56). He resolved to keep trying even though he knew his voice could not be heard above the 'stagnant water of the present' and for now had to bubble 'under the rocks, because it cannot out' (s1, 47, 51).

To push his poetry beyond imitation of Wolker, Havel emulated the foreign writers he randomly discovered in translation. In its structure *Tremors* mimics the classical Chinese poet Li Po (Li Bai) through its compressed observation of 'moments/ of responsibility to nature' (s1, 69). But in its spirit, the cycle imitates American poets – first Walt Whitman, then Carl Sandburg and Edgar Lee Masters – whom Havel embraced in order to find beauty in a mechanized world and to celebrate the common man without recourse to socialist-realist stock characters (just as he took up Hegel in order to be dialectical without Marx) (s1, 373; s3, 50–53). Havel emulated the Americans through images of simple working folk, around whom the 'consciousness and mystery of nature/ containing all the infinite wisdom of the world' dwell in a small, carmine-tinted cloud (s1, 43) or a cricket in summertime (s1, 49) or a melted snowflake (s1, 63). In his most Whitman-Sandburgish piece, a forsaken solitary walker looks out from a hilltop, experiences ecstatic communion with millions of toiling, singing, muscular workers and is infused with 'a powerful wave of faith/ that my life, my work are not and will not be pointless' (s1, 29–30).

The appreciation of American poetry was part of Havel's ongoing aesthetic education, now taking place through direct contact with eminent Prague poets, mostly born between 1900 and 1915 and blacklisted after falling out with the Communist Party they had once supported. One was Jiří Kolář, a woodworker who had started writing poetry only in his mid-twenties and, with Havel's future confidant Zdeněk Urbánek, translated those American poets Havel admired. Havel tried to imitate Kolář's poems in their free verse and compactness, their registers ranging from biblical to colloquial and their methodical progression along a premeditated sequence, often in the form of diary entries (s3, 74–6). Havel also valued their objective witnessing of the tragic horrors as well as the delights of everyday city life; to Kolář, the 'mission of literature and art has been the same from ages past to today, boundlessly simple in its complexity: DO NOT LIE!'[29] That unflinching candour got him into trouble; before Havel met him in April 1955, Kolář had undergone eight months of interrogation in the Ruzyně prison for writing his masterpiece, *Prometheus's Liver*.

Kolář was often irascible, inscrutable and intoxicated, but he was at least part of a circle (Group 42) and held court at the Café Slavia around a Stammtisch to which Havel and Paukert were admitted. Far less sociable, to the point of agoraphobic, was another poet Havel summoned up the courage to visit, Vladimír Holan. Like many of his generation, Holan had been jolted by the traumatic events of the 1930s into using two alternating genres: epic cycles that sometimes followed metre and rhyme in homage to national and Russian traditions (to protest German aggression) and free-verse, diary-style observations in the form of eyewitness documents or compact, gnomic meditations.[30] At war's end, he had expressed his elation in tributes to the Red Army, which the young Havel extolled to Paukert: 'Now, that is poetry! It is humanity itself!'[31] But Holan's own passions had quickly cooled, and in 1949 he was banned after he and another poet were overheard complaining in a café about the Communist regime's dogmatism. By the time of Havel's first visit, in May 1954, Holan had been readmitted to the official writers' union – the approximately 600 authors the state either most favoured or most wanted to manipulate – but he had signalled, in the poem 'To Enemies', that henceforth his self-respect would come before service to a cause.[32] Holed up in his Baroque villa on Kampa, an island on Prague's left bank, he was steadily producing new verse – which would be published only in the more permissive

1960s. Havel was at first intimidated by Holan's appearance: 'long hair, mighty figure, tanned, his eyes two lumps of coal, dressed in overalls'. But Holan also displayed a greater compassion than Havel had ever encountered. He returned to the villa a dozen times, roughly every fortnight, bringing along Paukert and a schoolmate from Poděbrady days, the future film director Miloš Forman.[33]

Under the influence of these and other Prague writers, the poems in Havel's 1955 cycle *First Notes* (in the promissory sense, like a bond or debenture) were longer and unfolded as vignettes or overheard conversations, with less of the directly personal voice of *Tremors*. But writing itself, especially poetry, remained the main subject, and a problematic one at that. The longest of all Havel's poems, 'History', tells a tale of a young worker who, by meeting a girl who works in a bookshop, acquires a taste for literature and tries his hand at verse. But he begins to be consumed by the drive to write, in the process becoming estranged from his workmates and even from his girlfriend, whose own tastes are far simpler (s1, 97–103). In 'He and She', a poet and his lover are troubled by a funeral procession for another poet who cracked up and drank himself to death (s1, 114–16). Elsewhere, poetry is likened to a parasitic worm, a hydra, a moth drawn to a lamp and unable to land, a taunting laugh disrupting pleasant dreams.

One commonality that Havel noted in Holan and Kolář, as well as most contemporary poetry, was the fragmentation of time into multiple parallel experiences. Havel attributed this device initially to the influence on the poets of T. S. Eliot but ultimately to modern physics' revision of Newtonian principles (s3, 141–2). Havel made this phenomenon, rather than the agonies of being a poet, the central theme of his next cycle, *Spaces and Times* (1956). In many of its eighteen poems, the speaker connects events happening at the same time in different places, and Havel first stated what would become, over the years, his deep faith in the potential for small actions to have world-changing consequences.

The word 'fate' (*osud*) appears fourteen times in some form, but is clearly not meant as fixed destiny; rather, it is the residue or sum of countless minor moments. In 'Saturday' (s1, 146), he carefully checks his appearance in the bathroom mirror before going out,

> And suddenly my future son is standing beside me,
> inquisitively examining every gesture of his father.
> He knows full well that everything I do
> I contribute unavoidably to his fate
>
> and thus to the future of humanity.
> For where is it written, that my son will not be
> a new Hitler or new Einstein?
> And where is it written, that it was they
> who decided the fate of the world?

Spaces and Times, like Havel's previous cycles, referred to real events, used snippets of overheard conversation and yearned for fellowship in ways reminiscent of Whitman or Sandburg: 'we are determined as much by the roar of Pittsburgh/ factories as by the drilling rigs of Baku./ The whole world is inhabited by everyday man' ('Spring Night', s1, 142). The pantheism of Havel's Thirty-sixer essays finds voice: 'And each of them carries within/ something originally mine, of each of them/ I carry something within me ('Before Sleep', s1, 157). But the connections being made flow not just from the natural ability to wonder what someone somewhere else is doing at this very moment, but also from awareness of the wider world, courtesy of modern communications, through which the poet can learn about a war in Africa, a superpower summit in Geneva and a royal wedding in Monaco. In these poems the narrator not only gazes down on Prague from his fourth-storey window (that globe on the roof just above his head) but reads the newspapers, talks on the telephone ('the confessional of the twentieth century,

Olga Šplíchalová and Havel at the Café Slavia in the late 1950s.

the last/ redemptive idea' [s1, 155]) and imagines families huddling around the newest arrival, television. In 'On the Observation Tower' (s1, 173), when a girlfriend asks, 'Where is the heart of this world?', the speaker looks down from Petřín Hill and replies,

> I don't know, perhaps over there on that bench,
> or down below in the hospital, or somewhere in Pankrác [prison],

or perhaps on a battlefield in Vietnam,
or in Strahov [stadium] during a match, perhaps
in a New York or Moscow
skyscraper . . .

The woman in this and other poems in *Spaces and Times* would
become the subject of Havel's last cycle, *On the Cusp of Spring*, also
written in 1956. Olga Šplíchalová was three years older than Havel,
from a very different part of Prague – the eastern working-class
section of Žižkov – and a very different household. Her parents'
marriage ended after Olga's mother, frustrated by her knacker
husband's absences, took up briefly with a younger man. Olga's
childhood had alternated between unsupervised freedom on the
streets and the responsibility of caring for her older sister's five
children; ice cream on the Barrandov Terraces was a memorable
treat.[34] She had had a limited education – her apprenticeship in
shoemaking ended when a press mangled four fingers on her left
hand – but she was an avid reader with an independent, no-nonsense
streak (neither a Communist nor a Christian), and like Havel had
absorbed the values of the Scouting movement.[35] Her love of theatre
led her to take an acting course, during which she befriended a
woman who worked in the same laboratory as Havel and introduced
Olga to him at the Café Slavia in 1953.[36] At first he seemed too young
for her liking, and his mother did not approve of Olga as a match for
the 'clean-handed son of a family/ from the city centre' ('Return', s1,
148). Havel persisted, and by 1956 had at last prevailed with Olga.

She attracted Havel, as he later explained in a letter to her from
prison, by being so unlike him:

I am inclined to sentimentality, self-flagellation, a lack of
self-confidence, etc.; I would not say that I am not a firm
person (on the contrary, in some ways I am obstinate to the
point of obsessive), but in many regards I am at the very

least insecure and perhaps a little unmoored existentially
(my long-held feeling of being outside the order of things,
the longing to be accepted into it, and lack of confidence in
the genuineness of my acceptance). What could be a more
perfect opposing pole and thus a more ideal complement of
such a character than your merciless matter-of-factness, total
unsentimentality, harsh and often rude candour, and immovable
inclination to unmask completely anything false? (s5, 701)

That Havel gravitated to Olga somewhat selfishly as a grounding,
nurturing force finds expression in the uncharacteristically ordered
structure of *On the Cusp of Spring*, which consists of eleven untitled
poems, each with four quatrains. Presented to her as a birthday
gift on 11 July 1956, they were as close as Havel could come to love
poems, as he was never comfortable with outpourings of affection.
He had told Paukert that 'the heart is contained in a box of heavy,
ideally oaken wood', which may lend friendship an outward
formality ('the coolness of its shell') but ensures its longevity,
lest like a candle it burn down too quickly. In this regard, Havel
claimed to be following Wolker, for whom love was primarily a
'work of habit'.[37] That Olga might have periodically welcomed more
effusive expression from a man supposedly skilled in language is
acknowledged in Havel's play *The Increased Difficulty of Concentration*
(1968) when the main character, using Havel's own term of endear-
ment for Olga (*broučku*, my beetle), assures a lover that he has
feelings for her even if he does not know how to put them into
words (s2, 268).

The poems also suggest that Havel found in Olga a way to break
out of his parents' world and broaden his social horizon. Looking
back on poems written before Olga, such as *First Notes,* he was horrified
by their 'spasmodic, exhibitionistic and bombastic knottiness and
godforsaken literary egocentrism'.[38] With Olga, he could make
that long-desired connection to the common (wo)man:

You, a daughter of Žižkov, me, a still untested
frequenter of literary cafés. We two
somewhere on the cusp of spring.
(s1, 185)

Spring at the time meant more than just the bloom of early
adulthood; there was also a political thaw in the Soviet bloc, bringing
a promise of greater freedom and acknowledgement of the crimes
of Stalinism.

It was fitting that *On the Cusp of Spring* bears the imprint of
another native of Olga's Žižkov quarter, Jaroslav Seifert, who in
April 1956 took fellow writers to task for failing to live up to the
'noble tradition of Czech literature and, of course, of literature in
general, that it was the poets who, knowing the truth, expressed
it sooner than the politicians'.[39] Seifert could say such things, for
he was, with Nezval, the most popular poet in Czechoslovakia,
although he had had his own brushes with the censors – he
was the poet with whom Holan was overheard complaining
about dogmatism in 1949. Seifert had also been the first writer
Havel visited, in March 1954, in search of advice, and in doing
so discovered his role model as an artist – someone who by all
appearances was normal, happy, with a wife and family, able to get
published and, to use Whitman's 'proof of a poet', to be absorbed
by his country as affectionately as he absorbed it.[40] When, thirty
years later, Seifert won the Nobel Prize in literature, Havel praised
him not just for his poetry but for his 'attitude to the world',
which meant a 'writer's responsible civic stance' (s4, 606–7).[41]

Havel was gaining confidence in his own 'attitude to the world'
and 'civic stance'; as the defensive introduction to *Spaces and Times*
declares, 'each person has a different way of thinking about the basic
facts of the life that surrounds him' (s1, 141). Already in June 1955 he
was reporting to Paukert that he had 'fought with Holan, waged a
battle with Kolář' and 'I think that I am really starting to do my own

The poet Jaroslav Seifert mobbed at a book signing, 1955.

thing.'[42] The problem for Havel was nagging uncertainty as
to whether poetry was the right vehicle. So far none of his poems
had been published, and those he had written showed he had talent
but were no assurance that he could fulfil – as his motto for *First
Notes* announced – 'the secret wish of everyone living illicitly off
poetry: to be something for someone' (s1, 88). As the promising
spring of 1956 turned to summer, Havel felt a need to move on:

> I feel involuntarily for my pulse.
> It ticks. My clock ticks. Time ticks.
> It is flying from one place to another. And all at once
> I have the feeling that it is flying by awfully fast.
> ('Sunday', s1, 163)

There was one other role Havel could still play in the context of poetry: rather than seek success as a writer of verse, he could conceptualize what good verse might be and campaign for its availability to the public. His role model in this capacity was Jindřich Chalupecký, the house theorist of Kolář's Group 42, whom Havel had begun to visit in 1956.[43] In autumn, as Soviet forces threatened to intervene in unruly Poland and Hungary, Havel told his friends that the time had come for 'our invasion into literature', and proposed as their target the periodical *Květen* (May).[44] The new monthly was staffed by writers born in the 1920s, former Stalinists now producing poetry that depicted unheroic people enduring everyday hardships, although still within 'a broader optimistic framework'.[45] Havel was unimpressed by their reinvention of the kind of poetry Group 42 had long practised (and been denounced for). Privately, he told Paukert that so far *Květen*, which in 1955 had rejected poems from his *First Notes* cycle, had 'done bugger-all for literature'.[46] He sensed, however, that it was now the place most likely to provide him and other new writers with a home.

An opportunity arose when the journal invited readers to contribute to the development of a new, post-Stalinist but still Marxist programme. Havel's submission chided the journal for thinking that a whole generation of writers would subscribe to a manifesto, especially one still to be infused with the forced joyfulness of socialist realism (s3, 55–9). To his surprise *Květen* printed his reproach and even paid him a respectable 100-crown honorarium, which he promptly spent on drink ('Olga had to get me home completely off my head,' he told Paukert).[47] Better still, this first publication won him an invitation to attend a conference in November 1956 at Dobříš, a Rococo chateau at the disposal of the literary establishment. His remarks there sketched out the kind of writer he, at the age of twenty, admired and aspired to be: embedded enough in his society to be a walking index of its hopes and flaws, in most regards ordinary but exceptionally able to feel more intensely and express what the ordinary person experiences. Using terms learned from Šafařík and Group 42 and anticipating his future definition of a dissident, Havel presented the modern poet's lot as a moral challenge – to live and describe life as the poet feels it ought to be lived, rather than according to external standards. The implication was that good writing would come neither from the eccentric or lunatic unable to relate to his surroundings nor from the state-coddled laureate who praised the masses but whose average day was not remotely like theirs (s3, 60–66).

This attack on privilege not only ruffled feathers, much to Havel's delight, but seemed to help him in his quest to win space in *Květen* and, by the end of the year, a mention in the flagship weekly *Literární noviny* (Literary News). There was talk by early 1957 of allowing a whole new periodical just for 'non-ideological modern realism', work that embodied Havel's ideal of 'substantial art' depicting life in complex truthfulness (s3, 126). He toyed with potential journal titles, such as *Pábení* (Palaver), a term beloved of Kolář and Bohumil Hrabal, an emerging master of the short story and, to Havel, the consummate everyman able to experience life with rare intensity (s3, 105–14). Hoping to eclipse *Květen* with a playful mix of poetry, prose, theory and artwork, Havel solicited contributions from beyond his familiar Group 42 and Thirty-sixer contacts; a slightly older poet noted in his diary that 'Havel at that time was constantly organizing something, chasing something down, putting someone together with someone.'[48] In March 1957 this emerging network of literary, musical and visual artists was able to hold a performance on Prague's Střelecký Island, with Havel presenting their core theses.[49] But in the wake of the Soviet Union's brutal suppression of unrest in Hungary, Czechoslovakia began to retighten the bolts on its intelligentsia. *Pábení* never materialized; *Květen* became inhospitable and in 1959 shut down altogether.

Looking back from the more relaxed spring of 1968, Havel assessed the long-term importance of the circumstances in which he came of age:

> The state of society at the time of our first awakening, at the time of our first attempts at political and personal self-realization, determines our basic outlook for the rest of our lives. For my part . . . I shall always be in some sense linked to the pseudo-dialectical tension between dictatorship and the thaw, between Stalinism and de-Stalinization, which was characteristic of the year 1956 when I was twenty years old.[50]

It was also time for a change of direction, as he had hit a dead end: he had finished night school in 1954, tried repeatedly but unsuccessfully to be accepted to a university arts programme, and was dropping out of the technical school he had entered in 1955 to study transportation economics, which bored him witless. He even considered learning Russian so that he could study literature in the Soviet Union, but was told that owing to his class origins he would never be allowed to go.[51]

No longer enrolled in higher education, Havel would be called up in autumn 1957 for two years of military service. Before then, he and Olga travelled to Poland – his first trip abroad – and around Czechoslovakia to escape their families' crowded flats and Božena's reproaches. One of their stops was Český Šternberk, a medieval castle at which Paukert, now an art history student, was working over the summer break. At one point they were playing on a terrace with a red ball, which was somehow sent flying over the ramparts. As Paukert recalled later, 'The ball bounced several times off the rocky cliffs and disappeared somewhere into the rapids of the Sazava river, and with it went our first youth, the period of our first intimacies with the Muses, the time of our first tremors, our first notes' (s1, 384).

Havel with his parents during his military service, 1959. Prague Castle is in the background.

3

Into Theatre and *Politič̌nost*
(1957–69)

At the beginning of November 1957, seen off by Olga at Prague's
Main Station, Havel reported for military duty. He had schemed
unsuccessfully to avoid it on medical grounds by feigning
depression, but now, as on many future occasions, he rationalized
this setback as potentially positive. After all, he told Paukert,
almost all men their age had to go through it; when it was over
he would be 23 and would have 'something behind me and many
things ahead'; and 'maybe at home they will have a different
attitude to me', as he was tired of being told '30 times a day' that
he had failed in life.[1] 'They' were his parents, who came from
families in which men had rarely had to serve in Habsburg armies
and now suddenly were sending both sons to the front line of the
new Warsaw Pact. Ivan was being dispatched to eastern Slovakia
and Václav to an artillery unit at České Budějovice, in southern
Bohemia, where he was assigned, like all conscripts of suspect
background, to the non-combat sappers.

The two years that followed were, on the whole, an arduous waste
of Havel's time, but they had two redeeming qualities. First, although
Havel was familiar with military discipline and communal quarters
from his days at the Poděbrady school, the army was his first exposure
to Czechoslovak society in all its diversity. One friend later reflected,

There is something completely Old-Testamentish about it,
that military service lasting two years makes a real man out

of a kid. A real man has to deal with people he'd otherwise never talk to in his life, he would avoid them. In those two years he learns to bear the fate of this world. Vašek [Havel's diminutive] can handle a lot of things today because he was forced to prepare for them. He was forced to in life many times, but it started in military service with the sappers.[2]

The other saving grace was that the army gave Havel his first taste of the theatre. Even before he was called up, several forces were nudging him in that direction. His grandfather Vácslav had been a patron of the National Theatre and on close terms with its demiurge, Jaroslav Kvapil, widely regarded as the founder of modern Czech theatre and himself a poet turned playwright.[3] Poets whom Havel loved or respected, such as Wolker and Nezval, had also written plays, or, in the case of Group 42 and Edgar Lee Masters, had blurred the line between verse and drama (s3, 148). The sociality of theatre appealed to Havel's outgoing personality and would allow him to bring space to life, as his father and grandfather had with the Lucerna and Barrandov Terraces (s5, 203, 402, 470). Olga was already stage-struck, and Ivan was toying with the idea of a play composed in a made-up language.[4]

To escape from tedium, toil and (now genuine) depression, Havel co-founded a regimental theatre group. In spring 1958 they staged *September Nights* by Pavel Kohout, a socialist realist born in 1928 who had turned from poetry to playwriting. Set in an infantry unit on manoeuvres, *September Nights* resembled the *Květen* poetry that was depicting ordinary people and their problems but did so swaddled in sentimental optimism. When it debuted in 1955 the play caused a sensation simply because any unheroic depiction of men in uniform was still taboo, but it was allegedly blessed by the president, Antonín Zápotocký, who had literary pretensions and believed that a bit of 'constructive criticism' could help revive faith in the Communist project.[5]

Havel's production competed in army drama tournaments, and its success emboldened him and co-founder Karel Brynda to write their own play. Titled *Life Before You* – in the spirit of *September Nights*, when a character describes himself as having his 'head held high, thousands of plans, everything before you'[6] – the play can be read either as a romp about a drunken soldier who falls asleep on duty while his rifle is used by another officer to kill an intruder, or as a deeper drama of a man whose integrity is at stake when he is compelled to live in truth despite the consequences.[7] Havel himself coyly summarized it as a 'lightly socialist-realist play, but [one] which at the same time was somewhat critical'.[8] Whatever its purpose, when the play was presented at regional contests Havel had his first, pleasing experience of audience reaction, including a positive review in the army newspaper, until political commissars decided that an author with his class background should not enjoy such acclaim.[9]

As his military service neared its end, Havel decided to apply for a place in the dramaturgy programme of the Academy of Performing Arts. He was one of five applicants (out of a hundred) who made the cut after three days of exams in June 1959, but the panel's decision was subject to review by a political commission, and on 1 July he was told that there was no place for him.[10] At this point his father, who had tended to intervene less than Božena did in their son's affairs, sought help from one of the family's show business contacts. Jan Werich happened to live in the same villa on Kampa as the poet Holan, one floor above, but in a very different world. As half of an avant-garde vaudeville act with Jiří Voskovec (V+W), Werich had started out in the 1920s by performing at the Lucerna, where Miloš Havel was promoting a mix of Berlin cabaret and American jazz. The duo's success enabled them to move around the corner and take over the 800-seat Liberated Theatre, where they produced 25 shows using 'a basic revue pattern . . . that moved toward musical comedy or, indeed, drama with musical interludes, with political satire as its core'.[11] Their clowning earned them comparisons to Aristophanes and Charlie Chaplin, but they occasionally needed Miloš's financial help to stay in business. Werich, like Nezval, remembered his debt and after the war lobbied in Miloš's defence and visited him in exile, acting as a messenger for the family.[12] Voskovec had also emigrated, so Werich founded a new Satire Theatre. It was there that Havel was taken on as a stagehand.

Work in the wings during the 1959–60 season gave Havel a feel for theatre's dynamics while he figured out the kinds of drama and acting he liked or disliked. He found an outlet for his thoughts in reviews he wrote for the monthly *Divadlo* (Theatre), among the first of which was a profile of Werich's new sidekick, Miroslav Horníček. The two men, in the V+W tradition, would interrupt the evening's show to conduct semi-scripted banter known as *forbíny*. While Werich had always represented the earthy side, the more cerebral Horníček impressed Havel as a practitioner of estrangement, pushing commonplace notions or bureaucratic formulas to absurd extremes and forcing the audience to look at them anew (s3, 270–80).

Havel also liked what he was seeing at Werich's theatre (now named the ABC) because it was not satire as defined under socialism. Satire had made a quick comeback after Stalin's death; the first send-up of Communist jargon and cronyism, Václav Jelínek's cabaret *Scandal in the Picture Gallery*, opened in October 1953 and became the most popular show of the season.[13] Skittish officials all the way up to Communist leader Antonín Novotný welcomed satire if it 'severely drove out everything old [bourgeois] in our life' and acted 'on the side of social progress and truth'.[14] A conference in November 1954 circumscribed acceptable satire as humour that 'defends the interests of the people, the interests of building socialism, when it can properly distinguish the Party and institutions from particular phenomena and functionaries who violate the Party's correct line' and do so

KONSTRUKTIVNÍ SATIRA

100%	100%	100%	100%	100%	100%	100%
100%	100%	100%	100%	100%	100%	100%
100%	100%	100%	100%	100%	100%	100%
100%	100%	100%	100%	100%	100%	100%
100%	100%	100%	100%	100%	100%	100%
100%	100%	100%	100%	100%	100%	100%
100%	100%	100%	100%	100%	100%	100%
100%	100%	100%	100%	100%	100%	100%
100%	100%	100%	100%	100%	100%	100%
100%	100%	100%	100%	100%	99%	100%
100%	100%	100%	100%	100%	100%	100%
100%	100%	100%	100%	100%	100%	100%

'Constructive satire', a Havel typogram from 1964.

from an 'optimistic perspective'.[15] Havel mocked this co-opted 'constructive satire' in a visual form of poetry, the typogram, which he started playing with after leaving the army (s1, 258).

State-defined satire also did not appeal to Werich, who even in freer interwar conditions had preferred a timeless Aesopian approach; V+W plays written in response to problems of the 1930s could be restaged twenty years later and still resonate in Czechoslovakia and abroad (an East Berlin tour in 1958 received thirty-minute ovations).[16] Furthermore, there was always the risk that even an artist with impeccable leftist credentials such as Werich might find himself in trouble; when he opened his Satire Theatre in 1955, an official encouraged him to 'shoot hard and bravely' like a footballer, to which Werich replied that 'in football I, my opponent, the spectators and the referee can see where I was aiming and where the ball landed. Whereas in theatre I shoot and only the next day do you draw the lines.'[17] Reviewers' carping that he was not delivering the satire that the Party expected prompted Werich to change the theatre's name to ABC in 1957. Havel seems to have learned here from Werich: while his poetry had clearly been set in Communist Prague and its environs, his plays would not be.

Havel was one of the few critics to appreciate the ABC's ground-breaking production in 1959 of *The Visit of the Old Lady* by the Swiss playwright Friedrich Dürrenmatt. Although the young Havel is often said – with reason – to have been influenced by Eugène Ionesco and Samuel Beckett, Dürrenmatt should be factored in as well. In *The Visit*, a wealthy woman, Claire, returns to her hometown to exact revenge for a wrong committed decades before. The inhabitants have been reduced to a poverty that, unbeknown to them, Claire has orchestrated, so that when she demands the sacrificial killing of a former lover, they comply, disturbingly able to silence their consciences through eloquent rationalizations. The play can be read as a cautionary tale, a tragicomic projection of Western civilization's drift towards a 'pragmatic and materialistic but basically soulless age of technocracy'.[18] Havel, in an unpublished review titled 'Ethics and Life', warned that the play's events should not be assumed to be inevitable or possible only in a capitalist society. In its preoccupation with providing quantifiable creature comforts, socialism was also failing to foster 'social responsibility, responsibility for work and towards fellow citizens, or for their own human growth' (S3, 301). The problem was not that socialism could not match Western commercial success; it was that it wanted to at all.

Havel knew that he was hardly the first to detect the regime's mixed messages and their unintended consequences; as he

70

began work in earnest on his own plays, he sought a way of addressing those issues that would differ from how they were already being depicted on stage. As in his poetic years, his rivalry would be primarily with writers born in the 1920s. Kohout, the author of *September Nights*, would be easy to surpass, because subsequent plays such as his *The Third Sister* (1960) lacked a dramatic conflict containing 'something general, generally interesting and generally applicable' (s3, 359). Kohout was guilty of 'exhibitionism', overloading his plots with too large a cast and showy devices that felt 'unhealthily deliberate, artificial, self-important' (s3, 331). Also in his immediate sights was Jaroslav Dietl, whose *Once There were Two* at the ABC Havel derided as 'quite bad' because it could not express its purpose dramatically, relying instead on the 'ground-floor humour' typical of Dietl's 'shallowness' (s3, 339, 475).

Less easily dismissed were plays from better writers, such as *An August Sunday* by František Hrubín. Havel had liked Hrubín's poetry but described his Chekhovian play to Paukert as an 'unsuccessful attempt at a Czech disillusioned frustrated modern "atmospheric" drama'.[19] Havel was more generous towards his friend Josef Topol, a poet who had staged his first play in Prague at the age of twenty. Topol had followed up in 1959 with *Their Day*, one of several new works at the National Theatre with present-day philistinism as their subject.[20] Although *Their Day* had the trappings of a tale of restless youth, the enemy was not the older generation but any 'state of self-satisfaction, a life without dreams and goals, without responsibility to oneself or to society'.[21] Havel praised Topol for providing the best depiction to date of the socialist careerist content to live a 'de-ethicized, mechanical life' (s3, 302), but he could have chided him for burying the core conflict between a young musician and his pragmatic father beneath the banter of the many other characters. The play's horizon was also limited by its setting ('a small town in central

Bohemia on the road to Prague'[22]), its reference to identifiable institutions and its dialogue in the slangy vernacular of the time.

Havel was also finding fault with much of the acting he observed. In general, he favoured restrained performances, like those of Miloš Kopecký at the ABC, which he likened to the nimble caricatures of Saul Steinberg, an American cartoonist of Romanian origin.[23] He feared that actors of his own generation, even his friend Jan Tříska, too often relied on bursts of anger or anxiety without regard for the 'order, structure, perspective, analysis, control and command' that a good play needed (S3, 505–16). A strong directorial hand, of course, could keep actors in line, as Havel saw when he filled in as an assistant to Alfréd Radok at the Chamber Theatre. Radok's goal was

Miloš Kopecký and Miroslav Horníček, performing in 1962.

a 'living theatre', with the audience experiencing not a bravura display of acting skill but something that was as near as possible to an authentic human presence, the characters alive and in real dialogue with each other (s3, 416–61). Radok was driving actors to abandon their hallmark gimmicks and tap their innermost emotional memories, using methods that he himself could not explain and which Havel later compared to shamanism or alchemy (s4, 656–60). Not all directors subscribed to Radok's method, as Havel knew, so his own plays would embed restraints on the actors in the very text.

Havel's first post-army piece, *A Family Evening* (1960), was a 'little study of the banality' of the petty-bourgeois life being passed on to the young under socialism (s3, 315). In seven short scenes he depicted a dull gathering of three generations, but to prevent the play itself from becoming dull he adopted the devices of French absurdism. He hoped that an estranging distance from reality would sensitize the spectator to the vacuity of a life reduced to shopping and planning holidays (s3, 316). The chit-chat dialogue, when not falling into long silences, often turns to the subject of television. The ageing grandmother dozes over a game of cards, as in a recent Czech film, *The Wolf's Lair*, which Havel believed had 'perfectly symboliz[ed] the whole absurdity and deadening character of the lifestyle of bourgeois domesticity' (s3, 249). As if to underscore both the play's message and the acting style Havel wanted, the family's surname is Pokorný (humble, meek), their canary Felix lies dead in his cage, and the play ends with all the characters falling asleep as a radio drones (s2, 9–35).

At the time he wrote it, Havel did not have a place to stage *A Family Evening*, and he sensed that the ABC was in decline, no longer trying 'to express some truth about the world' (s3, 469). Werich quit at the end of 1960, worn down by bad reviews and illness due to cancer. Shortly before, Havel himself had left to work at the Theatre on the Balustrade, a new house that was at most a quarter of the size of the ABC. He had won a place there in the same way he had won the invitation to the Dobříš conference in 1956: by publishing an article on the smaller venues that were then mushrooming around Prague. While full of praise, he cautioned their writers and directors to curtail the tendency to end their shows with a didactic moral. A good play, Havel advised, has a 'deeper ideational meaning' but lets it creep up on the audience, taking them unawares as they laugh (s3, 304–11). The Balustrade's artistic director, Ivan Vyskočil, was struck by Havel's remarks and asked for other samples of his writing. Havel submitted *A Family Evening*, and was offered employment as a stagehand on the understanding that it would lead to more creative opportunities. Soon Olga would also find work there, as an usher.

For the next two years Havel operated in the vibrant chaos of the Balustrade under Vyskočil. A psychologist specializing in deviant behaviour by training, Vyskočil was initially drawn to theatre as therapy for institutionalized adolescent girls. The idea of drama as a clinical tool stayed with him as he moved into the world of Prague's nightclubs and small theatres in the late 1950s.[24] He developed the genre of the semi-improvised 'text appeal' (a play on the English phrase 'sex appeal'), usually an ensemble of faux-lectures and vignettes on a timely subject, such as hitchhiking, which was spreading with the rise in car ownership. Vyskočil liked that topic because it could be used to poke fun at the persistence under socialism of prestige derived from property, and it presented the kind of situation with which his previous shows had often ended: a moment when one character has to decide whether to join his fate to another's and enter into dialogue.[25]

Vyskočil opened *Hitchhiking* with a statement by a professorial Demonstrator, followed by three scenes. As he encouraged collaboration and constant revision, he invited Havel to draft variants of two of the scenes. In one, *Motomorphosis*, members of a society against 'motorism' – a disease causing people to turn into cars – begin to see its virtues and yield to its symptoms.[26] (Havel himself, like many of the men in his family, was a car enthusiast.) In the other, *Hela, Ela and Stop*, two respectable women have a go at hitchhiking and abandon their dignity, first by arguing over old boyfriends and then by dancing and singing to attract drivers. When one does stop, they envelop him in what would become a standard feature of Havel's plays: a rhythmic, assonant verbal fugue consisting at first of lists of possessions, then strings of vaguely Russian-sounding nonsense. The fugue accelerates to a crescendo before slowing to a whisper as the scene, like in *A Family Evening*, peters out.[27] Both scenes contain the quintessential questions of all of Havel's early plays: whether a person is grounded in an identity and can express himself through the language, to use Šafařík's terms, of personally avouched truth.[28]

Neither of Havel's variants was used in the show when it ran at the Balustrade in March 1961; they differed too starkly from Vyskočil's free-form style. Havel favoured traditional composition, for if theatre was to be a dialogue, then it needed all involved – those on stage and in the seats – to be clearly distinguished. At times Havel punctured the illusion of the play as a self-contained world, but only by having characters address the audience – never by bringing the audience into direct participation (as director Jerzy Grotowski was doing at that time in Poland). Havel would later be very dismissive of 1960s 'happenings', 'because where everything is permitted, nothing surprises' (s3, 773; s5, 415). As a rule, Havel wrote dialogue in the bookish language 'of meetings, state speeches, trials, ceremonies, press conferences, lectures, philosophical debates, funerals', which he defended as the source of his plays' tension: the audience never knows whether to take a character's fine talk at face value, for it always has an 'undertone of mendacity' (s4, 1012).

Vyskočil recommended that Havel enlarge *A Family Evening* into a tale of careerism, connections and generational strife. Havel set to work on *His Day*, a working title that must have been intended as a

reference (or riposte?) to Topol's *Their Day*: both involve an office
party and an attempt to advance someone's career by entertaining
a powerful official.[29] Like *Their Day*, *His Day* originally had three
acts, the first of which introduces the Houks, who seem very like
the residents of Engels Embankment 78.[30] An anxious family
whose social status has changed quickly over one generation, the
Houks are terrified of slipping; when it seems that an important
guest is not coming, the parents panic, the wife wailing, 'We find
ourselves in isolation!'[31] They are counting on their younger son
Hugo to protect the family by rising through the ranks of the state
'liquidation office', and they urge him to ingratiate himself at its
upcoming garden party. They have written off their elder son Petr,
a black-sheep intellectual, who moans that he is 'suffocating in
this musty bourgeois domesticity!' When Petr announces that he
would rather do his military service than put up with home life and
that he will become 'a poet of the everyday', the father recalls how
much better it was when his sons were still boys and 'wandered
in the grass, caught butterflies, read history in the evenings'.

The characters' names were publicly ironic and privately
barbed. The parents were first called Karel and Blažena, but
Havel quickly changed them to Oldřich and Božena. For Czechs,
that duo evokes the medieval romance of a prince and a peasant
girl whose son Břetislav would go on to safeguard the Přemyslid
dynasty and expand the Bohemian realm. Their legend was
popularly known from chronicles and puppet plays, and a 1953
comedy updated them as stalwart collective farmworkers.[32]
Among those who knew Havel, however, the appearance of his
own mother's name in connection with the use of her father's
name for the younger son must have raised eyebrows.

In the second act of *His Day*, Hugo dutifully goes to the
office party and, succumbing to his parents' paranoia, fears
that he is about to be replaced by a relative of the director.
He temporarily undergoes a hallucinatory loss of self, but

in the process sets in motion events that seem to put him on track for promotion. When his parents learn in the third act of his apparent success, they break into song:

> Anything can be achieved through a social call,
> Only through connections can you get ahead,
> And you have to be able to weave intrigues
> And be schooled in bribery.

The final twist comes when the parents learn that the great task with which Hugo will be entrusted is to liquidate the very office of liquidation, thus putting himself out of work, a consequence Hugo is too naive or addled to grasp. The parents' anguished screaming is drowned out by rock music as the curtain falls.

This first version relied heavily on the comedic conventions of misunderstandings and a young man's quest for recognition. The main twist was to have the awaited guest, the director of Hugo's office, at first represent an off-stage *senex iratus* (the older man whom the hero has to challenge), then turn up as a *deus ex machina* (bearing the glad tidings of Hugo's special task), and finish as a tragic nemesis. In its initial form, *His Day* was probably good enough to be staged but not remembered, especially if compared to better, very political plays on offer in 1961–3 from Topol (*The End of Shrovetide*), Milan Kundera (*The Keepers of the Keys*) and his cousin Ludvík (*Total Cockcrow*), and even from Dietl (*The Accident*, in which a junior official protests the scapegoating of a section head for the bureaucracy's flaws, only to find himself made the new section head).[33]

Fortunately for Havel, Vyskočil left the Balustrade in 1962 after his methods triggered a mutiny by cast and crew. The new artistic director was someone Havel had long known from Kolář's Café Slavia crowd, Jan Grossman. It was Grossman who, in the 1950s, had introduced Havel to Franz Kafka's writing before it became fashionable, and *His Day*, like *Motomorphosis*, has many Kafkaesque touches. But with Havel the Kafka elements, like those from French absurdism, were made less devastating. Havel had already set a respectful distance from Kafka in 1958 when reviewing a Hungarian film, *Master Hannibal*, in which a mousy, Chaplinesque schoolteacher is destroyed by the inscrutable forces of a fascist society. While Havel saw obvious similarities to Kafka's *The Trial* and *The Castle*, he identified a crucial difference: Kafka's stories were rooted in an eternal, 'original ontology', the protagonists' fates reflecting the 'general tragedy of man in the world', whereas *Master Hannibal* indicted a specific regime, in which ideology falsified reality and debased human conduct, making everyone – even the teacher – co-responsible (s3, 227–42). Like Dürrenmatt's *Visit of the Old Lady*, Havel's plays would show a worst-case, but not inevitable, world.

Under Grossman's guidance, during summer 1962 and spring 1963 Havel radically reworked *His Day* into *The Garden Party*, such that the premises survived but the dialogue, pace and tone changed utterly. He gave the family a different surname (Pludek) and reduced the role of Petr (himself) to a brooding silence. He deleted the musical numbers that interrupted the original text, and converted a long interlude into a fourth act. In the process, the play became less a comedy of errors and more a study of the crisis of identity and communication. Accordingly, Hugo was made into an empty vessel standing apart from the rest of the characters, who remain the grotesque archetypes found in the first draft.[34] Whereas in *His Day* Hugo speaks in his own diffident voice, in *The Garden Party* he can only parrot the jargonized discourse of others. He advances through institutions just as he plays both sides of a chessboard in the first act, besting others in feats of formulaic, unavouched speech and mixing divergent viewpoints into the meaningless sludge Havel derided in an essay as 'dialectical metaphysics', not true dialectical confrontation (s3, 619–29). By the end, Hugo has so adjusted himself, synthesizing the identities of others, as to be unrecognizable to his family.[35]

The rewriting was necessary in part to get past the censors, but the result was a superior work more universal in its appeal. It was noticed by West German critics within days of its ebullient premiere on 3 December 1963, and by the following spring Havel was negotiating the rights to a German translation and production in West Berlin. In the process he forged a lifelong partnership with the publisher Klaus Juncker, without whom, Havel later surmised, he would never have become internationally famous (s5, 505). Translations into other languages followed, although the first English version took liberties in the belief that the text had to be made more accessible to British audiences.[36] No Czech dramatist had had a comparable breakthrough outside the Soviet bloc since Kohout

Stefan Wigger as Hugo and Lu Säuberlich as his mother, Božena, in the production of *The Garden Party* at the Schiller Theater in Berlin, 1964.

```
V A Z B Y



/1/

a  n  i  d  o  R          R  o  d  i  n  a
n           O          O              n
i    ...on  D          D  ona...      i
d           I          I              d
o           N          N              o
r  o  d  i  n  A       A  n  i  d  o  r


/2/

      R  a  d  i  n  A
   O                  N
   D           ...ona I
   I  on...          D
      N              C
      A  n  i  d  o  R
```

'*Vazby*' (1964).

six years earlier, and in coming decades royalties from the West
would be a lifeline for Havel and for the dissident community.[37]

    Eleven years after the Thirty-sixers held their founding session,
Havel was at last a published, performed and praised writer. And
eleven years after he first met Olga Šplíchalová at the Slavia, they
were at last married on 9 July 1964 in the town hall of her Žižkov
neighbourhood, with just two witnesses (one being Grossman).
After a meal at the Moskva restaurant – chosen, Havel later
alleged, because it was the only one serving meat on a Thursday
afternoon (s3, 602) – they honeymooned at an inn near the West

German border. Only then, five days after the event, did Havel notify his father, in a letter of searing candour. Havel defended their elopement as a command of his conscience to eliminate the 'schizophrenia, the kind of alienation, in which I have lived until now', too afraid to formalize the de facto marriage that had existed for eight years. He hoped he would now 'be truly taken seriously at home for the first time', otherwise he could not feel that he was taken seriously anywhere.[38] The language of the letter anticipated his later explanation of the dissident activities that forced him into confrontations he would rather have avoided but he felt he had to undertake to be true to himself: 'I married not in protest against my family, but in protest against my own half-heartedness [*polovičatosti*].'[39] The letter was directed not so much at V. M. as at Božena, who only slowly came to accept her daughter-in-law.[40] Havel rendered the fraught process into a typogram that played on the multiple meanings of the Czech word *vazba* (confinement, binding, coupling), as he (*on*) and she (*ona*) are at first separated by family (*rodina*) and then achieve an imperfect fusion (s1, 230).

Success in the theatre made Havel a very public figure overnight. Not yet thirty, he was now someone whom periodicals would call when canvassing intellectuals on issues and trends. Perhaps the most telling sign of his status was that he was now a target for parody: J. R. Pick, a past contributor to *Květen* and Vyskočil's early 'text appeals', rendered scenes from *Romeo and Juliet* in the style of several contemporary playwrights, such as Kohout and Kundera, and ended with the Capulets' reaction to their son's death as if they were the Pludeks from *The Garden Party*.[41]

Celebrity was not yet taking Havel into politics, for which he would have had to join the Communist Party or one of its satellites. But because his fame came from theatre, he was necessarily drawn into what he called *politićnost*, a sensitivity to 'the problems of man as a member of the human polis'. To Havel, theatre had a uniquely organic connection to social and political undercurrents, and thus a responsibility to provide an aesthetic reflection of 'how the world is organized' (s3, 819–21). That obligation was not, he stressed, a licence to browbeat audiences in the manner of Bertolt Brecht; the author need only make an appeal, posing a question without a ready answer but which otherwise might not occur to the spectator.[42] As the somewhat estranged observer, Havel preferred to take in the politics of his surroundings and 'witness it . . . report on it' matter-of-factly, hence his decision to publish his first plays and typograms under the title *Protocols*.[43]

Havel's next play, an exaggerated but not unbelievable bureaucratic horror story, was a perfect example of *politčnost*. Although generally regarded as his second major work, *The Memorandum* was really his first, since it had been in progress to some degree since Havel left the army. Its overlapping gestation with *The Garden Party* can be sensed in the plot of the first draft, from June 1960. Xiboy Rutvet, a young man living with his mother, receives a letter in an indecipherable language and traipses through a bureaucratic maze in futile search of an explanation. In despair, he goes to the river to commit suicide, but meets a kind secretary who translates the document for him. It instructs him to report to the very office that earlier turned him away, and he obtains a leading position in a new department. The secretary then seeks Xiboy's help when she is fired for having provided an unauthorized translation, but he ignores her plight.[44]

The strange language of the letter, Ptydepe, was based on an idea Havel got from his brother Ivan and to which he was already alluding in *His Day* and *Hela, Ela and Stop* (the women's fugue degenerates into words that include 'ksiboj', a homonym of the character's name). In *His Day* and then in *The Memorandum*, Ptydepe is presented as a highly precise artificial language designed to eliminate any ambiguities from official correspondence, but which no one knows how to read. With its elements of Kafka and *Faust* (the forsaken secretary is a Gretchen type that would

recur in many of Havel's plays[45]), *The Memorandum* was already
a more menacing work than *The Garden Party*. Havel was advised
by Vyskočil, the actor Miloš Kopecký and others not to pursue
it, since the early 1960s were not yet ready for such a work.

Buoyed by the success of *The Garden Party* and a belated but
palpable cultural thaw, Havel returned to *The Memorandum*. The
version that debuted at the Balustrade on 26 July 1965 retained
the premise of a man – now called Josef Gross – bewildered by
the receipt of a letter written in Ptydepe, but the story is situated
entirely within the nondescript office of which he is already the
director. It takes place in twelve scenes divisible into four segments,
each of which moves through three locations (Gross's office, a
Ptydepe class and a translation centre); this process gives it the feel
of an Expressionist 'station drama'.[46] The first six scenes depict
Gross's steady downfall at the hands of his deputy, Baláš, who
seems to have mastered Ptydepe, followed by a reversal and Gross's
equally steady re-ascent as it emerges that no one apart from a kind
secretary, Marie, actually understands the language. She interprets
the letter Gross received, which turns out to be an order to liquidate
Ptydepe. The play could have ended as a conventional comedy, with
Gross's apparent triumph over his rival and his new romance with
Marie, but this is Havel: Gross fails to come to Marie's defence when
she is fired for giving him unauthorized assistance – he offers her the
trite comfort that 'you are still young, you have all of life before you'
– and learns from his nemesis Baláš that a new artificial language,
Chorukor, is being introduced. We are left with the feeling that the
twelve-scene sequence is about to repeat itself as a *perpetuum mobile*.

Gross differs from Hugo in terms of essential flaws: whereas
Hugo is so lacking in identity as to be almost mechanical, Gross is
all-too-human, capable of love but even more capable of betrayal
in order to keep his job.[47] Like the townsfolk of Dürrenmatt's *Visit
of the Old Lady*, he has a knack for silencing his conscience in a
soliloquy of diabolical eloquence, and is thus more dangerous

than the brazenly cynical Baláš.[48] In the political switchbacks
of coming years Havel would be dismayed by how many of his
acquaintances were capable of Gross-like self-deception (s4, 400).

Like *The Garden Party*, *The Memorandum* was popular –
six regional theatres staged productions after its debut at the
Balustrade – although critics were more impressed by concurrent
offerings, especially Topol's *Cat on the Rails*, for which Havel's
friend Jan Tříska, in the male lead, won accolades.[49] Domestic
reception, however, was only part of the picture: Havel knew
that there would be an immediate West Berlin production, and
the text of *The Memorandum* was not shackled to a Czechoslovak
setting, despite its allusions to recent Communist purges and to
former president Edvard Beneš, whom Havel called the 'Gross of
Czechoslovak politics' (s4, 399). The male characters' identities
are not particularly Czech: Josef Gross could belong in a Kafka
novel; his rival Baláš's name is probably a derivative of Balthazar/
Belshazzar, common across central Europe (and occurring in the
Havel family); and the Ptydepe instructor, J. V. Perina, is J. V. Stalin
in his capacity as the author of *Marxism and Problems of Linguistics*.[50]

As always, Havel was having many personal experiences of
the bureaucracy that *The Memorandum* lampoons, but he was
also learning how to prevail under changing circumstances.
When the authorities denied the Balustrade troupe permission
to attend the West Berlin production of *The Garden Party*,
Havel and Grossman threatened a mass walk-out, which got
results: for the next five years, Havel was allowed to travel
almost at will. In 1965 alone, he went to West Germany,
Austria, Hungary and Yugoslavia; in 1966 to West Germany,
Sweden and Finland; to France, Britain, West Germany and
the United States in 1968; and to West Germany in 1969.[51]

Less happy but still instructive was the fate of a periodical
on whose editorial board he was invited to serve, *Tvář* (Face,
Visage). The monthly had been founded in 1964 to be, like

Květen, a platform for younger, less orthodox writers. *Tvář* soon ran into trouble, not only with the old guard but with moderately reformist Communists who were trying to take over the weekly *Literární noviny* and viewed *Tvář* as a sop to be thrown to the hardliners. To preserve its identity, *Tvář*'s board members tried the kind of quiet lobbying that Havel's parents had used to varying degrees of success, but also bolder methods, such as the formation of an informal pressure group (about sixty artists joined, with Havel as their leader), petition drives (for which Havel's connections were enormously helpful) and statements of solidarity solicited from university students.[52]

Havel also polemicized with a bête noire of the *Květen* years, the poet Jiří Šotola (born in 1924), who was now secretary of the writers' union that controlled the publication of literary journals. In June 1965, in the middle of the fight over *Tvář* and shortly before *The Memorandum* opened, the union held a special conference to mark the twentieth anniversary of the end of the Second World War. Šotola's opening address horrified Havel as an example of the muddied 'dialectical metaphysics' he had lampooned in *The Garden Party*, whereby an official acknowledges that socialism has had its problems but then deflects attention to its many achievements or to the shortcomings of the capitalist past or West (s3, 666–84). For this 'evasive thinking' Havel had coined the word *akorátismus*, which could be translated as 'yes-but-ism' or 'on-the-one-hand-on-the-other-hand-ism' (s3, 624). In remarks to the anniversary conference and in a series of related essays, Havel asserted that truth and good art emerge when people counterpose distinct, authentic representations of their experiences of reality, and do not rely on pretence, as he said Šotola's poetry did (s3, 686–93).

Šotola's peevish rejoinder was as evasive as the speech Havel had critiqued, hitting the mark only when it accused Havel of faddish enthusiasm for the 'authenticity' espoused by Jean-Paul Sartre or Martin Heidegger (whose essay 'Hölderlin and the Essence of Poetry' *Tvář* had just printed).[53] But in this battle it was not the quality of argument that mattered; the union in whose name Šotola spoke, and the Party ideologues breathing down his neck, had the upper hand. At the end of 1965, *Tvář*'s editors shut the journal down rather than make the changes demanded of them. The episode was a valuable trial run of tactics that would be used by dissident groups in the 1970s and '80s, in full awareness of their unlikely short-term success but potentially greater impact later. What he had put poetically in 1956 (see 'Saturday' in Chapter Two) Havel put analytically in an interview about *Tvář* in 1968:

> Very often a small task successfully carried out can have far-reaching consequences, because it can serve as a model or catalyst for further action . . . Thus the struggle for relatively unimportant and 'nonpolitical' goals can, under certain circumstances, have a very great – and political – significance.[54]

Owing to the international success of his plays, Havel enjoyed a grudging respect at this time among Communist apparatchiks: when denying him permission to attend the International PEN Congress in New York in 1966 for fear that he would draw attention to the fate of *Tvár*, they felt a need to mollify him by letting him jump the queue to buy a new car (a Fiat).[55] Even the Czechoslovak secret police, the StB, at first hoped to make him an accomplice rather than a target. In June 1965, after the writers' conference, Havel received an anonymous anti-Communist leaflet. Following his father's custom and Grossman's advice, he assumed it was a hoax to test his reaction and reported it to the police. Pleased, the StB dispatched two officers on 23 June to interview Havel at his home. The conversation was cordial and turned to his impressions of West Germany, to which Havel replied that while the standard of living was obviously higher, he did not care for the Western simplification of life's purpose to 'a full stomach and driving a car'. Even more pleased, the StB opened a file on Havel as a candidate for recruitment, to spy on an American professor of Russian literature who was coming to Prague.[56]

Before inviting someone to collaborate, however, the StB had to vet candidates for three months, and during that time they received too many conflicting signals to consider Havel suitable. Instead, in November 1965, they began looking for evidence that Havel was working with anti-Communist émigrés, in particular the publisher Pavel Tigrid in Paris and his primary contacts in Czechoslovakia, the writer Jan Beneš and the literature scholar Václav Černý (the original leader of Group 42). From February 1966 until March 1968, Havel would be under surveillance by means of a telephone tap and bug in the family apartment (recording 7,548 hours of conversation) and informers. At times of heightened interest he was tailed in the streets, on eighteen days in 1966 and fourteen days in 1967.[57]

When Jan Beneš was imprisoned in 1967, Havel was called as a witness and then undertook the kind of publicity campaign on behalf of a persecuted intellectual that would become all too common in coming decades. Havel was careful not to do anything that would be grounds for arrest, but ominously his request for permission to travel in western Europe and the United States in 1967 was rejected (although he was included in a delegation that toured the Soviet Union for three weeks in May, about which he wrote almost nothing other than a postcard to Šafařík from Lake Issyk-Kul in Kyrgyzstan[58]). From StB files it is clear that by the end of that year the regime was getting ready to frame a group of intellectuals as puppets of Tigrid and American diplomats, with Černý as the alleged mastermind and Havel as his adjutant.[59]

Fortunately for Havel, the ageing leader of the Communist Party – the same Antonín Novotný who had once defined the terms of acceptable satire – was forced by his colleagues to step aside in January 1968. Under his younger replacement,

Alexander Dubček, StB surveillance and censorship ground to a halt, more from confusion than by a direct order. One of the first new theatrical works staged in these suddenly freer conditions was Havel's next play, *The Increased Difficulty of Concentration*. Like its predecessors it had been through lengthy planning and revision, but in a different context: one of the benefits of Havel's association with the Balustrade was that he had finally been accepted, in 1962, to a part-time university course in dramaturgy. Although he was presumably reading widely in literary theory, and now preferred British over French theatre (he singled out Harold Pinter, Ann Jellicoe and a young writer of Czech origin, Tom Stoppard, as 'among the most influential playwrights in Europe'[60]), his new play was more faithful than ever to early sources of inspiration such as Shklovsky, Šafařík and Kolář.

Šafařík, to whom the play was dedicated, was no longer just the philosopher who wrote *Seven Letters to Melin* but also a friend and a sounding board for playwriting. He had attempted a few dramas of his own, including a troubling dialogue between a jailed writer and a prison warden about culture, fear and sex, which Havel read in 1966 while writing *Increased Difficulty*.[61] Šafařík was also producing a stream of essays, including one on 'Man in the Machine Age', for which Havel arranged a public reading in February 1967. An excursus on the inability of science to grasp the essence of being human, Šafařík's lecture had warned that 'precision is not truth. The living body – and thus art too – takes no pleasure in exactitude, because a number cannot be the key to its mystery.'[62]

The futility of trying to pinpoint what it means to be a person is symbolized in Havel's *Increased Difficulty* by the attempt of a well-meaning researcher, Dr Jitka Balcárková, to devise a battery of questions that would isolate an individual's unique or random attributes from those rooted in bigger patterns and regularities. This impossible endeavour is stressing her talking computer, Puzuk, to breaking point. (By coincidence, the play opened five days after the release of Stanley Kubrick's film *2001: A Space Odyssey*, with its similarly humanized and overtaxed HAL). No less absurd is Balcárková's selection of Huml, the play's central character, as a test subject. Born in 1928 and some sort of social theorist, Huml converses over the course of the play with his wife, his mistress and a secretary, whom he also tries to seduce while dictating a blandly sweeping treatise on values and happiness. He speaks to each woman with apparent sincerity but, when seen in the round, is not a consistent, concentrated person who can be summed up. Is he a thoughtful man looking for love? A lothario? A rapist? He initially takes Balcárková's questions seriously for fear that she and her team are secret-police officers in disguise, until he grasps that they are indeed scientists and explains with heartless but faultless reasoning that their project is doomed to failure. Reduced to tears, Balcárková is now just another erotic object to be conquered.[63]

Huml's inability to do anything but react to what his day throws at him is underscored by his given name – and the play's original title, *Eduard*, which recalls another hapless social scientist, President Beneš. Huml's unstable identity is reflected in the play's very structure, the most elaborate that Havel ever attempted, in the mould of Jiří Kolář. Thinking musically, Kolář had organized his poems as cantos in a sinfonietta, following each other in a careful, deliberate sequence.[64] But like many colleagues in Group 42, Kolář always thought visually as well, and after 1952 returned to his original medium, collage, as a reaction to the Stalinist debasement of language, to his visit to Auschwitz (seeing the assemblages of personal belongings, each representing a fate defying description) and to his growing feeling that 'man's destiny could never be explained and seized from a single point, or within a single perspective.'[65] His collages or 'crumplages' often contained printed words cut into strips or mashed, as 'when events and explosions of destiny crumple one so abruptly and profoundly that one is never able to smooth or iron out the consequences of those sudden storms'.[66] Anticipating the wave of visual poetry across Europe that inspired Havel's typograms, the collages also represented the fracturing of time that occurred in the poems of T. S. Eliot, in the poetic-realist films Havel had loved in the 1950s (such as Marcel Carné's *Le Jour se lève*) and in the stories of Alain Robbe-Grillet, which Havel listed among his favourite recent discoveries (s3, 157–66, 712).[67] Disruption of linear time was then common in Czech plays, but Havel would take it to extreme lengths.

In the thesis for his dramaturgy degree, Havel explained that he wanted his new play to explore the same questions as his previous works but do so in a way that would be less familiar and predictable to audiences and critics (s3, 711, 716–17). *Increased Difficulty* shows one day in a man's life, but if Havel had let the play run in a straight line, from breakfast to supper, it would have turned into a sex farce, like the comedies Werich adapted from Nestroy, rather than the hellish beehive Havel intended (s3, 725–6). Instead, it splinters time at 21 points according to Huml's encounters with the four women. Each relationship was coded as a separate plot line, usually with four to five scenes inserted out of order but following a geometric progression, in the spirit of Walter Benjamin's precept that 'the description of confusion is not the same thing as a confused description' (s3, 744). But as Havel revised the play between 1966 and 1968, he took out details that had enriched his initial draft, such as the questions Balcárková puts to Huml (when she asks him whether, under favourable conditions, he could be a good leader, Huml replies that he doubts it very much).[68] The finished work was colder than the essays of Šafařík, which took delight and comfort in rubato, the slight but perceptible variation in the rhythm of musical performances that symbolized the uniqueness of each person.[69]

Huml's deranged day was a Kolář-crumplage of the life Havel had been living for several years.[70] Even after his success with *The Garden Party*, Havel still had to perform a mix of jobs at the Balustrade, from the menial to highly conceptual.[71] Balancing

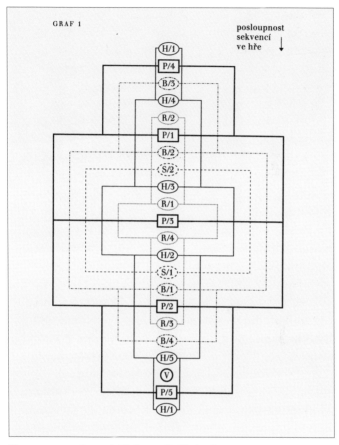

posloupnost
sekvencí
ve hře ↓

H/1
P/4
B/3
H/4
R/2
P/1
B/2
S/2
H/3
R/1
P/3
R/4
H/2
S/1
B/1
P/2
R/3
B/4
H/5
V
P/5
H/1

The arrangement of scenes in *The Increased Difficulty of Concentration* as set out in Havel's dramaturgy thesis, 1966.

those duties with writing, coursework, friendships, Olga and *politicnost* drove Havel to heavy smoking, alcohol (he crashed a car while drunk in 1966) and phenmetrazine, a stimulant he had discovered at the ABC.[72] Although the drug had fewer side effects than amphetamines, it stoked the tendency of his plays to descend into delirium.[73] (Baláš refers to phenmetrazine in scene nine of *The*

Olga and Havel, 1967.

Memorandum as a tool in the development of Ptydepe [s2, 170]).
It is also likely that the state of Huml's marriage corresponded
somewhat to the author's; when reporting his wedding by letter to
his father (who, biographers imply, was himself a loving but not
always faithful husband), Havel admitted to having already enjoyed
'the physical favours of other women'.[74] A screenwriter's diary
records Havel attempting a seduction in March 1967, although 'as
usual he did not succeed, as he is so terribly decent and polite.'[75]
A deletion from the final draft of *Increased Difficulty* was Huml's
revelation to Balcárková that he and his wife had had children who
had died; it may have been a tacit or unconscious acknowledgement
that Havel and Olga were unable to conceive a child of their own.

By the time *Increased Difficulty* opened on 11 April 1968, the
events known as the Prague Spring were in full flow. Havel regarded
the Communist Party's attempt at a controlled reform with
scepticism, as its success would depend on insiders who had lost
their Stalinist illusions, like the Kohouts and Šotolas he had been

baiting since the 1950s. Only months before, Havel had struggled in vain to get them to speak in defence of their fellow writer Jan Beneš, and at the union's congress in 1967 their belatedly demonstrative criticism of the government had upstaged his bid to revive *Tvář* (the StB recorded Havel griping that 'these writers are still Communists in sentiment'[76]). Havel took advantage of the collapse of censorship in 1968 to express his concerns in an essay published a week before the premiere of *Increased Difficulty*. He systematically dismissed as inadequate all forms of check on its power monopoly that the Communist Party was willing to entertain (such as by public opinion, media pressure or interest groups); nothing less than competition with a new political party would suffice. The scope of the opposition Havel had in mind was limited by Western standards: there would be underlying consensus on a 'national programme' of a humane, just society, with the new party focusing on the 'spiritual starting point', 'moral renewal', less bureaucracy and more compassion (s3, 838–40). The appeal was drenched in Šafaříkian talk of guarantees and avouching, but the language of Josef Ludvík Fischer and V. M.'s efforts to elevate the interwar republic to a 'quality democracy' could also be heard.

Havel then departed, without Olga, for a six-week trip abroad, in part to do research on Czech émigrés. He also attended the opening on 5 May of his first American production, *The Memorandum*, at Joseph Papp's Public Theater in New York; he stayed with Werich's original partner, Voskovec.[77] When he returned to Czechoslovakia via Paris, events were approaching a critical stage: as Havel had feared, many of the top reformers in the Party were having cold feet about what they had set in motion and Soviet leaders were signalling a readiness to prevent 'counterrevolution' by any means. At this point, Havel crossed the line from *političnost* into politics, for which Communist Party membership was briefly unnecessary. He threw himself into the reform of the writers' union, aiming to convert it into a loose constellation of autonomous grouplets; chaired a Club of Independent Writers and co-founded a society of non-Party intellectuals; endorsed the refounding of the social-democratic party that in 1948 had been forced into a merger by the Communists; chaired the board of the revived *Tvář* (although quarrels with other members lessened his appetite for the job); and agreed to serve as an editor, like his grandfather Hugo, of the long-defunct daily *Lidové noviny*, which was set to resume printing in the autumn.[78]

After a summit of Soviet and Czechoslovak leaders at the beginning of August seemed to reduce the threat of military intervention, Havel and Olga, like many Czechs, went on holiday. On the morning of 21 August they were visiting friends with the actor Jan Tříska in the northern town of Liberec when they learned that a massive invasion by the USSR and its allies was under way. They joined the local civil resistance, for which Havel wrote fiery appeals that Tříska read on underground radio and television, directing the people to stymie the occupiers, shun or arrest collaborators, and prepare for a campaign of sabotage and clandestine communications (s3, 857–65). The appeals displayed an instinct for operational detail that eschewed violence in order to claim the high ground against illegitimate force, a skill that would re-emerge when Havel contributed to the formation of dissident groups in the 1970s and the revolutionary movement of 1989.

Although they used the language of moral superiority, Havel's Liberec addresses were at pains not to lull listeners into inaction; in this regard his broadcasts were very different from the radio speeches his grandfather Hugo had given in 1938 during the Munich crisis, in which capitulation had been rationalized as a Christ-like self-sacrifice 'for the salvation of Europe'.[79] The similarity to the earlier crisis lay only in the people's willingness to resist; as Havel told one Czech émigré shortly thereafter,

> It was maybe the only week since 1938 when the whole nation was really united, when all were courageous, everybody

Havel in New York's Central Park, 1968.

spoke the truth, when people were very kind to each other, when the smartest ones became natural leaders, when true democracy existed, and all social barriers disappeared.[80]

In 1968, it indeed seemed that 'the discipline of conscience' might prevail over the 'discipline of the pistol' (s3, 864). Like most of the country, therefore, Havel was baffled when Dubček returned from talks in Moscow with only a vague promise to salvage what little he could in return for public acceptance of 'normalization' – in effect, reform's slow death at the hands of those who had introduced it.

For the rest of the year and into 1969, Havel argued strenuously against the idea that only one path of 'realism' could be taken at such times, the reactive path of tactical retreats; reality, Havel told a gathering in November, was not just the presence of several thousand foreign soldiers on their soil but also the wishes of fourteen million Czechoslovak citizens, who through history had often been more willing than their leaders (for example, President Beneš) to take risks.[81] In his first published meditation on what it means to be a politician ('False Dilemma', in December 1968), Havel reminded the country's leaders that they always retained some power to shape the conditions in which they operated, and with that power came responsibility. In turn, citizens had a duty to develop a 'positive programme' of 'being for something or for oneself or one's true interests' (s3, 866–74). As he told a university magazine, 'If someone says that we can do nothing because the world is divided, that would be as absurd as if someone said that we should all commit suicide because at some point we're going to die.'[82] When shortly after that interview a student, Jan Palach, in fact chose an especially horrific form of suicide – burning himself on Wenceslas Square – to shock the country into action, Havel went on television to plead that no one follow suit. However, he interpreted Palach's act as an 'appeal' and 'truly moral and political message' to be heeded, especially by collaborators with the invasion, whom Havel named and urged to leave public life.[83] Havel also inserted references to Palach into an acoustic collage of snippets of speeches, conversation and music that he was compiling with the help of a radio studio in Liberec.[84]

Because intellectuals had a prominent role at such turbulent moments in Czech history, Havel was horrified by the seductive reasoning of Milan Kundera's Christmas essay, 'The Czech Lot'. The two writers' relations had always been uneasy. Kundera was part of the Kohout-Šotola generation and Havel had already taken a swipe at him in 1956 in *Květen* (s3, 58). In 'The Czech Lot' Kundera praised his compatriots for their resistance to the invasion – 'the week the nation suddenly beheld its own greatness, in which it had not dared to hope' – and subsequent refusal to break ranks and allow a new 'police regime'. That conduct alone had earned a place in the history books, and he saw no reason to press Czechoslovakia's beleaguered leaders to stay on the course of reform, because the destiny of the country would be decided, as ever, by greater powers. In one all-night sitting, Havel drafted a riposte that defended the people's right to insist on assurances of liberties, on taking responsibility and deciding one's fate. To make the general more personal, Havel argued that Czechoslovakia was located within the Soviet sphere not by blind geographical necessity but because people like Kundera in his youth had put it there (s3, 894). Like Šotola four years before, Kundera parried ad hominem, alleging that Havel was a moral exhibitionist whose identity as the victim of class warfare depended on adverse and 'abnormal' conditions. Kundera then fell silent, but Havel and others continued the exchange in ways that anticipated debates that would take place a few years later on the purpose of dissent.[85]

In the last hurrah of the Prague Spring, writers gathered in June 1969 to reorganize their union in line with the only constitutional change that the Soviets would tolerate: the conversion of the centralized unitary state into a federation of the Czech and Slovak

Havel with miners at the Klement Gottwald works in Ostrava, June 1969.

republics. Slovak writers had long had their own branch, and now the Czechs had to create a counterpart, with the poet Jaroslav Seifert as their chairman. Although by this point censorship had been reinstated and all progressive journals had folded or would do so soon, Havel made a rousing appeal for the Czech union to use every lawful means at its disposal to challenge acts of the state and to forge a united front with workers and students. He knew those moves would make little immediate difference, but he feared the longer-term moral consequences if writers forgot Seifert's injunction to tell the truth (s3, 902–9).

Havel was far from alone: the students and workers to whom he referred had persisted doggedly in various forms of protest. On 19 June 1969 he appeared at a packed rally of miners in Ostrava, a major industrial centre in northern Moravia. Such gestures, much as they would have pleased the younger Havel reading Whitman and Sandburg, were increasingly in vain. With the approach of autumn, Havel had the minor consolation of knowing that, as twelve years earlier, he and his brother were both about to go away, this time to America. Ivan would be starting doctoral work in computer science at the University of California at Berkeley. Havel had definitively turned down, on 26 August 1969, the offer of his own academic base as a writer in residence for a year at the University of Iowa, in favour of a grant of almost $10,000 from the Ford Foundation that would allow him and Olga to spend six months meeting 'with American directors, playwrights, critics and theater historians'.[86] The itinerary had yet to be worked out, but Havel had proposed a month in New York, followed by a road trip 'opposite to the clock-hand direction [*sic*]' that would take in Harvard, San Francisco and Berkeley, Hollywood, Las Vegas, New Orleans and Cape Kennedy.[87]

They would first travel on 10 September to Vienna to collect an Austrian state prize for literature, and then fly two days later to New York. At the last minute, however, only Ivan was allowed to leave. As Olga later recalled, she and Havel had thrown a going-away party at their new farmhouse 130 kilometres east of Prague:

> Vašek and I were sleeping on the floor on straw mattresses
> – we let our guests use the beds – and suddenly at around
> six in the morning a man appeared, pulled Vašek by the
> leg and said, 'Passport control!' It was the police, they'd
> come to take away our passports. Vašek was apparently
> dreaming right then that we were on a boat to America
> and someone was checking our documents.[88]

Havel and Olga decided that if they could not leave the country, then for the time being they would not leave the countryside.

4

To Hrádeček and Dissent (1970–79)

In the early 1970s, Havel and Olga had several reasons to avoid the city to which they were so intimately connected. The first was that Havel had been tipped off to the resumption of StB surveillance of Engels Embankment 78. After the turmoil of the Prague Spring, when many StB officers had sided with Dubček's reforms, there was capacity at first to monitor only around a dozen households intensely, but Havel's was one of them: the electronic bug removed in March 1968 was reinstalled in November. One of the technicians, however, got word to a painter, who in turn met Havel in a church to pass along the details.[1] With the help of Olga's nephew, Havel staged the discovery of the device on 21 January 1969 while mounting a new ceiling light. He called witnesses, filed a formal complaint and demanded a police investigation, all of which he recounted in a literary weekly (s3, 880–86). This highly legalistic approach fitted the Havel family's custom of making at least pro forma appeals against state decisions, his own disposition (he often described himself as a pedant with bureaucratic tendencies) and his post-invasion resolve to take action. In the larger scheme of things, it anticipated what would become the main strategy of dissent in coming years: pressing the regime to honour its legal commitments and embarrassing it if it did not.

Even if the exposed bug was temporarily disabled, its discovery added to the reasons to dwell elsewhere. Havel and Olga had joined a building cooperative, at the time the only option for private citizens

outside the state construction monopoly. They would have a floor
of a plain row house, Number 4 in U dejvického rybníčku, a quiet
side street in western Prague. The process was slow and the flat
would not be ready until 1970. In the meantime, they emulated the
thousands of other urbanites who were finding refuge in the country.
One such was Andrej Krob, whom Havel knew from military service
and backstage work at the Balustrade. Krob owned one of the half-
dozen cottages at Hrádeček ('little castle'), so named for its proximity
to the ruins of a fortress, in an area cleared of its German residents
at the end of the Second World War. Havel and Olga had visited
in 1966 and the following year bought an adjacent farmhouse.[2]
At first they used it for weekends and summer entertaining – a
Havlov for less glamorous times – but as they progressively fixed
it up, it became a year-round alternative to the quarters they had
been sharing with Havel's parents, brother and his bride. A friend's
diary records, 'At the beginning of June [1970] we were at Hrádeček
staying with Vašek Havel. He doesn't go to Prague, at most for
two or three days out of every fourteen.'[3] Another visitor, a British
drama critic, filed this impression of the farmhouse in late 1969:

> A record of *Hair* was loudly pounding away inside. The
> whole place was a defiant temple to Yankee decadence,
> with protest buttons and psychedelic posters on the walls,
> and a Flower Power sticker on the outside privy. Havel
> met us at the door, much fattened with potatoes from his
> garden, wearing an old West Point sweater he had bought
> in New York for a dollar. He clearly is not giving in.[4]

Admittedly, the situation at Number 78 was changing: Ivan
and his wife were in the United States, and Božena died of cancer
on 11 December 1970, two weeks after having attempted suicide
to end her agony.[5] But it was not just the living arrangements
in Prague that were off-putting. By March 1969, after a year of

increasingly political involvement, Havel found that it was only at Hrádeček that he could even try to write, because in the capital he was diverted by unceasing 'talks, meetings, duties and various pressing activities' that he felt obliged to undertake out of the 'stupid feeling' that they might influence the course of events.[6] His connection to the Balustrade had ended, in part because he wanted more independence (which royalties made financially possible), and because the theatre's manager no longer wanted to be associated with him, with Grossman or even with Olga. Havel was facing his first indictment for subversion, owing to his signature on the 'Ten Points' petition of August 1969, which had appealed to the country's authorities to return to the path of reform. His trial was cancelled at the last minute in October 1970, since he was not one of the petition's organizers; his absence from Prague may also have been taken as a sign that he would avoid such gestures in the future. The charge, however, was left pending.

In his study in the back of the farmhouse, looking out onto a Chekhovian landscape of a 'softly rising slope dotted with fruit trees' and a birch copse beyond, Havel tried to focus on continuing as a world-renowned playwright.[7] But he could not just follow the formula that had worked in the first half of the 1960s. Critics had feared it was growing stale even before Havel lost the connection to the Balustrade, with *The Increased Difficulty of Concentration* stuck in a 'one-sided poetics' leading to a 'dead end'.[8] This defect was not unique to Havel but symptomatic of a general crisis of Czechoslovak theatre, which since 1965 had been drifting into inward, often highly allegorical or fairy-tale motifs.[9] Havel realized that the Soviet invasion and Dubček's eventual downfall had marked the end of the world that he had entered around 1956, a world that had been easy to navigate, 'a bit comical, a bit wobbly, and very Biedermeierish'. The new world that had suddenly replaced it was 'Asiatically tough' and Havel at first was experiencing it too directly as a participant to be able to assess it with his characteristic 'irony, grimace or cool

Havel in his study at Hrádeček, 1974.

analysis'. The theme of identity in crisis would remain relevant, but without the 'oral juggling' of the early plays; there could be no joking about liquidation offices at a time when real purges were again sweeping through. The 'fun was over' (s4, 151–2).

For this darker time Havel found guidance in the work of the German-born psychologist Erich Fromm, who had lectured in Prague in 1966 and whose book *The Heart of Man* was translated into Czech in 1969. What had disturbed Havel in the years since the Soviet invasion was not the intimidating presence of foreign armies so much as the ease with which many Czechs and Slovaks had convinced themselves of the need for 'order', 'normalization' and 'consolidation' rather than freedom. Fromm had studied this mindset in the context of fascism, from which he extrapolated a general type, the necrophile, 'a new type of man; he can be described as the *organization man*, as the *automaton man*, and as *homo consumens*', a personality with an unhealthy attraction to mechanistic, quantified, bureaucratized order.[10] For the necrophile there exists a fundamental polarity, 'the powerful and the powerless', and the necrophile is erotically drawn to the powerful because they can dominate, hurt and kill.[11]

The idea of the necrophile's flight from freedom informed Havel's first post-invasion play, *The Conspirators*. It focuses on five characters, four of whom represent the coercive state (police, general staff, procuracy and censor), and they have recently taken part in a revolution to overthrow a colonial dictator, Olah. They are not accustomed to the hurly-burly of democracy, and too quickly start to fear that Olah will exploit student unrest and the prime minister's waffling so as to orchestrate his return from exile. In their overreaction, they form a 'committee to defend freedom and democracy' and set in motion precisely the sequence of events they wanted to prevent. In his commentary on the play, Havel stressed that the group undertakes every step sincerely, but in doing so they allow an evil to emerge that always lurked in their necrophilic need for undue assurance. Their lack of avouched truth is reflected in the stilted speech even of their private conversations. When the prime minister reports word of an organized conspiracy against the democracy, the five lack the self-awareness to realize that the rumour has been spawned by their own meetings; they are 'like a dog barking at the echo of its own barking' (s4, 27). It is a dark take on the comic gag Havel had anatomized in an earlier essay, an action boomeranging back on the agent (s3, 412).

In response to the rumour, the five characters resolve to form an even smaller and more secretive 'revolutionary council'. In vain they cycle through nine of ten possible three-person configurations, each one undermined from within by the characters' lack of discernible intentions and trust. As one of the conspirators notes, none of them can take power alone but each can thwart the taking of power (s2, 404). In line with Fromm's Freudian analysis, the driving force is the Eros of the widowed Helga, who never seeks power for herself but for whichever man of the moment she finds attractive, to the point of sadomasochism. (This is Havel's only full-length play in which a woman tops the list of characters, but one of several in which the sex is rough.) At wits' end, the five welcome Olah back to save them from themselves.

The play naturally reflected recent events in Czechoslovakia set in motion by the brutal dispersal of a student protest in late 1967 that precipitated the downfall of Novotný, and ending several months later with the decision of several of the very men who overthrew him to invite and abet the Soviet invasion. There are also traces of the more distant past, such as the crisis restrictions on liberties enacted in interwar Czechoslovakia (see Chapter One); Havel described the character of the prime minister as a Benešite 'politician of appeasement' (s4, 47). But Havel did not want foreign audiences to take the play as a parody of Ruritanian intrigue, just as *The Memorandum* was not an office farce. To emphasize its universal themes of identity crisis and automatism in discourse, Havel located it in an unnamed country that could be in the Middle East, Latin America or Africa, and the characters' names are a mix of biblical, Teutonic and Ptydepic (including a judge called Xiboj, Josef Gross's forerunner).

After the actor Jan Tříska tried and failed to get permission to stage *The Conspirators* in Prague, Havel could only hope that a Western theatre would take it. One promising lead came from Kenneth Tynan, the literary manager of the National Theatre in London, in February 1971. Tynan had met Havel in Prague and wanted to commission a new play, in which Laurence Olivier could appear. Havel eagerly offered *The Conspirators*, which was already roughed out. Initially pleased with the play's premise, Tynan was disappointed by the final draft that arrived in October 1971, which he felt dwelled too much on dynamics within the group and not enough on the tension between the group and what they think is an Olahist conspiracy (but is just their echo).[12] After Harold Pinter turned down an offer to direct it, the play languished until it was staged in West Germany in 1974.

This tepid reception, so different from what Havel was used to, reinforced the doubts about the play that he expressed in his 1972 commentary (S4, 59). What Havel as a young reviewer had said of someone else's play – that it sounded like the 'transcript of a congress of people who are pathologically over-politicized' (S3, 357) – could be said of *The Conspirators*. Havel's misgivings caused others to place it beneath his earlier work.[13] But author and critics were too harsh; even if it is not an easy play to perform, it deserves no less than any of his to be read, as does his commentary, which represented the first of five major political essays he would write over the next fifteen years. It certainly holds up better than another play Havel was writing off and on in the early 1970s, *Mountain Hotel*. A throwback to pre-invasion tastes, bearing a strong resemblance to his cousin Jan Němec's allegorical film *About the Party and Guests* (1966) and to Robbe-Grillet's screenplay for *Last Year at Marienbad* (1961), it was a mechanical assemblage of interchangeable persons and verbal fugues that confirmed the exhaustion of Havel's stock techniques.[14]

Mountain Hotel was written for himself, the one-time lab technician, to test the limits of his 'anthology of dramatic principles' (S4, 157; S5, 120), and Havel admitted that he was at a disadvantage when he could not visualize a specific group of actors or attend rehearsals. Fortunately, even in the bleak 1970s he had a few opportunities to write in more encouraging conditions, with commensurate results. The first was an invitation to adapt John Gay's 1728 satire of politics, commerce and collaboration, *The Beggar's Opera*, for Prague's Drama Club. Havel took to the commission with gusto, as one of the club's leading actors, Pavel Landovský, was a longtime drinking companion. Havel had already developed a taste for British eighteenth-century humour, with Laurence Sterne's Tristram Shandy one of his (and Olga's) favourite literary characters (along with Don Quixote, Meursault from Camus' *The Stranger* and Pierre Bezukhov from Tolstoy's *War and Peace*).[15] He preserved the characters and London location of Gay's original and its premise of the moral equivalence of the criminal underworld and polite society, while mapping its plot twists of double-crossing and dissembling on a grid of careful symmetry (two halves of seven scenes each).[16]

To transform the operetta into a fully Havellian work, he converted the original's songs into the apologias of his earlier plays, in which a male character eloquently rationalizes a decision to ignore the commands of conscience.[17] The language is incongruously erudite and legalistic, a smokescreen behind which the characters try to ascertain each other's true intent, set traps and strike pre-emptively. Although universal in its theme, Havel's *Beggar's Opera* ingeniously captured the mood of early 'normalization', a time of prevarication as the StB rebuilt its informer networks and Communist Party members waited to see who would be expelled. The play's absurdly bureaucratic criminal organizations mirrored the restoration of central planning, which before 1968 had been scaled back to make way for market forces; the only positive male character, Filch, is a freelance criminal who refuses to join a bigger outfit and avouches his authenticity by going to the gallows. Šafařík read the play in draft and praised Havel for pushing the 'dramatic principle and technique' of his earlier works up to, but not beyond, their 'maximum effectiveness and load-bearing capacity'.[18] Of all the plays Havel derived from classic inspiration, his *Beggar's Opera* was the best, and was perhaps also the best of all his plays.

For years Havel lamented the lack of a translation that would allow his *Beggar's Opera* to be staged in Britain and the United States 'so that the excessive reception of my other plays be balanced by greater attention to this seldom-performed play of mine, about which I have – which is a bit comical – fewer reservations than any of my other plays' (s5, 496). He would have to wait almost thirty years until one was undertaken by Paul Wilson, the most astute of Havel's translators into English. Havel did not have to wait so long to see the play performed in Czech, although this was not at the Drama Club, for which it was now too risky. Instead, Havel's Hrádeček neighbour Andrej Krob obtained the approval of the local authorities on the very edge of Prague, in the suburb of Horní Počernice, for his amateur troupe to stage it in a tavern's social hall. It is not clear whether the officials grasped that the text would not be Gay's, nor would it be another famous adaptation, Brecht's. Havel had observed secret rehearsals at Hrádeček and provided Krob with pages of detailed advice, so he was delighted with the performance that took place on Saturday, 1 November 1975, before 300 guests. Olga remembered it as the best theatrical night of her life, and it may have been Havel's as well.[19]

The authorities soon knew about the performance – a local official had come to watch and alerted the StB – but the resulting retaliation might not have been so severe had Radio Free Europe, an American-funded station broadcasting from Munich, and the West German weekly *Der Spiegel* not reported the show as part of a new 'offensive' by intellectuals to which the regime had so

The cast of *The Beggar's Opera* at Hrádeček, 1975. Havel is leaning against a tree on the left.

far responded 'sheepishly'.[20] Havel signalled to the government that he would get foreign journalists to stop crowing if Krob and the cast were left in peace; although he apparently held up his side, the authorities did not, and all involved were fired or expelled from universities. Actors whose only offence was to have been in the audience – such as Landovský and Tříska – were let go from theatres with which they had been long associated.[21]

The use of Hrádeček as a rehearsal site was not uncommon at the time; Havel and Olga often hosted informal arts festivals and mini-congresses of banned authors there as a way to overcome their social isolation and channel their theatrical energies. At any time in the summer of 1975 the house had at least ten guests, for whose amusement Havel started to write a trilogy of one-act plays that drew on recent personal experience. The first was inspired by the need to make money owing to a legal dispute with DILIA, the Czechoslovak copyright agency, which levied confiscatory fees on foreign royalties. His earnings were down in any event, as there had been fewer productions and translations since 1970; for the first time in years, Havel felt financially straitened. After several unsuccessful enquiries, in February 1974 he found a brewery in nearby Trutnov that was willing to take him on. Like his military service, the work was menial but socially important, as it re-exposed Havel to the daily lives of ordinary, apolitical people. He was relieved that he got along well with his workmates, whom he impressed when a famous but also blacklisted singer, Marta Kubišová, dropped by to see him.[22]

After nine months Havel no longer needed to work in Trutnov – he successfully sued DILIA – but drew on his impressions to write *Audience* in June 1975. In the play, Vaněk, a banned playwright working in a brewery, is summoned by his foreman, Sládek (which can be both a surname and a title, Maltster). Sládek appears to like Vaněk but his own record of petty crime is being used by the police to make him an informer, so in a spiral of increasing inebriation he begs and browbeats Vaněk to give him some titbit that he could pass along. Vaněk politely but firmly refuses; Sládek dissolves in self-pity. The play ends ambiguously, with the empathetic Vaněk restarting the dialogue from the beginning but perhaps willing now to give Sládek what he needs. In essence a V+W *forbína* between a clown and a straight-man, *Audience* was written in two days with no grand design; it is the Havel play that most directly imitates everyday life and – probably for that reason – the one that most deeply wormed into the Czech psyche, such that Havel would hear its tag lines parroted back to him by diners in restaurants or by hitchhikers on the road to Hrádeček (s4, 578). It owed this popularity to a bootleg recording made in 1978 of Havel reading Vaněk and with his friend Landovský cast perfectly in the role of Sládek, one of the few Havel wrote that allowed an actor to shine.[23]

Encouraged, Havel quickly wrote another one-act play, *Vernissage* ('sneak preview', 'private viewing' or 'unveiling'). This time the intellectual, referred to only as Bedřich (but presumably Vaněk again), visits a couple, Michal and Věra, at their newly refurbished apartment. It is a ghastly ensemble of knick-knacks, gadgets and antiques straight from Havel's essay 'Notes on Being Half-educated' (1964), which lambasted people who felt the need to appear cultured through a feverish, random accumulation in line with 'the most varied, most incompatible and wholly incoordinate values' (s3, 636). Bedřich's hosts have thrown themselves into their nest and their work as an escape from reality; they neither support 'normalization' nor see the point of resisting it. Like Sládek, they claim to care for Bedřich but cannot accept him on his terms: they urge him to ditch the company of outcasts, father a child and enjoy life as they claim they do. Like Sládek, they lurch from smiles to tears to rage as Vaněk's taciturn intransigence pushes them towards awareness of an existence as vacuous as the one Havel depicted in *A Family Evening*.[24] It is not even clear why they have invited him: Michal at one point seems to tempt Bedřich into a fling with Věra – might it be a police-ordered honeytrap for blackmail, or a symptom of the couple's dependence on external validation? Bedřich resists but, as in *Audience*, avoids a complete rupture: he makes to leave, only to return. As the curtain falls Michal subjects him to the pop tunes of Karel Gott, a fate almost as gruesome as the murder of a nonconformist poet by his hosts at the end of Topol's *Nightingale for Supper* (1967) or the mutilation of a dramatist, Vavák, in Havel's radio play *Guardian Angel* (1963).[25]

The third Vaněk play, *Protest*, was not written until 1978, but was based on events from six years earlier. After the 'Ten Points' manifesto of 1969, the opposition to the post-Dubček regime was limited primarily to a fringe farther left of Havel, consisting of purged Communists and Trotskyites. By 1972, almost fifty of them were in prison. Pavel Kohout, the poet-playwright who had turned into a fierce critic of the system he once served, organized a petition asking President Ludvík Svoboda to include these prisoners in his customary Christmas amnesty. Havel, one of six signature collectors, approached other writers, who produced every conceivable excuse not to sign – that it was futile (Kundera); that it would endanger his latest television serial (Dietl); that in the current geopolitical situation Czechs should not engage in pointless heroism (Zdeněk Mahler, a screenwriter born in 1928). Šotola, the former chair of the writers' union, at first agreed to sign but then backed out. In the end, around 35 people did put their names on the petition, which the president ignored.[26]

That episode, and the meetings with Dietl and Mahler in particular, were transformed by Havel into a dialogue between Vaněk and Staněk, a writer approaching fifty (thus born around 1928) who harbours no affection for the post-1968 regime but has adjusted to it so that he can continue to work. He has contacted Vaněk for help in pressing the authorities to release a detained singer, who has impregnated Staněk's daughter. Vaněk reveals that a petition is already in the works but that it is not too late for Staněk to add his name. To avoid doing so, Staněk puts Vaněk on the defensive, as Sládek, Michal and Věra had done, suggesting that it is Staněk who has the harder lot as someone toiling within the system to improve it – a claim that rings hollow in his well-appointed home. Staněk delivers a feat of exculpatory rationalization like the flawed men in Havel's previous plays, but taken to extraordinary lengths – five pages in the collected works (s2, 665–70). News then arrives that the musician has been released and the petition is no longer needed. Staněk is off the hook, but in Vaněk's catalytic presence he has revealed himself as someone capable of titanic self-deception in order not to jeopardize his access to the public. From the dialogue it is clear that Staněk works in television, a medium Havel, in an essay of 1975, derided for its stupefying illusion of mass intimacy, 'making a new animal species out of us, the *herded televisual human*' (s4, 111–12).

Of the people Vaněk visits, only the maltster Sládek is quite so dulled; they are all well-meaning and consider themselves to be no less conscientious and responsible than Vaněk, whom they regard – as Kundera did Havel in 1969 – as a moral exhibitionist. Indeed, over time, it was these pragmatic opportunists who hollowed out the socialist system, paying lip service to its doctrine while pursuing their selfish ends with countless unintended consequences.[27] But it was also they who, by their automatism, kept the system going up to the point of its sudden collapse. They represent the path Havel did not take after 1968 but could have, as symbolized by the few letters that separate Vaněk's surname from Staněk's.

It was at this time, between working at the Trutnov brewery and writing the first Vaněk plays, that Havel reached an important decision about his own options. He could no longer merge smoothly back into the system as Staněk (or Dietl) had done unless he undertook a humiliating public recantation; some writers, such as Šotola and even Havel's beloved Bohumil Hrabal, did so in 1975 in order to get published again. Another option, the one chosen that year by Kundera, was emigration to the West; with his uncle Miloš's fate in mind, Havel did not entertain it. A third option was to carry on in Hrádeček's endless weekend, rising at midday after long nights of carousing or reading forbidden books from émigré and underground publishers or struggling to write without the impetus of a director or deadline. While that existence had had its appeal, as a respite from the frenzied Balustrade days, by the middle of the decade it had run its course. Just as ten years earlier he had married Olga to end the torment of avoiding what he felt a duty to do, so in 1974 he prepared to end the unsatisfying limbo of the banned but unmolested (and forgotten) writer.[28] As before, he would set out his reasons in writing to a male authority figure – not his father this time, but the general secretary of the Communist Party.

The phenomenon of the letter to a country's top officials was hardly new in the Soviet bloc: Polish and Russian intellectuals had been writing them since the mid-1960s, and other Czech and Slovak dissidents had already issued several since 1970.[29] Havel himself had written one, to Alexander Dubček in August 1969, at a time when the personification of the Prague Spring was no longer leader of the Party but was still visible as speaker of the federal legislature. Havel feared that Dubček was too loyal a Communist to object publicly to the increasingly harsh 'normalization' unless others pressed him 'to vouch personally for his truth' (s3, 926). At that point, approaching the first anniversary of the invasion, Havel knew that Dubček could not alter the country's direction; instead, he was thinking about the long-term benefits to morals and morale if a respected politician acknowledged his co-responsibility for a deplorable situation: 'The sudden assertion of genuinely human criteria in a dehumanizing world of political manipulation can act like a flash of lightning that brightens the obscured landscape' (s3, 929). Dubček did not follow Havel's advice but kept his own counsel, neither defiant nor repentant, as he steadily fell farther from power and into his own limbo as a forestry official in his native Slovakia.

In late 1974, Havel began to compose an even sterner reminder of a politician's responsibility to Dubček's successor as Party leader, Gustáv Husák. Like many, Havel had had mixed feelings about Husák's rise to power in April 1969: he already disliked Husák's fondness for tough talk (and had said so in a telegram to President Svoboda, urging him not to let Husák push the country back into 'police terror') but privately admitted that he considered Husák more competent than Dubček.[30] Husák posed as something of an intellectual (a lawyer by training, a historian by fancy); his first wife had been a theatre director and he had spent the 1950s in prison as a victim of Stalinist power struggles.[31] While pledging never to take the country back to conditions that had caused him great suffering himself, Husák was committed to reimposing firm control, especially on the media and intelligentsia, in order to revive the centrally planned economy.

By the time Havel was finalizing his letter in spring 1975, Husák could claim to have met his goal, and was about to cap it off by ousting the ailing president Svoboda and taking his place in Prague Castle. With the additional title would come even greater responsibility, which Havel saw as grounds to caution Husák that the country's outward calm was based on indifference, opportunism, surveillance and fear – not the terror of the 1950s but the 'existential pressure' of losing the life chances valued in a modern society, such as access to education and meaningful employment. It was a fear that could be felt not just by a Staněk, Michal or Věra, but by everyone from Sládek up to the highest official. Marxist ideology had been reduced to a 'conventionalized ritual-communication system', masking the consumerist escapism that the regime quietly encouraged owing to its distracting, stabilizing effect. Although Havel had long denounced socialism's attempt to replicate Western materialism, in his earlier essays he did so from beyond its reach; now, in middle age, it was a more personal matter of renouncing the life he and Olga had been leading as the homemakers of Hrádeček.[32]

Using Fromm's framework of necro- and biophilia, Havel contrasted the entropy of the mechanistic, homogenizing state against nature's instinct for diversity, novelty, self-organization and 'the transcendent'. The language of his letter was appropriately organic, likening the regime's impact to castration, ravishment, enfeeblement and anaesthesia, and the concomitant moral crisis to impotence, sterility, boils, pus, vitamin deficiency, carbon monoxide and lava. At some point, he warned, the irrepressible forces of life would erupt in a 'tornado' and take leaders by surprise because censorship had muffled the arts and the press – society's early-warning system (s4, 67–108).

Havel posted the letter to Husák on 10 April 1975. Hunkered down at Hrádeček, he waited for reprisal, but none came – even after the Party leadership, the Præsidium, discussed the letter and were advised that Havel had committed subversion by sending copies to Western press agencies, which had begun to print excerpts within days. He may have been spared again because his abstract social-moral analysis – his second, after the *Conspirators* commentary – troubled the Præsidium less than the more concrete complaints

Havel and Olga in the kitchen at Hrádeček.

issued at that time by Dubček and other expelled Communists, whom they feared as a rival leadership in internal exile.[33]

For the time being the brunt continued to fall on leftists outside the Party and on underground cultural movements that enjoyed no international protection. During the 1960s the authorities had tolerated (or been powerless to suppress) a proliferation of rock and pop bands, but in the early 1970s began to insist that only groups licensed by the state could perform. A few of the 3,000 that failed to get permission, such as The Plastic People of the Universe, persisted in playing and by 1972 were under intense StB scrutiny. Ivan Martin Jirous, an art historian who acted as manager and lyricist for The Plastic People, was sentenced in 1973 to the first of the five prison terms he would eventually serve. Havel was already acquainted with the other minds behind The Plastic People's deceptively coarse music (such as Jiří Němec, a psychologist and Catholic philosopher, and Egon Bondy, a poet-philosopher inspired by Marx, Fromm and Buddhism) but he did not meet Jirous until March 1976.[34] The Plastic People and nine other underground bands had just put on a festival, using Jirous's wedding as cover, and now he and 21 musicians and concert organizers were facing prosecution for 'disorderly conduct'. The crackdown quickly provoked an outcry from Amnesty International, but Jirous also sought a show of solidarity from Havel and other Czech intellectuals.

Although he had grown out his own hair and a moustache, Havel was straight-laced in comparison to the unwashed Plastics, and his musical tastes ran to mainstream Anglo-American rock and Czech 'tramping' ballads sung by scouts and nature walkers. However, he immediately sensed the importance of defending the underground as a matter of artistic freedom and authentic self-expression; Šafařík had warned in *Seven Letters to Melin* that sometimes the true creators of culture seem to lead 'uncultured' lives.[35] Havel can be faulted for romanticizing the Plastics as noble savages; from his version of events it is not apparent that these were skilled musicians familiar with the verses of William Blake, Edmund Spenser and Jiří Kolář, and that some were ardent Christians.[36] They were the free-spirited youngsters of Topol's *Their Day*, now grown up and creating a chiliastic community indifferent to 'the material security that the Establishment offers'.[37]

But Havel was not a disinterested witness; he was a combatant in a public-relations campaign against the state media's depiction of the accused as crazed drug addicts.[38] Havel's account of the trial of Jirous and three musicians in September 1976 is a masterpiece of estrangement, describing it as Tolstoy did Natasha's visit to the opera in *War and Peace*: the proceedings are viewed from a naive remove in order to expose the judge's bias and the prosecution's ill-prepared case, which even a Communist apparatchik described to Husák as 'a fiasco'.[39] With its normally intimidating conventions defamiliarized, the trial becomes the confrontation of those who avouch their own truths and those who rely passively on the 'collective vouching of colossal social power' (s4, 136–41).

Havel was also getting caught up in the underground's penchant for mythology and self-mythologizing, and his essay on the trial was an origin story for the dissident community that was coalescing around the Plastics' cause.[40] He first had to overcome friction with the musicians' principal advocate, the philosopher Němec, which dated back to their days together at *Tvář*; once the air was cleared, they recruited around eighty other philosophers, scholars and writers to sign declarations in support of the Plastics and to seek similar statements from famous Western intellectuals. Their efforts seemed to pay off, in that charges were dropped against all but seven of the arrested; those who were tried received sentences that, while still unjustified, were not as stiff as they might have been.[41] The atmosphere of the courthouse in Prague's Malá Strana district intoxicated Havel, as dozens of supporters whose paths would not normally have crossed mingled in the corridors and stairwells. Old divisions between once- and never-Communists melted away. As part of his own journey in this unfolding fairy tale, Havel felt that he was now crossing over for good: 'All at once I was appalled by a whole world, in which – as I realized at that moment – I had still had one foot', a world of emergency exits through which a half-hearted person could always duck out (s4, 140).[42]

After the trial, strolling around Malá Strana as the Thirty-sixers once had, Havel and Němec deliberated on the best way to convert their ad hoc coalition into a lasting form of advocacy. As was the case with open letters, there was nothing novel in this: a Society for Human Rights (SLP) had been founded in May 1968, with Havel a member, and it survived a year.[43] In the autumn of 1976 the SLP founder, Emil Ludvík, noticed that the Czechoslovak government had finally promulgated the United Nations International Covenant on Civil and Political Rights and its sister Covenant on Economic, Social and Cultural Rights, which had been signed by Czechoslovak diplomats in 1968, approved by the federal legislature and ratified by President Husák in 1975. They had taken effect on 23 March 1976, but it was their appearance in the government's gazette on 13 October that made their expansive guarantees easily citable. Ludvík pointed out this opportunity to another former SLP member, Ladislav Hejdánek, a philosopher and recently freed political prisoner. Hejdánek in turn brought up the UN covenants at a strategy meeting in Prague on 10 or 11 December (sources vary about the date) that brought Havel, Němec and Kohout together with expelled Communists such as Zdeněk Mlynář, a lawyer and one of the architects of the Prague Spring.[44] Over the next ten days a rather dry but mutually acceptable statement was composed, pointing out the many ways in which the Czechoslovak government violated its covenant obligations. It also announced the formation of Charter 77, an 'informal and open society of people of various persuasions' that would seek 'constructive dialogue' with the state by documenting and reporting violations of rights, suggesting remedies and offering its services as a mediator.

The Charter's founding document was not a pure Havel text; he provided the first draft, but the final one – like the Barrandov Group's manifesto of 1933 – was deliberately a collective work. As noted above, Havel did have a legalistic streak, and the new group's mission to research, record, report and try to redress wrongdoing fitted his nature as the fourth-floor poet gazing on the city below. However, the initial statement lacked reference to finding and telling the truth as a moral undertaking that wells up from a person's intense experience like poetry or good acting; that perspective would be provided by one of the Charter's first spokesmen, the philosopher Jan Patočka.[45] Havel's connection to Patočka was long in the making: at sixteen, he had gone to great lengths to obtain, and read 'with feverish excitement', Patočka's seminal 1936 essay 'The Natural World as a Philosophical Problem' (S4, 171). Later he attended some of Patočka's lectures and heard him speak as Ivan Vyskočil's guest at the Balustrade. As a non-Marxist phenomenologist Patočka had an uneasy place in academia, at times allowed to teach, at others only to work in research institutes even as his international reputation grew. In 1972 he was forced into retirement but continued to hold private seminars, often in artists' studios, and he had been keen to come to the defence of the Plastics in 1976 (as were the poet Seifert and the literature professor Václav Černý, who also signed the Charter). When it was decided that Charter 77 should have three spokesmen, so as not to put the burden all on one, Patočka, like Havel, was a natural choice. He did not hold the position for long – he died in March 1977, his already poor health undermined by flu and several long police questionings – but he managed to produce two essays on the Charter as an ethical as well as legal enterprise.[46]

Although Havel welcomed Patočka's moralization of the Charter and contributed to the veneration of the late philosopher as part of the group's narrative, Patočka's influence on him should not be exaggerated.[47] Of the philosopher's enormous, difficult corpus,

Havel may have been familiar with just the works that appeared in the mid-1970s from underground presses, in particular the *Heretical Essays* ('a "history of the soul" from ancient Greece to the modern era that highlighted the struggle to transcend creaturely life'[48]). The 1936 essay on 'The Natural World' had not opened the adolescent Havel to new ideas so much as it reinforced inclinations he already had. Its singular impact was to provide the elements with which Havel developed his idea of home (*domov*), but even here he did not follow the philosopher slavishly. For Patočka, home was a part of the world that mankind experiences bodily and imprecisely, in contrast to the abstract world of scientific measurement; for Havel, home grew out of a modesty before nature, in contrast to the drive to master and manipulate it through technology and modern agriculture.[49]

In terms of Havel's intellectual development, Šafařík was always the greater influence, but by the mid-1970s their friendship was under strain: Šafařík believed that Havel should just write plays and neither compromise with nor antagonize the authorities.[50] When Ivan Havel asked him to sign the Charter, Šafařík refused, but not from cowardice: he had recently endured months of StB interrogation for involvement in an informal writers' circle and knew how badly harassment could disrupt an artist's work. As he said to Paukert, who was also being questioned, 'If everyone is going to be doing politics, who will be left for culture, who will create?'[51] Havel indirectly replied to this question in prison in July 1980, by reflecting on the Polish film *Con amore*:

In essence, it was about there being situations when an artist has to put aside his art in order to do something good in life, perhaps something inconspicuous, by which he does not earn a place in history but which is an expression of some moral imperative or simply of love for people. The film also contained the rather optimistic idea that the artist

Havel entertaining important friends from his youth at Hrádeček. From left to right: Olga, Ondřej Hrab, Havel, Jiří Paukert (Kuběna), Josef Šafařík, Josef Topol, Anna Šafaříková and Zdeněk Urbánek.

who is capable of putting aside his art for the sake of life – at least for a while – is ultimately, in at least a certain regard and for at least some people, a more interesting artist than one who would sacrifice anything for his art – that kind later sacrifices his art too, because he strips it of meaning. (s5, 142–3)

Patočka, born in the same year as Šafařík (1907), was thus a surrogate provider of the validation Havel needed while taking such a momentous step.

When news of Patočka's death reached him, Havel had already been in police custody for two months. The drafting of the Charter's text and the collection of 241 signatures had gone surprisingly smoothly, either because they took place away from sites normally under surveillance and over holidays when fewer officers were on duty, or because the StB wanted to let the group emerge so that it could then crack down on it.[52] In any event, once Havel and others began to distribute copies of the Charter on 6 January 1977, the StB sprang into action, starting with a hair-raising car chase around Prague that became part of the Charter's lore. Over the next week, Havel was called in for hours of questioning in Ruzyně prison as prosecutors (and Husák's Præsidium) tried to come up with legal pretexts for suppressing the Chartists. By 14 January they felt they could make a case against Havel by linking him to the smuggling of manuscripts to émigré publisher Pavel Tigrid via a courier who, it turned out, was an StB informer. Havel at first feigned ignorance; only when witnesses implicated him did he confess, on 25 January. Havel had handled hostile questioning in the past, in connection with Jan Beneš's arrest and the 'Ten Points' manifesto, but never before had he been caught in a lie.[53]

Despite the confession, the StB did not yet have enough evidence to establish a connection to Tigrid that would stand up even in a kangaroo court. They kept Havel in indefinite detention, questioning him for six hours at a time, at first daily but then weekly as the sessions reached the limits of their utility. With no prospect of a resolution and Olga not allowed to visit until 25 March, Havel fell into depression, requested sedatives and rapidly lost weight.

By April he was ready to work out an understanding, whereby he would live at Hrádeček – he had never felt at home in the new Prague flat and loathed its heavy, 'bourgeois' furnishings (s5, 43) – and would dedicate himself to writing plays. He would not publicly renounce his views or actions to date but he would cease to act as a Charter spokesman and do nothing that could be used in the domestic or foreign press to foment conflict: 'I consider myself a writer, and while I have and can have views different from official views, I do not consider myself a "dissident", that is, some sort of professional opponent of the regime.'[54] Any advocacy on behalf of a person or cause would be conducted privately or by litigation, unless an extreme case required more visible methods. In essence, he would return to his pre-1975 hibernation, but he would do so on his terms.[55]

At the insistence of his interrogator, Havel outlined this offer in writing on 6 and 22 April, but asked that the regime not publicize it after his release. While he was in detention the state-run media had subjected the Chartists to the same character assassination as they had the Plastics in 1976. In March Havel was singled out for attack in a highly tendentious account of his life, broadcast on the radio and then reprinted in several newspapers, that relied on anecdotes from a minor writer who had informed on him in the mid-1960s. The regime's propaganda strategy was to accentuate the Chartists' small numbers and lack of social base, in contrast to the mass protests that had recently shaken neighbouring Poland. At the end of January 1977, hundreds of smartly dressed entertainers, writers, musicians, artists and architects assembled at the National Theatre in Prague to hear a proclamation committing them to 'creative deeds in the name of socialism' and denouncing the 'little group of recreants and traitors' that 'isolate themselves from their own people, its life and true interests'. In coming weeks many more – perhaps 7,500, or about thirty for every Charter signatory – signed it at their workplaces. The names, published in column after column of the daily press, included celebrities such as the pop singer Karel Gott, the screenwriters Dietl and Mahler and the poet Šotola, but also people closer to Havel such as Karel Brynda (the co-author of his army play) and, from his ABC days, Miloš Kopecký, Miroslav Horníček and Jan Werich.[56] Some, such as Werich, claimed that they had not realized the ulterior purpose of the proclamation as an 'Anti-Charter' and regretted their association with it. Havel was always outwardly forgiving, as he knew that everyone was conditioned to sign whatever officials shoved at them lest their careers suffer (S4, 528). But he did not want his discharge from prison to be part of this media onslaught.[57]

A savvier StB or Party Præsidium would have honoured his request and let Havel slip back to Hrádeček and into obscurity, but they could not resist the temptation to exploit the material he had given them. On the day he walked out of Ruzyně prison, 20 May 1977, the state press agency issued excerpts of his 6 April statement, edited to sound more penitent than it actually was. The report appeared the next day in the Communist Party's paper next to the equally devastating news that Zdeněk Mlynář, the most important ex-Communist in the Charter, was emigrating to Austria. As planned, Havel relinquished his position as a Charter spokesman and returned to Hrádeček, but did so at a loose end, learning belatedly the lesson of his uncle Miloš that it was vanity to think he was clever enough to do a deal in private and control how it would play out in public.

Rebuked by several (but not all) prominent Chartists, Havel now felt released from the terms he had offered his captors and obliged to make amends. On 1 June he sued the informer cited in the media attacks on him in March, and by 18 June had conceived of three new Vaněk plays (*Protest* was the only one he completed).[58] In October he hosted a festival of underground music in the barn at Hrádeček; an even larger gathering was held there the following April.[59] In the summer of 1978, Havel and several other Chartists met covertly in the nearby Krkonoše mountains with representatives of KOR, a Polish committee for legal aid to workers arrested after the protests in 1976. Out of those encounters came a commitment to produce a joint collection of essays on dissent, for which Havel would write the introduction.[60] By the time the text was completed in October, it had become his third major socio-political analysis, 'The Power of the Powerless'.

The most famous of Havel's essays, it was also the longest and most ambitious iteration of the critique of modern culture he had been developing over 25 years. He was now writing under the influence of Patočka's *Heretical Essays*, Ivan Sviták's humanist-Marxist exposés of totalitarian manipulation,[61] Aleksandr Solzhenitsyn's 1978 Harvard address, and the *Der Spiegel* interview with Martin Heidegger published in 1976 (and translated by Patočka).[62] Owing to its intended reach beyond Czechoslovakia,

'The Power of the Powerless' downplayed the responsibility of individual leaders and focused instead on the effect of ideology. By ideology, Havel understood what in the cybernetic/structuralist heyday of the 1960s he had called 'the code', a form of communication that had originally imparted information but over time became automatized and fetishized, reliant on bureaucratic nomenclatures and unspoken connotations, a self-serving ritual rather than a means to natural discourse (s3, 697–8). The purpose of modern art, Havel had said, was to disrupt stultifying conventions and re-expose authentic facts, as underscored by the title of a collection of his typograms, *Anti-codes* (1964).[63]

'Power of the Powerless' accordingly defamiliarized the everyday practice of ideology, in part by utilizing a dozen metaphors (ideology was like a pair of gloves, a low-rent home, glue, a veil, an alibi and so on), in part by deconstructing gestures of acquiescence in the same way Havel had anatomized the comic gag and the trial of Jirous and the musicians.[64] The essay's most cited passage, regarding a greengrocer's placement of a sign reading 'Proletarians of all countries, unite!' in his shop window, is another feat of estrangement, deciphering the sign's message not as an endorsement of the regime and its principles, but a 'talisman'[65] that really says, 'I, greengrocer xy, am here and I know what I must do; I behave in the way that is expected of me; I can be relied upon and am beyond reproach; I am obedient and therefore have a right to a quiet life' (s4, 231). Ideological language allows people to send these humiliating signals in ways that preserve their self-respect while creating conventions enforced from below and from within, which Havel called 'mutual totalitarianism, that "self-totalitarianism" of society' (s4, 244). Just as Havel's letter to Husák had said that everyone, even the country's leaders, was trapped in fear, so were they imprisoned by this ideology, no matter how powerful they might think themselves. Just as Havel in 1958 had said that even the meek schoolteacher shared responsibility for the fascism depicted in

Master Hannibal, so in 1978 was everyone an accomplice in 'normalization', no matter how powerless they might think themselves.

But it was precisely that 'self-totalitarianism' that Havel saw as grounds for hope. The system depended on mass compliance, and thus could be undone in countless ways by ordinary people. If the greengrocer is the oft-mentioned culprit of the essay, the overlooked protagonist in section fourteen is Jan Špalek, a master brewer Havel met at Trutnov in 1974.[66] Špalek took his craft very seriously and wanted his coworkers to do likewise. His proposals for improvement, however, were resented by the complacent director, who had Špalek demoted and denounced. Simply by demanding a higher-quality production of beer, Špalek had exposed the limits of the system and been thrust, willy-nilly, into dissent. This fate could befall anyone with a shred of integrity, and these initially unseen, unreported incidents could snowball into a more structured, independent 'life in truth' (s4, 280–84).

Havel knew from the experiences of the now 800 people who had signed the Charter that the consequences of living in truth were more easily borne in community. This, too, Havel turned into a virtue: the self-help networks that arose under socialism represented a form of *polis* that the West could also learn from, as they protected persons from a whole way of life – the manipulative consumerism found on both sides of the Iron Curtain (s4, 289–90). Rather than despair, like Heidegger in the *Spiegel* interview, that 'only a god' could save humanity from the 'planetary predominance of the unthought essence of technology', Havel wagered on the 'moral reconstitution of society' through small, open, ad hoc groupings, which relied not on formal procedures but on the 'full existential avouching of each member' (s4, 326). Havel hoped to see these fluid grouplets evolve into an authentic 'humane order' very much like that found in his teenage optimalist writings: a 'post-democratic' politics without a bureaucratized state and mass parties; an economy of employee-managed enterprises; a culture of unmuzzled expression (s4, 319–27).

The delivery of 'Power of the Powerless' to Warsaw in November 1978 coincided with Havel's return to acting as a Charter spokesman and his involvement in the Charter's heated internal debate about its mission and methods.[67] It was also a time when the StB was trying either to prevent visitors from reaching him at Hrádeček or, when he was in Prague, to keep him under house arrest at the apartment in U dejvického rybníčku, where his car was vandalized and phone disconnected (s4, 335–44, 368–74). The pressure was part of an StB umbrella operation launched in January 1978 to intimidate Chartists into silence or emigration; by 1985 at least twenty, perhaps dozens more, had left the country as a direct result.[68] Violence to persons and property was common, and Havel's friend Pavel Landovský moved to Austria in January 1979 after his leg was broken in a ferocious attack. Landovský had had an earlier scrape with the police exactly one year before, when a group of Chartists attempted to attend a publicly advertised ball held by railway workers in Prague. Once the StB realized what was afoot, they and the police intervened with undue force, and took Landovský into custody. Havel came along as a witness on his behalf, only to end up arrested for allegedly insulting an officer. He was taken again to Ruzyně prison and detained for six weeks until the state conceded it had no case (s4, 205). Kept this time mainly with men, many of them Roma, who were being charged with 'parasitism' for not being conventionally employed, Havel found it easier to bear captivity and felt no need to make concessions to get out.

Several Chartists, some with their own experience of imprisonment, had created a body to demand the release of Havel and Landovský, and in April 1978 they converted it into a permanent Committee to Defend the Unjustly Prosecuted (VONS). Like KOR in Poland, VONS would be a combined legal-aid charity and publicity campaign on behalf of individuals – on

Havel and Olga, 1978.

average two people a week for the next ten years – whose plight
otherwise would get no attention.[69] While less central to its
creation than he had been to the Charter's, Havel did his part by
drafting the brief announcement of its founding, raising awareness
of cases, facilitating financial support from abroad and giving
money to the families of prisoners.[70] When the government
decided to suppress VONS, Havel was one of ten representatives
it targeted for arrest on charges of subversion, for allegedly
trying to undermine public confidence in the justice system.

The police raid on their residences occurred at dawn on
29 May 1979, but at U dejvického rybníčku no one was home.
A team descended on Hrádeček but found only Olga, who said
she did not know her husband's whereabouts. She probably did,
but the truth would have been awkward to admit. Havel was in
Prague, and had stayed out the whole previous night dining with
other VONS members and watching The Plastic People of the
Universe film a video near the Vyšehrad citadel (Havel had a go
on an improvised drum set of pots and oil barrels).[71] Around noon

the next day, he headed not to his flat but to one at Matoušova street 12, directly across the river from the Engels Embankment and belonging to Anna Kohoutová, the ex-wife of the playwright and Chartist Pavel Kohout. Anna was not Havel's first mistress, and Havel's infidelity was not unique; few marriages withstood the strain of dissent, and it was customary to seek new sexual partners within the network. Olga remained the intellectual and practical crutch she had always been, but accounts suggest that, starting with Kohoutová, Havel was transferring marital emotion into parallel relationships; he later described 'Andulka' as 'a rare creature, full of love and incapable of hate' (s5, 250). Like Olga, she was older than Havel (by four years) and he pursued her as he had Olga, starting in July 1978 at a fiftieth-birthday party for Kohout. Anna, like Olga, at first resisted; however, being a single mother struggling to get by as an underpaid assistant on Dietl's television serials, she welcomed his affection. They became lovers towards the end of the year, by which point Kohout had left for Austria with his third wife.[72]

After the police tracked Havel down at Anna's flat, he was taken to his own to witness an official search for 'writings of an anti-state character'. While it was in progress Havel asked whether he should add one pack of cigarettes or a whole carton to the prison kit bag he always kept ready; an officer advised him that he was going away for a long time. Havel, characteristically, thanked him, and at 8 pm was officially delivered into StB custody.[73] He would not be back for almost four years.

5

From Trial to Castle (1979–89)

In the summer of 1979, awaiting trial in the 'permanent sauna' of Ruzyně prison (s5, 11), Havel sent the first of what would eventually be 165 letters to Olga. Under prison rules he could write no more than one per week; they had to focus on 'family matters' and avoid mention of politics. Ever the micromanager, Havel advised (and nagged) Olga on the upkeep of Hrádeček, the content of the parcels and letters she would be sending him, and her preparation emotionally and physically for the one hour, four times a year, that she would be allowed to see him. There were also words of tenderness, many of them omitted from the collection that would later be published, as he made an effort to repair the marriage he had damaged by his philandering. Through these letters, however, he also spoke to Anna Kohoutová, for whom he still had unconcealed affection; to his brother; and to the many well-wishers who sent him postcards. His letters were thus doubly public documents, in that they would be scrutinized by the state before delivery, and by the dissident community with which Olga would share them upon receipt.[1]

Like open letters, prison letters were a well-established literary genre in central Europe, and like Kolář's diary-entry poems Havel's weekly messages would have a careful order.[2] They can even be read broadly as '*explications du texte* for all the rest of Havel's writings . . . a metaversion of his other texts, the underlying code for the more concrete and context- or genre-specific manifestations of his thinking'.[3] The imperative of the first letters was to assure his wider readership that he was in good spirits and not about to repeat the mistake of 1977, for which he felt fated to atone. He knew that the prison sentence, when it came, would be a long one, punishment not so much for his relatively marginal role in VONS as for all his other deeds since 1969. He assured Olga that he would bear it 'without harm to body or soul' and that it would be 'mostly just an awful drag'.[4]

Two events disturbed the wait for the trial. The first was one Havel had been dreading since the death of a parent at the start of the decade: the death of the other, on 22 July 1979, from a pulmonary embolism. Havel was allowed to attend his father's funeral, which he feared would disrupt the emotional equilibrium he had achieved in prison. To his surprise, he felt fortified, returning to his cell all the more convinced that 'I am not here pointlessly and that everything has some sort of meaning'.[5] The other development was the regime's offer of emigration, thanks to an invitation from Joe Papp's Public Theater to come to New York. The vivid dreams Havel was having in prison mostly took place in childhood locations but were populated by adult friends in exile, such as Landovský, Jan Tříska and Miloš Forman, who in real life were encouraging Havel (through Olga) to accept Papp's offer. Havel had now been in custody as long as he had been in 1977 when he offered to slip into internal exile, and he wanted to avoid a similar lapse of judgement (S5, 35). After discussions with Olga and Ivan, he resolved that he would go abroad only if he was sentenced to five or more years; at the VONS 'monster trial' in October, the judge gave him four and a half.[6]

Havel could now focus on the 'new sense of time and altogether new concept of life' that prolonged captivity entailed (S5, 51). He adopted the attitude he had taken to military service twenty years earlier: if it could not be avoided, then he would make the best of it – as an opportunity to study English and German and work on a new play and as a rupture that would allow a 'certain calming down' at home on his return (s5, 14). If anything, he welcomed the forced sabbatical from the nerve-wracking life of a dissident: 'I am somehow returning to earlier times, I will be thrown into the world in the same way as when I was a lab technician, a stagehand, a soldier, a student. I will have my number, I will be one of many, and no one will expect anything from me or notice me in some exceptional way' (s5, 64–5). He even delighted in his convict's haircut, which symbolized both his anonymity and the goal of regaining the ebullience of his youth (s5, 84).

Although he insisted that the planned 'self-consolidation' and 'reconstitution' were not as 'pathetic, nor as absurd, nor as religious' as what an imprisoned hero in a Dostoevsky novel would undertake (s5, 52), Havel's letters did steadily acquire a more philosophical and spiritual quality. This development was a consequence of the derailment of his original plans for study and playwriting, owing to conditions at the first prison to which he was sent, Heřmanice, near Ostrava (where he had rallied with miners in 1969). He had the company of two other convicted VONS members, and did his best to follow both the formal rules and the folkways of the 400 inmates. Largely petty criminals, on the whole they were well disposed to the exotic political prisoners and, like Sládek in *Audience*, were impressed by Havel's personal acquaintance with celebrities (s5, 167, 223). To his jailers, Havel's demeanour was 'to a certain degree ingratiating, refined' but also 'not self-critical', and they delighted in disciplining him eight times over eighteen months for minor infractions (almost all of them involving books, letters or photographs).[7] Punishments ranged from temporary loss of privileges (receipt of parcels, access to television and films) to stretches of five to fifteen days in harsher confinement. By all accounts Havel was never physically abused, but the frequency of these sanctions, combined with the impossibly taxing work he was expected to do as a welder at the nearby ironworks, quickly took its toll.[8]

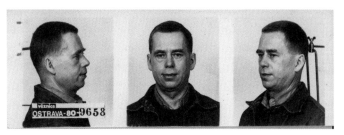

Havel after his assignment to Heřmanice prison, 1980.

Havel, as was his wont, made the most of legal channels, and in September 1980 won assignment to more suitable work with a cutting torch. He came to like it, looked forward to it on dull Sundays, and even tried to win distinction as a 'model worker' (he fell short, impeded by tendonitis). He also developed a defensive 'self-care' regimen during the summer of 1980, to strike a balance between detachment and engagement with his surroundings. He focused on diet, sleep (with the help of a secret supply of diazepam), yoga, a daily tea ritual and a detailed cataloguing of his moods and ailments (s5, 165–72, 255–330). Given that, at around 170 centimetres (5 ft 7 in.) in height, he was not physically imposing, Havel liked to think of this mind-calming 'self-mastery' as 'true manliness', and he commented to Olga about fellow prisoners who outwardly looked tough but were prone to breakdowns and 'thus are not real men at all' (s5, 221, 249).

In the course of these self-ministrations, Havel scaled down his ambitions: he would be content just to leave prison approximately the same person he had been when he entered, show that he could endure his lot and regain the trustworthiness he feared he had jeopardized in 1977 (s5, 331, 490). Memories of the people and simple pleasures of his pre-prison daily life – his 'concrete horizon' – lingered like an amputee's phantom limb, but he tried to turn more to the unseen 'absolute horizon' that was the 'source of my hope, the reason for my sacrifice' (s5, 198–9). Without his library or the company of learned friends, these first meditations were tentative and unsustained, drawn from memory of Šafařík and Patočka's *Heretical Essays*; Havel feared that they would earn no place in literary history (s5, 161). During the first half of 1981, according to informants in Havel's midst, he was anxious, cautious and withdrawn, trying to decipher from newspapers what was happening in the outside world, especially Poland. He was rattled by the transfer in April of the other VONS defendants to different prisons, and by the detention of Ivan and Olga for several days in May over their involvement in underground publishing.[9]

For a big change to take place in Havel's psyche and letters, a moderate one first had to take place in his circumstances. At the end of July 1981, nearly halfway through his sentence, he was moved to Bory prison, in Plzeň, 100 kilometres west of Prague. Although Bory had been notorious for its cruelty during Stalinism and Havel had visited his suffering uncle Miloš there, he found its nineteenth-century, panoptic star layout more to his liking (s5, 339).[10] Assignment to work in the prison laundry gave his aggravated lungs and elbows some relief, and a haemorrhoidectomy in September 1981 temporarily ended 25 years of intermittent torment. As he recuperated and adjusted to the new surroundings, Havel produced what in effect was a second draft of his ontology. He dipped back into Erich Fromm's lexicon to posit an entropic, homogenizing 'order of death', which responsible persons resist through the 'order of spirit', a virtual permanent record of every human attempt to find meaning in life, especially through art. He ended the year with a series of reflections on theatre as a focal point (*ohnisko*) uniquely able to take its participants – the playwright, actors and spectators – down an unpredictable path of spiritual adventure, unlike Dietl's television serials (s5, 405).

Even this second cycle of metaphysical letters, however, did not please Havel; his observations on theatrical community were just a restatement of claims he had made long before, as in his 1968 essay 'Special Features of Theatre' (s3, 801–29). To dislodge him from these furrows, a change also had to occur in the messages being sent to him by his brother. Ivan's first 46 letters were mostly brief and, to conform to prison rules, focused on family news and his own professional interests (artificial intelligence, theoretical physics). However, as he got a sense of what his brother needed and what would be let through, from December 1981 Ivan became a conduit for essays written or translated by members of seminars he held at Engels Embankment 78 and attended in apartments near the Kampa island that had been home to Werich and Holan, who had died within months of each other in 1980. The 'Kampademy' combined outcast professors and curious autodidacts united by attraction to Patočka, Plato, Carl Jung and Catholicism; the member who would engage the most keenly with Havel, Zdeněk Neubauer, was a microbiologist by profession and a theologian by calling.[11]

Exposure to Kampademic discourse, which in Neubauer's case was so eclectically erudite as to verge on the incomprehensible, at first deflated Havel. But then, on reflection, he regained confidence and resisted their pressure to translate his experience of the 'absolute horizon' into conventional religious terms. He had had this debate once before when, as a teenager with Voltaire's *Philosophical Dictionary* to hand, he had explained to Jiří Paukert why he was neither a materialist nor a Christian:

To wit: I am primarily against the word 'god'. I can't help it, it is a personification, making God in a human image. All human qualities are attributed to him, the necessary consequence of which is that they all take the form of superlatives – the greatest good, the most just, etc. . . . I prefer to call it – I don't know who proposed it – the 'world reason' that governs the universe, or the rationality concealed within the Universe, the Absolute, the summation of ideas (Platonic, of which I am an avid devotee), an absolute truth unknowable to us, a summation of abstract laws governing the universe, all the causes and effects, the timeless summation of truth, which is divided by matter into time and understood by (material) man in time, an abstract 'truth of the past', objective reality, things in themselves, etc. etc. All one supra-material principle, which takes concrete shape in the material, relative world, our world is its image and is governed by it. But unlike you I call it not 'someone' but 'something'; 'someone' was created by primitive religions, when people willy-nilly attributed inexplicable things to a being that was similar to them but, of course, was 'the most . . .'. And Christianity took on this idea. And I would dare to say that that a religion of 'something' could someday become the successor to Christianity.[12]

Writing almost thirty years later, Havel explained to Neubauer via Olga that a term like 'God' misrepresented the absolute horizon by reducing it to an ultimate source, prime mover or creator. He preferred 'Being' (*bytí*) because it was a verbal noun, and thus more fluid and more easily associated with duration, presence and omnipresence.[13] (*Bytí* is the most frequent noun in the published letters, occurring 446 times.) Havel's absolute horizon was eternal, judging ceaselessly without a Last Judgement. It had more in common with his grandfather Vácslav's astral plane, V. M.'s Masonic cosmology, Havel's adolescent pantheism and his more recent taste for best-sellers by American doctors on near-death experiences.[14] And much of what Ivan's philosopher friends were saying, Havel noted with wry satisfaction, suggested they were simply coming around to where Šafařík had been decades before.[15]

A still stronger push came courtesy of the 'flying university' of Western academics who were able to enter Czechoslovakia and hold secret seminars. A Dutch scholar, Theo de Boer, lectured on the French thinker Emmanuel Levinas in March 1982, and Ivan took detailed notes. Suspecting that its title would appeal to Havel, Ivan obtained a translation of Levinas' short essay 'Without Identity' and copied it over the course of two letters in April.[16] It immediately sent Havel into his third and finest sequence of meditations.[17] While ironing sheets in the prison laundry, he worked out sixteen instalments – letters 129 to 144, from May to September 1982 – that would supersede all his previous efforts (s5, 515). He told Olga that he wanted the sequence to be 'a "dramatically" (or "musically"?) composed whole, having an effect at once by its substance and its expressivity – and the substance and expressivity of a wayside chapel, not the particular bricks of which it is constructed' (s5, 686). In effect, Havel was applying to his letters the process of his poetry and revisiting his poetry's theme of the tension between individualism and belonging. He arranged his thoughts around poetic moments of sudden encounter, be it with the natural world (a distant treetop that at first enraptures and then unnerves, as in Holan's poem 'Reminiscence II'); with another person in a moment of vulnerability (a television weather announcer on whom the sound relay has failed); or with a voice that commands him to put a crown in the fare box when he rides alone on an empty night tram. These moments of what Patočka in the *Heretical Essays* had called 'naked man . . . man placed before his own bare existence'[18] to Havel were 'expressions of a single integrated Being' (s5, 579) and the sort of inter-subjective connection he imagined in *Spaces and Times* and *On the Cusp of Spring*. As in a poem or his plays, these vignettes reprise in symmetrical locations: the tale of the muted weather announcer, for example, opens the second letter in the sequence and then the penultimate.

What distinguished Havel's current outlook from his earlier pantheism was that the longed-for union with Being was now seen as unattainable except in death – a topic he had studiously avoided in his poems. Once humanity has become self-aware and is no longer 'unproblematically participating in Being "from within"' as other animals do, there is no going back, just as there is none for the infant who has realized that her mother and surroundings are separate

Olga on a night tram in the 1980s.

from herself (s5, 542–4, 547). Our sense of responsibility to others is a residue of a prehistoric, seamless connection to Being, but now must take a non-utopian, 'mature' form, avouching to discrete persons. Otherwise, it would degenerate into either a fanatical drive to cure all ills by extreme means or trifles and projects that wreck the natural world (s5, 548–76, 586–9) – what Patočka called the 'orgiastic demonic' and 'the anonymity of everydayness'.[19]

Despite the prison constraints that gave his letters a clenched, gnomic quality, Havel was able to build to a rousing call in letter 143 for an existential revolution and 'renewed community' of values such as love, compassion, friendship and tolerance (s5, 599–600). As Ivan noticed, the cycle could be mapped onto the structure of a classically constructed play, in which the concluding letters represented the *katastrophē* following the cathartic crisis of 1977 revisited in letters 138–9.[20] Havel agreed, likening letter 143 to the lofty monologues delivered by the male lead near the end of almost all his plays (but in this case meant sincerely), followed by a 'soft landing' in letter 144 that returns to the sequence's beginning (s5, 686–7).

The sixteen letters were a breakthrough that inaugurated a five-year stretch in which Havel's theoretical and analytical skills were at their peak. By this point Havel knew that he was writing for a potentially large readership: previous letters had found their way into exile periodicals, and by the end of 1981 Ivan was circulating a compilation of excerpts. In March 1982, Havel had agreed to a more complete collection under a title that would honour his wife and echo Kafka's *Letters to Milena*.[21] When *Letters to Olga* appeared in 1983, the letters were edited to end on an upbeat note – the last line taken from letter 144 reads, 'In short, I feel fine and I love you' – but the impression was misleading. From the omitted postscript and subsequent 21 unpublished letters it is clear that Havel had been staving off a severe depression, which then hit with full force. His elbows were inflamed again, he was developing tooth, skin and vision trouble, and he was dismayed that Olga took no interest in his philosophizing. Even though he now needed a sedative to cope with the crowded cells, he rejected an offer of early release in November 1982 because it was conditional on pleading for clemency. Suspecting that he was being set up as in 1977, he resolved to serve out the remaining year of his sentence.

At times Havel dared hope that he might be freed on medical grounds, but when indeed he was, it came as a surprise. He had had numerous bouts of flu and one of pneumonia at Heřmanice, and after he was transferred from the Bory laundry to work with cable insulation, his lungs were again at risk. On 23 January 1983 he was hit by pneumonia so severe that he was transferred to the hospital wing of Prague's Pankrác prison. Once on antibiotics, he began slowly but steadily to recover, and by 5 February was well enough to write to Olga with a powerful, slightly valedictory message to the dissident community, urging it not to despair that its efforts so far seemed fruitless. Nothing in the letter hinted at anything other than his eventual return to Bory. By this point, however, Havel's welfare was an international cause, thanks to Olga and Ivan, their many friends in exile, Havel's German publisher Klaus Juncker and Western human rights groups. The Vaněk plays had been performed in solidarity by dozens of foreign theatres, and a gala event in Avignon, France, in July 1982 staged tributes to Havel by Samuel Beckett and Arthur Miller.[22] He may not yet have grasped that in captivity he had attained something like the renown of the exiled Russian writer Solzhenitsyn, and the Czechoslovak government wanted to avoid embarrassment. On 7 February 1983, Havel was suddenly told that he was being paroled. He would continue his recovery in the civilian hospital below Petřín Hill that the narrator of his poem 'On the Observation Tower' (1956) had said might be the heart of the world (another possibility being Pankrác prison).

The illness that Havel feared might kill him secured not only his release but a gentler transition to life on the outside: he was allowed to convalesce in hospital for a month, receiving visitors in controlled numbers. It was very much what he wanted, because other prisoners had warned him that the shock of freedom could be overwhelming (s5, 508). In late 1982 he had begun minutely planning, day by day, meal by meal, how he would slowly reintegrate, first just with Olga and then with a gradually wider circle of friends, during a six-to-eight-week 'incubation'. He was determined – as when marrying Olga and writing to Husák – to embark on a 'new phase of life', one driven more by his sovereign wishes than the requests of others, exploring the world with the 'phenomenological curiosity' of his pre-fame youth.[23]

Even in hospital, however, Havel already felt stunned by the 'information explosion' of catching up on what he had missed, and after his discharge on 4 March he struggled to cope with the restored privacy, space and freedom he had craved in prison.[24] (An émigré contact arranged a shipment of an anti-depressant, Laroxyl.[25]) He was drawn back into the practicalities of keeping the small Charter community afloat, and in vain he protested: 'I have already been through enough dissident flitting-about, I haven't written a play because of it, new fighters have to step up.'[26] Havel agreed to research and draft Charter statements on drug abuse and on the state's regulation of pop and rock music as subjects he considered important but also likely to attract new, younger signatories.

Some duties he took on in reciprocation, such as when he was asked in April to supply a short play for an event in Sweden for Charter 77 like the one held for him in Avignon; in two hours, he wrote *Mistake*, about the hierarchical prison gangs described in letter 47 to Olga (s5, 167). The authorities could count on such sub-groups to keep inmates in line and enforce norms, as shown in the play by the roughing-up of a foreign newcomer, to whom his cellmates' detailed instructions are as unintelligible as Ptydepe (he is called Xiboj, like the original protagonist of *The Memorandum*) (s2, 679–84). Havel offered *Mistake*, in the spirit of Beckett's tribute to him, as a general warning against the 'danger of self-appointed totalitarianism present today in every society in the world, big or small'.[27] The prison gang's 'king' and his underlings are thus the tattooed kindred of the greengrocer of 'The Power of the Powerless'.

In mid-May Havel decamped from Prague to Hrádeček, and could initially report 'absolute peace and quiet' and feeling 'anchored in my true home'.[28] But even there he struggled both to fend off demands on his time and to make progress on a new play; he returned to Prague in December plagued by his 'horror at blank paper and a priori aversion to everything that I might eventually write on it'.[29] Instead, the coming winter would be arranged around the need to write an acceptance speech for the doctorate he was going to be awarded in May 1984 by the University of Toulouse in France.[30] He welcomed this assignment, as he had already been planning a long essay reflecting his post-prison drive to enlarge his knowledge of philosophy. He canvassed his friends for suggested reading, and one new name that kept coming up was that of Václav Bělohradský. A Czech in Italian exile, Bělohradský had synthesized the ideas of his teacher Patočka's *Heretical Essays* with those of Hannah Arendt, Michel Foucault and Max Weber. The result was a genealogy of modern power as impersonal discipline and technique from which conscience had been stripped in the Western pursuit of morally neutral, rational bureaucracy. The intention in the time of Machiavelli and the wars of religion had been admirable: to bring peace and plenty by putting the state above conflicts of world view. The unintended consequence in the twentieth century, however, was an officialdom that carried out orders and enforced laws without questioning their legitimacy, resulting in the Shoah and Gulag.[31] Havel was so impressed that he wanted Bělohradský to attend the ceremony in Toulouse, where Tom Stoppard would read Havel's acceptance text, 'Politics and Conscience'.[32]

Written in February 1984 while he hid for nine days at the Hotel Růže in the picturesque town of Český Krumlov, 'Politics and Conscience' was Havel's fourth major sociopolitical critique since the Soviet invasion. It took many of the premises of 'The Power of the Powerless', a détente-era document, and revised them in light of two developments: growing awareness of environmental devastation, which Charter 77 had been highlighting in recent reports, and the renewed Cold War, marked by the deployment of Pershing II missiles in West Germany, the suspension of arms talks and uncertainty about the Soviet Union's future (its leader, Yuri Andropov, died while Havel was in the middle of writing). Havel read the essay to a gathering of banned writers in Brno, and while most liked it for imparting the received wisdom of dissident circles to a Western audience, a few did not:

> [Karel] Pecka says that I should write plays and not get mixed up in things that should be left to experts, and it's just 'Kundera-like quackings'; Eda [Kriseová] said that it was boring and I'm just repeating things that Patočka and Bělohradský said; Lenka [Procházková] said that it is written in some sort of specialist language unsuited for a writer and that I should write personally and humanly . . . that Solzhenitsyn said the same thing better in his Harvard address.[33]

Havel's critics failed to grasp how his warning to the West differed from Solzhenitsyn's. At Harvard commencement in 1978, Solzhenitsyn lifted terms from that university's Pitirim Sorokin to lament the West's moral decay owing to its 'irreligious humanistic consciousness', which left it unwilling and unfit to resist the mortal danger posed by Soviet communism.[34] Havel had certainly enjoyed reading Sorokin in his youth and cited Solzhenitsyn's Harvard speech in 'Power of the Powerless' and 'Politics and Conscience' because it tallied with his own call for a meaningful life not reduced to material consumption. It also fitted his hostility to appeasement: in messages to the many peace congresses that were seeking his opinion, Havel urged the West not to repeat the mistake made at

Munich in 1938 and think that it could prevent a cataclysmic act of violence by tolerating small ones (s4, 546–7). Unlike Solzhenitsyn, however, he did not summon the debauched West to gird its loins – if anything, Havel dismissed as a techno-rationalist delusion the thought that a few extra American missiles in Europe would make a difference (s4, 432, 436). The crisis of civilization instead required an attitude to the natural world more receptive to its unquantifiable mystery; an 'anti-political' politics of small deeds with potentially far-reaching consequences; and, as the Šafaříkian focus (*ohnisko*) of all social action, the 'autonomous, integral and dignified human "I", vouching for itself' (s4, 435–6, 441–2).

One unmistakable change in the tone of Havel's analysis – and one that probably did reflect Solzhenitsyn's influence as well as Havel's experience of prison – was a greater willingness to talk in stark terms of good and evil, especially the latter. 'Politics and Conscience' likened the disregard for the natural world to the Faustian pride that precedes a fall (s4, 420), and the impersonal power of the modern state, especially the totalitarian kind, to a 'truly diabolical temptation' because it offered to subdue humanity's quarrels (s4, 438). That choice of words reflected Havel's determination since 1977 to write something on the Faust theme, and all three of the plays he composed between 1984 and 1987 had Faustian elements.

The first, *Largo desolato*, presents an anguished philosopher, Leopold Kopřiva ('Nettles'), dreading a visit by the secret police because of his phenomenological works, which, judging by their titles, sound very much like Havel's prison meditations and 'Politics and Conscience'. Doctor Kopřiva paces his apartment as if already a prisoner in his cell but also like Doctor Faust in his study at the beginning of Marlowe's and Goethe's tragedies. Friends and well-wishers visit him, claim to admire and love him, and enquire into his poor mental and physical health, all the while pressing him to write yet another work that will get him into trouble. One tells him, 'You are clearly buffeted by great devils, only those devils are not driving you anywhere, they just circle around you' (s2, 713). Unconditional love is offered by a young philosophy student, Markéta, whom Kopřiva immediately tries to seduce, as Faust does Gretchen.

Largo desolato, like *Mistake*, clearly drew on the author's experiences and had elements of self-deprecation, but it was not to be taken as a self-portrait. Kopřiva is Havel's view of his pre-1979 self, living not only in expectation of arrest but almost wanting it, as a deserved punishment and respite from having to make decisions and meet the demands of others. Markéta, speaking from Havel's post-prison perspective, challenges Kopřiva's self-flagellation as a futile attempt to find meaning in a persecution that is fundamentally unjust and to flee from life's dilemmas. Kopřiva also has much in common with the protagonist of Saul Bellow's *Herzog* (1964), a novel Havel read in prison with great relish (s5, 502–3), and with the land surveyor K. of Kafka's *The Castle*, in that Kopřiva cannot be pinned down as courageous or cowardly, decent or swinish. When he falls to the floor at the end of the penultimate scene, begging the secret police both to leave him alone and to cart him off, the audience is unsure whether to admire, pity or despise him. But that quandary is itself an appeal to not pin our hopes on a superman or redeemer, for doing so only relieves us of our responsibility.[35] The play closes as it began, with Kopřiva alone onstage in a pantomimed limbo. Havel intended the play to be musical in its verbal fugues and repetitive action, and in how it unsettles the soul (s4, 498, 502). Its title is taken from the final movement of Alban Berg's *Lyric Suite*, which contains a coded reference to Baudelaire's poem 'De profundis clamavi' and its lines, 'I envy the lot of the lowest animals/ That can sink into a dumb sleep'.[36]

If the play was a depiction of Havel's life at the time of writing, it was so in regard to the state of his marriage. Kopřiva has a *družka* (companion or common-law wife), Zuzana, and a *přítelkyně* (girlfriend), Lucy. Although Kopřiva indicates that he would like

Zuzana to stay at home and have a proper supper with him, she is always going out for the evening with a male friend. Before she exits, she reminds him that she has made 'her position' clear (s2, 694, 743). What that position is can be inferred from the one Olga had made clear to Havel on his release from prison: whereas his letters promised a return to an emotionally warmer (but not necessarily monogamous) relationship, she had followed her mother's example and in her husband's absence taken up with a younger man. The lover, Jan Kašpar, was well known to Havel, as he had played Filch in *The Beggar's Opera* at Horní Počernice and helped Olga maintain Hrádeček, track down the items for her parcels to Havel and get to the quarterly prison visits.[37] He was a talented photographer, and unlike Havel snapped many remarkable pictures of Olga (and of Havel himself). It is not clear when Olga informed Havel of her affair, but it may have been as early as February 1983, when he was still in hospital. She did not want a divorce – her relations with Kašpar eventually returned to a practical friendship – and she would still care for Havel in a motherly or sisterly way, but she now had her own circle of friends and underground activities.[38]

This news did not fit the plan Havel had drawn up for his return, and added to his disorientation. He probably tried to resume his affair with Anna Kohoutová, only to find that she and Olga had become friends, and his passion cooled. Instead, he turned to Jitka Vodňanská, whom he had met briefly before his arrest (her ex-husband had signed Charter 77). In addition to having many of the attributes of other women he found attractive, she was a trained therapist – expertise that might help him cope with his post-prison mood swings. By the time Havel was writing *Largo desolato* at a crowded Hrádeček over four days in July 1984,[39] Vodňanská's presence was tolerated by Olga, in part because she had a young son and Olga happily hosted the children of other dissidents during summer vacations. The following month they all endured the largest police raid on Hrádeček when hundreds

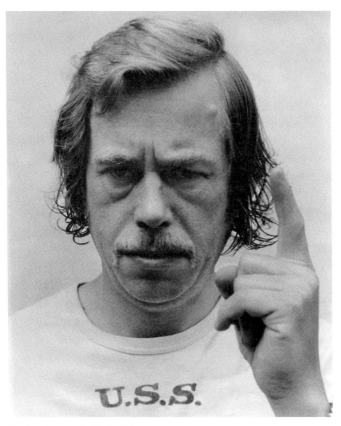

Havel as photographed by Jan Kašpar.

of books, journals and cassettes were confiscated, leaving
Havel with almost no copies of his own writings. Only when
Vodňanská became pregnant did the Havels' marriage approach
breaking point; the crisis was resolved by an abortion.[40]

Largo desolato did not exhaust Havel's interest in Faust; the next
play, *Temptation*, would be his long-promised full rendition. He was
familiar with the famous versions by Goethe and Thomas Mann,
but he wanted his to be seen as a 'loose variation' on an 'archetype',

The Kampademy at Hrádeček, summer 1983. From left to right: Zdeněk Neubauer, Martin Palouš, Pavel Bratinka, Radim Palouš, Václav and Ivan Havel.

resting on the Bohemian carnival and puppet traditions and on a recent scholarly history of the legend.[41] He consulted literature on magic and Hermeticism recommended first by Václav Černý and then Zdeněk Urbánek, a novelist and translator Havel had known from the Group 42 set at the Café Slavia. After the emigration of so many friends, Urbánek had become Havel's principal confidant, and his anti-clerical scepticism was a foil to the Kampademy symposia Havel hosted every June at Hrádeček with sessions on Jung, Tolkien and the jimson-weed shaman Carlos Castaneda.[42] In November 1984 Havel previewed the research and premises that would inform *Temptation* in an essay on myth in modern times. Borrowing the title of Michael Jackson's 'Thriller', in the video for which the singer metamorphoses into a werewolf and zombie, Havel scans news from around the world – as he did as a young poet in *Spaces and Times* – and sees beneath the rational, scientific veneer of modernity the enduring 'forces of night' in the human unconscious. Once explained and channelled by myth, they now have only violence as their outlet, on a scale far worse than in the pre-modern age and not sustainable if the human race is to survive. 'Thriller' showed that Havel retained the Sorokin-inflected faith of his Thirty-sixer days in a new ideational age to come (s4, 507) and that *Temptation* would be another enactment of Šafařík's critique of 'scientism'. (Šafařík had noted the persistence of the occult and astrology in his essay 'Man in the Machine Age' and in 1974 had written, for an anthology Havel edited, a 'Mephisto Monologue' that left its mark on Havel's letter to Husák and 'The Power of the Powerless'.[43])

Temptation was written in a ten-day sprint at Hrádeček in October 1985. It returns to the bureaucratic world of *The Garden Party* and *The Memorandum*, in this case an institute whose mission is to be an enforcer of rationalism and scourge of any interest in myth, magic or alchemy. One of its researchers, Jindřich (Henry) Foustka, is having doubts about his workplace's purpose, and expresses them eloquently to an adoring, innocent Gretchen figure (again named Markéta). At home, he dabbles in the dark arts. By the play's midpoint he has been denounced to his director, and fends off an investigation through a mix of lies, bargaining and self-deception

A scene from a production of *Temptation* in 1991 at the Theatre on the Balustrade.

– like Staněk in *Protest* he has his private heresy but does not want it to endanger his professional status and comforts. In the process he abandons Markéta and she descends into an Ophelia-like madness, babbling lines from Urbánek's translation of *Hamlet*. Foustka also alienates Vilma, his partner in sadomasochism, and she is wooed away by a ballroom dancer. Into the final scene it seems he will at least save his job and reputation, until he learns that all along he has been under surveillance by an informer, Fistula, as a test of his loyalty. His fate is left uncertain: the powerful may be content to keep him dangling like Kopřiva, or he might be spared but exposed, in Bělohradský's phrase of the time, as a man without scruples.[44]

Like all of Havel's plays, *Temptation* can be read in many ways, on many levels. In its immediately personal sense, it revisits the events that first drew Havel to the Faust story, when he thought he could talk his way out of detention in 1977. It could be an allegory for the methods of the secret-police state,[45] or for the sciences of human behaviour that displace belief in a soul: the provocateur Fistula speaks the language of psychoanalysis, Markéta is sent to a psychiatric ward, and Walpurgis Night festivities in the institute's garden are presented as 'modern group costume therapy' (s2, 830). (The two themes go together, in that mental hospitals were used in Soviet bloc states for political persecution; VONS had issued a statement in November 1984 on the abuse of psychiatry.[46]) *Temptation* also revisits Havel's evergreen themes such as the use of language either to communicate truth or to seduce, oppress and befuddle, depending on motives and circumstances; the tension between individual authenticity and conformity to power; and the danger of evading responsibility, which is also central to Marlowe's *Doctor Faustus*.[47] The play's Czech title, *Pokoušení*, is etymologically related to the *zkušenosti* (experiences) and *zkoušky* (tests, trials) that in prison letter 139 Havel said were preconditions for grasping the inevitability of responsibility (s5, 573). Whereas *Largo desolato* saddened its first Czech readers, *Temptation* was received with delight because of the moral delivered by the institute's director: that a person has to take a side and a stand (s2, 853).[48] It was, to use the title of a Havel essay on the dissident's life, responsibility as destiny (s4, 402).

By the time *Temptation* was written, there had been yet another death in the Kremlin, and the Soviet Union was now led by Mikhail Gorbachev. As he consolidated his power, he steadily unveiled reforms resembling those introduced or promised by Dubček in 1968. The similarity was lost on no one in Czechoslovakia, not least on the ageing leaders around Husák whose entire claim to power was that 1968 had been a dangerous error. Their refusal to follow Moscow's newly liberal line caused widespread frustration and impatience, which found expression in Havel's last major sociopolitical essay, 'Stories and Totalitarianism', in April 1987 (s4, 932–59). The Czechoslovak regime's inertia was presented as indicative of the suspension of time in a totalitarian system, leaving life with no sense of narrative flow. Behind the illusion of calm, however, a secret war was being waged on society by a pervasive 'nothingness'. (The essay honoured the philosopher Ladislav Hejdánek, a specialist in meontology – the idea of non-being.) Reaching back to Šafařík, Havel rooted this nothingness in a scientistic way of thinking about history as something that has laws, patterns, impersonal forces, no mystery and no identifiable villain; the country's leaders were as captive to nothingness as they were to fear in the letter to Husák and ideology in 'The Power of the Powerless'. People lived not through their own stories but vicariously, through cosy films such as the Oscar-nominated *My Sweet Little Village* (1985) that took place outside of historical time and context.

Nothingness deadened the experience of space as well: it homogenized all outward detail, imposing a single rhythm and inhibiting free movement and thus the opportunity to be a Šafaříkian participant. In the essay's more lyrical passages, Havel described the surly, careworn people he saw on the streets,

trying to meet their material needs – a struggle he also recounted in a short play about his attempt to acquire a pig for a customary slaughter and feast (*zabijačka*) at Hrádeček.[49] The blighted terrain of 'Stories and Totalitarianism' was exceptionally grim, without the humanizing touches of his poetry from the 1950s; it was akin more to Kolář's poems from the Second World War, full of graveyard gloom.

That connection between space and death became the basis for the new play that Havel wrote in two five-day bursts in October 1987, *Asanace*. This Czech word derives from the French verb *assainir*, to make healthy, to clean up or clean out; it had come to refer specifically to the demolition of cramped medieval neighbourhoods, such as the one in Prague at the end of the nineteenth century that had benefited Havel's grandfather. In the play, a team of architects has assembled in a castle to plan to level the old town below, replacing it with an estate

The deadened landscape of northern Bohemia, one corner of central Europe's 'black triangle'.

of prefabricated flats despite the attachment of the residents to their distinctive home (*domov*). As in *The Conspirators*, the location is not identified, the characters' names suggest a mix of nationalities, and Havel wanted some of the townsfolk to be black to remind Western audiences of their own injustices.

Death and nothingness stalk the architects in three ways (s4, 1005). The first is psychological: several members of the team are suicidal, and one, Kuzma Plechanov, does kill himself at the end – the only primary character to die in a Havel play. Plechanov differs from his colleagues in having a responsible personality, acting as a quiet conscience or moral memory. He kills himself at the end because he has given up hope not only that he can have an effect, but that a promising younger architect, Albert, might be able to. Albert, like Filch in *The Beggar's Opera*, defies impersonal power by questioning the *asanace*, and Havel originally intended that he should be the one to die (again, like Filch); the funeral oration at the end of the play reads like that for a young man, and comes very close to Havel's remarks on Jan Palach in 1969. However, the friends to whom Havel showed the first draft were not moved by Albert's suicide, as it seemed too formulaic; only Plechanov, they told Havel, had a right to be tragic, and only his death would illuminate the 'nonsense and powerlessness' of the other characters (s4, 1025–33). Instead, Albert is punished in the castle dungeon, where he endures the solitary confinement Havel experienced at Heřmanice. It is the sight of the broken young man on his release that pushes Plechanov into fatal despair.

The second form of death is architectural: the planned housing estate is denounced by Albert as an affront to nature and the landscape perpetrated in the name of hygiene and progress (s2, 878). Plechanov observes that architecture mirrors society, and Havel was using the *asanace* as a metaphor for totalitarianism and the rationalist-scientific thinking from which it sprang (s4, 1017). This leads to the third form of death in the play, the political. On three occasions the dialogue is punctuated by the intervention of two inspectors, who condense several decades of speeches by Communist leaders. The first speaks as a folksy, post-Stalinist liberalizer, who is then replaced by a 'normalizer', who then awkwardly has to adopt the language of Gorbachev's reforms. The first two interventions have a huge impact on the characters' behaviour and expectations, but by the time of the third, everyone is exhausted and indifferent to the exhortation to produce bold new ideas. The very title *Asanace* was a weary retort to Gorbachev's own architectural metaphor, perestroika (reconstruction).[50]

Structurally, the play uses a classical frame of five scenes but contains a postmodern melange of elements and references ranging from Czech puppet theatre to murder mysteries. Below the traces of Chekhov's *Seagull*, Ibsen's *Master Builder* and Hrubín's *August Sunday*, there is almost certainly mockery of a Dietl television serial, *The Man in Town Hall*, which had celebrated the razing of a decrepit city centre to make way for prefab flats.[51] Finally, the play rounds out Havel's treatment of Faust as the ruthless engineer of Goethe's Part II, in which he builds a great city with his palace at the centre, impeded only by the refusal of an old couple to yield their ancestral land, cottage and chapel. Faust directs Mephistopheles to transplant them to a better farm, but they die of fright; the book Havel consulted on the Faust story interpreted this scene to mean that 'if it is necessary to remove the outmoded mode of production – and of life – with the rise of modern society, with its progress and technology, then it is not possible without violence and victims.'[52]

By the time he was writing *Asanace*, Havel had moved into what with hindsight can be seen as a pre-presidential mode of operations. In February 1986, through a chain of property swaps, he and Olga returned to the fourth floor of Engels Embankment 78, which they shared with the now-divorced Ivan. But the move to the city centre had its downside, exposing Havel even more to demands on his time. Writing was already turning into the treadmill he would come to loathe during his presidency. When not working on the three plays – which together consumed only one month over three years – he was replying to the offer of an honorary degree or prize or to an invitation to a conference in the West that he could not attend, or marking an anniversary, a friend's birthday or death. By the spring of 1987, the man who as a young poet yearned to belong to the people now hated to find that he could not step into a pub for a quiet drink without being accosted by curious strangers. At his hotel hideaway in Český Krumlov, he thought about one thing:

What to do about the fact that I absolutely cannot play all my roles and execute my 'office'. The roles are representative, consultative, assisting, protecting, harmonizing, promotional, editorial, noetic, literary, and I don't know what else, it's all important, I blame no one, I just agonize over how to do

it all and at the same time be a normal person, who in his
old age fixes up the apartment and sometimes reads some
book just because he wants to and not because he must.[53]

To cope with these roles, Havel built up a cadre of assistants and
handymen, running them, as his father had run his businesses, on
strong personal loyalty and mutual respect. Although he remained
active in Charter 77 and its offshoots, Havel was becoming an
institution in his own right, and many of the people he was
grooming to take on some or all of his dissident duties would
instead soon follow him into the presidential administration in
Prague Castle.[54]

Havel was also unwittingly preparing for office in how he
presented himself. His major undertaking of 1986 was not a play
but a book-length interview with a Czech journalist based in West
Germany, *Questioning from Afar*, which systematically refuted the
slanderous version of his life told for years by Czechoslovak state
media.[55] He refined his opinions on disarmament, the division
of Europe, historical controversies and the role of market forces
in the economy. He dissociated himself from 'socialism' (a word
he now thought too debased to describe his preferences) but did
not like being claimed by conservatives (he was privately scornful
of Ronald Reagan); if he had lived in West Germany, he would
have enthusiastically voted Green.[56] He hosted summits of the
fast-proliferating opposition movements and in December 1988
spoke at the first public rally for human rights that the regime
allowed to take place. To the consternation of many fellow
dissidents, however, he was not eager to seek interlocutors in
the government; he felt it was enough to let something percolate
in the social subconscious. He was far more intent on expanding
his contacts in the official cultural sector, and was encouraged by
an invitation to a reception at the end of 1988 for the Theatre on
the Balustrade's thirtieth anniversary.

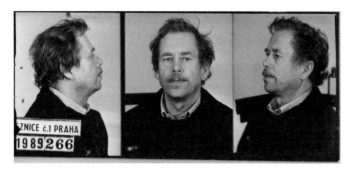

Havel after his arrest in January 1989.

Anniversaries, however, were also flashpoints, and there were many in Czechoslovakia at that time: on the twentieth anniversary of the Soviet invasion in August 1988 and the seventieth of Czechoslovakia's independence in October, crowds gathered without permission and were sometimes violently dispersed. Older dissidents such as Havel were reluctant to encourage the young to put themselves in harm's way, especially as the twentieth anniversary of Palach's self-immolation approached. Starting on 15 January 1989, members of Charter 77 and other civic initiatives tried to hold a commemoration on Wenceslas Square, but the police prevented them. In the following days, thousands of demonstrators attempted again to reach the square, and the police responded with escalating brutality. Havel did not want to be the centre of attention, but on 16 January he ventured out to get a look; he was recognized by police officers and arrested. He had been detained several times since 1985, but always released after 24 or 48 hours; this time the authorities decided to try him for 'disorderly conduct' in a bid to subdue the growing opposition. He was convicted on 21 February 1989 and sentenced to nine months.[57]

Havel's return to prison immediately caused an international outcry, and Czech friends organized two petitions for his release that attracted more than 5,000 signatures. Buoyed by the hundreds of postcards sent to him, he sensed that the regime was losing its nerve: the trial had not been the circus it was in 1979, and he was housed in relatively calm, comfortable conditions at Pankrác prison, in a wing normally reserved for foreigners.[58] His letters to Olga reported relief at time off from his 'office' as dissident-in-chief and from his excesses:

> I would gladly drink less on the outside too, alcohol
> perhaps bears responsibility for many of my sorrows.
> In general I have made several significant life decisions;
> for example, I do not want to be so subject to the female
> world and I want to live in a more orderly way – although
> appropriate visits to the pub I will, of course, not forego.[59]

From Havel's next letter it emerged that he was ending his affair with Jitka Vodňanská, but he asked Olga to remain hospitable to her and her son. In return, Havel promised Olga that in their old age they would take a trip around the world together, starting on New Year's Day in 2000.[60]

As he neared the halfway point of his sentence, in May 1989, Havel applied for parole. As he expected, it was granted. He was greeted by a massive homecoming party, with even Alexander Dubček dropping in. The more important new acquaintance on that occasion, however, was Jiří Křižan, who was exactly the sort of contact Havel wanted to cultivate – a screenwriter well positioned in official culture, but harbouring deep hostility to the regime: his father, like Havel's uncle Miloš, had escaped to Austria in 1950, been returned by the Soviets and then hanged for shooting a border guard. On the second night after his release from prison, Havel dined with Křižan and Havel's young assistant, Alexandr (Saša) Vondra, to work out a way to allow more people to signal their opinions without having to assemble on the streets or get involved with the Charter. The three men quickly devised *A Few Sentences*, a petition of seven demands that, although not brazenly political, would be transformative if they were met (such as allowing free association, speech and exercise of religion). During the summer they gathered 20,000 signatures, about twenty times more than the Charter had attracted in ten years.[61]

Havel sensed that 'classic' dissidence was drawing to a close, but in October 1989 his last essay before the end of the Communist regime cautioned that the situation was not yet ready for open politics. It was at root still a moral crisis, which could as easily be addressed by small, everyday acts that would lay the civic foundations on which a future politics could operate (s4, 1154–9). At Hrádeček around 10 November, he consulted Křižan and Vondra on a plan for a two-hour jamboree of signatories of *A Few Sentences*, who now numbered around 40,000, to be held on 10 December (Human Rights Day) on a square by the Engels Embankment. Brief political speeches would be interspersed with musical and theatrical acts, as if Havel were reviving the 'text appeal' cabaret of the Balustrade under Vyskočil.[62]

Rather than wait until Human Rights Day, however, a mix of official and informal youth groups used International Students' Day – 17 November – to hold their own rally. It quickly turned into a political demonstration and a march around Prague. By late evening, several thousand protestors were heading up the Engels Embankment, past the Café Slavia and towards Wenceslas Square, until they were boxed in and assaulted by riot police. The savagery was no worse, and perhaps even less, than that meted out to the Palach commemorators in January, but it came at the end of a year when Communists had ceded power in neighbouring states and the Berlin Wall had opened. When rumours (false) spread that a young man had been killed, students and theatres called for a general strike. In the month that Havel least liked – he had described November as good for nothing but illness and haemorrhoids – the country was being hit by the very tornado he had forecast in his 1975 letter to Husák (s4, 101–2; s5, 41, 72, 179).

Havel had planned to return to Prague from Hrádeček on 19 November, but was urged by his secretary to come a day earlier. His presence and the centrality of the flat on the Engels Embankment made him the focus of what followed. As when writing his Liberec radio addresses in 1968, Havel believed that the power of the people could be greater than that of guns and tanks but had to be directed and sometimes curbed, so as not to provoke a reaction like the Chinese regime's crackdown on Tiananmen Square that June. In the coming days, Havel would provide that discipline through the formation of Civic Forum, a concatenation of dissident and student movements, and through his speeches to the crowds that gathered day after day in ever larger numbers on Wenceslas Square, when he called for an inquiry into police brutality, for the resignation of compromised officials, for dialogue and free elections (s4, 1160–63). The political cabaret Havel had intended to take place on 10 December had to kick off nineteen days earlier, reprise almost every evening for a week in freezing temperatures and have its equivalents in cities all over the republic; that he could draw on friends who knew how to put on a show made the revolution possible and peaceful.[63]

The ensuing parleys between Civic Forum and Communist ministers from 26 November to 6 December allow us to see Havel in a new light, as a character in a comedic text rather than its author.[64] His secretary recorded and transcribed the talks, and the impression they give is of Havel as a politely firm and practical, albeit sleep-deprived, negotiator. He would allow ministers to bluster like an Inspector from *Asanace*, then turn the discussion to what Civic Forum wanted. His strategy was to play 'good cop' to the 'bad cop' masses whose patience would allegedly run out if the government did not meet the demands transmitted by Civic Forum. Havel presented his side as having to earn continuously its right to represent the people by getting results, which in turn would enable it to help the government keep order.[65] When deliberating separately

with other leaders of Civic Forum, he had a similarly canny way
of setting the agenda, honed from years of coping with Charter egos
and factions. He allowed others to speak their piece but, as the StB
reported on 22 November, it was Havel who had the 'decisive word',
decided when to end a discussion and which conclusions to draw
from it.[66] He conceptualized Civic Forum as the sort of ad hoc,
time- and purpose-limited entity he had idealized in 'The Power of
the Powerless', and not as an incipient political party. Like others
with VONS experience, he thought of it as an oversight body, vetting
and vetoing appointments to a provisional government of experts
and ensuring that they laid the ground for economic reform,
depoliticized the army and dismantled the StB.[67]

Soon, however, Havel realized that all year he had underestimated
the pace of change and that Civic Forum was caught between three
grindstones: the public, which wanted it to take power rather than
just supervise a shuffled cabinet; the Communist apparatus, which
wanted to discredit it by rushing it into co-responsibility for the
economy; and its own demands for resignations, including Husák's,

Havel shakes hands with a future prime minister and ally, Marián Čalfa, during talks on
26 November 1989.

that had not simultaneously proposed occupants for the vacated offices.[68] On 5 December, once Civic Forum felt compelled to nominate ministers and the next president, several influential figures suggested Havel for the latter. Havel wanted neither to appear eager for a position elected by the Communist-dominated federal legislature, nor to rule himself out. When it came time on 8 December to commit to running, he framed the presidency – perhaps with a touch of irony or dissembling – not as a reward but yet another wearisome diversion from his art, a cross to bear 'even at the cost of my wife Olga divorcing me, because she is opposed to this decision'.[69]

Havel then had to deal with the men to whom he had once written letters on leadership and responsibility: Dubček and Husák. Civic Forum had demanded Husák's resignation by 10 December, and at the last minute he complied, after appointing a new, multiparty cabinet headed by Marián Čalfa, a fellow Slovak. By convention the head of state and head of government came from different nations, so Husák's successor would have to be a Czech, which worked in Havel's favour and against that of his most likely rival, Dubček. Undeterred, Dubček was intent on the presidency as vindication for 1968, even though he was not endorsed by Civic Forum's Slovak counterpart, Public Against Violence, which feared he would trap the country in a Gorbachevian halfway house. It fell to Havel, backed by the students who started the revolution, to convince Dubček to hold off, as Havel intended to serve only until the election of a new legislature in June 1990. Havel privately promised to support Dubček if he sought the presidency later, and was willing to say so in public, but was advised by Civic Forum's lawyers not to commit himself.[70]

The challenge remained of getting a legislature chosen in sham elections in 1986 to vote for Havel. The Communist Party's leaders had overnight become ardent democrats and wanted a direct presidential election, in which their candidate would have an enormous organizational and media advantage. Civic Forum, only three weeks old and unready for a state-wide contest that would be divisive and disruptive, found itself having to defend the traditional parliamentary route. Prime Minister Čalfa, a Communist eager to adapt and survive, assured Havel he could deliver the vote. Indeed, he kept his promise too well: on 29 December, in Prague Castle's Vladislav Hall, all 323 members present raised their hands for Havel as the sole candidate, to the chagrin of Civic Forum figures wanting at least a few 'no' votes as a sign of change.[71] But there would be plenty of them soon enough.

6

The Presidential Great Work
(1990–2003)

In private on 9 December 1989, Havel had said he had no intention
of 'sitting on my backside in the Castle for five years' and would
serve only until the first parliamentary elections to act as a guarantor
that they be free and fair.[1] But after those elections passed smoothly
on a turnout of 95 per cent, Havel was easily persuaded to serve
another two years, as guarantor of the drafting of a new federal
constitution. (Dubček, back in his old position as speaker of the
federal legislature, offered no competition.) When the federation
broke apart at the end of 1992, Havel was willing to act as guarantor
of the building of a separate Czech state. And in 1998, he was
willing, although less so than before, to serve a final five-year term
as guarantor of the Czech state's integration into NATO and the
European Union. Already in May 1991 he confessed that he was
becoming more suspicious of his motive for staying in office: that it
was not just a sense of duty and sacrifice but a longing for influence
on the world (s6, 362). He saw no sin in this; politics did not have
to be 'dirty work' and could be just as honourable an undertaking
as dissent had been (s6, 367, 521, 526; s7, 37).

The office Havel inherited from Husák at the end of 1989 was
mostly to his liking, neither robotically ceremonial nor bogged
down in everyday governance, but it suffered from what its first
occupant Tomáš Masaryk had called the 'presidential problem'
– a lack of consensus about powers, duties and expectations.[2]
Masaryk himself had wanted something akin to the presidency

of the United States, where he had ended his peripatetic wartime exile, but other authors of Czechoslovakia's first, provisional constitution preferred the Swiss collective presidency, British constitutional monarchy and, most of all, the French model of a president elected by the legislature and sharing power with a prime minister. During the shift to a permanent constitution in 1919–20, Masaryk was able to win a few American-style enhancements, such as the power to have his own staff, appoint and remove ministers, chair sessions of the cabinet, provide an annual report on the state of the country and propose legislation. He failed, however, to get direct election, and in practice his ministerial choices had to reflect the wishes of the parliamentary factions. Once the political system settled into new routines and Masaryk's health faltered, the prime minister and party cartel moved to the fore.[3] In the Communist period, the presidency was diminished in prestige so as not to overshadow the general secretary.

Havel's immediate priority was to build up the presidential staff and acquire direct control of the Castle precincts in which it was housed, as the Communists had minimized the former and run the latter through the interior ministry. After six months, Havel felt he now had a 'modern political office' at his disposal (s6, 226). At its core were the men and women he had recruited since the mid-1980s, above all Křižan (now lead adviser on domestic politics) and Vondra (foreign affairs). They were joined by a press secretary, Michael Žantovský, and a series of chiefs of staff that included Prince Karel Schwarzenberg.[4] Full of former dissidents, writers and artists, the presidential administration at the peak of its influence was also at its most chaotic. Havel had never liked formal command; when put in charge of his prison cellmates in November 1982, he complained to Olga that 'I definitely do not know how to give orders and be "badass", but unfortunately that's the way it has to be.'[5] It was thanks instead to Žantovský, a clinical psychologist, that the office settled into a more professional pattern, although

Havel (back to camera) with several of his advisers, including Saša Vondra (in glasses) and Jiří Křižan (third from right).

it was also subsiding in importance: many of Havel's advisers eventually dispersed to ministerial jobs, party leaderships or the diplomatic corps.[6] Over the coming years Havel supplemented the input from his staff by convening 72 seminars at a villa near the presidential country residence at Lány, to which 2,000 specialists, activists and advocates were invited to speak, and speak freely.[7]

The Castle itself was a continuous project, since Havel wanted to make the massive citadel more accessible to the public (he opened many gardens, galleries and ramparts that had long been off-limits); more hospitable for events (he founded a summer Shakespeare festival in 1994); and a less grim place in which to work. Masaryk had done something similar, commissioning the great Slovene architect Josip Plečnik in the 1920s to add classicist flourishes to the Castle's Gothic-Baroque expanse. Havel had a team of designers at his disposal, but like Masaryk enlisted an outsider, Bořek Šípek, a returning émigré, for the most delicate assignments: the president's study and the entrance in the Second Courtyard to the presidential administration. Šípek emulated Plečnik in many respects and the results, like Plečnik's, were not to everyone's liking, but they were to Havel's.[8]

In most respects, however, Havel looked not to Masaryk's example for guidance, but to the present-day German president, Richard von Weizsäcker. Havel quickly developed a close rapport with him and adopted his conception of the office as a moral command point and a quiet constant, ensuring constitutional stability and continuity. On becoming president of the Czech Republic in 1993, Havel announced that he did not want to be responsible directly for state decisions but 'be felt in the background as a certain guarantee of the legitimacy of those decisions', as a stimulator, integrator and 'watchman of political culture' (s7, 31–2). Havel had been allowed to mark up a draft of the Czech constitution in late 1992 – its affective parts, such as the preamble, are largely his handiwork – and he won a few of the changes that he had sought unsuccessfully as federal president that restored the office to what it had been before the Communist takeover. This revision boiled down

Havel in his office in Prague Castle.

to the elimination of the legislature's power to vote him out of office (a trial for treason or gross violation of the constitution must take place instead) and the addition of the suspensive veto, the right to return legislation with suggested changes. The interwar presidency had had this power, and its absence from the Communist-era constitution became problematic in October 1991 when the federal legislature passed an Act for 'lustration', the systematic vetting of officials for past ties to the StB. Havel supported the idea of lustration but objected to certain details, and felt he could resolve this quandary only by signing the bill while immediately proposing a raft of amendments (s6, 585).[9] Under the new Czech constitution he could no longer initiate legislation but could withhold his signature and send a bill back, forcing the legislature either to rewrite it or override his veto by a vote of at least half of all its members. Over ten years Havel, like Masaryk, used this veto sparingly, against only 27 of the 821 bills the legislature passed, and it was usually overridden, but he could use his veto messages to accentuate ideals such as the rule of law, pluralism and social justice.[10] Havel also influenced public law indirectly through his power to appoint (subject to Senate consent) the justices of the constitutional court, to which he referred nine major Acts for review, and monetary policy through the governing board of the central bank, in the naming of which he had a free hand.

That Havel did not seek to increase his office's formal powers came in part from his realization that at least '50 per cent' of political success derived from psychological savvy rather than the constitution (s7, 38). Politics, he concluded, did not require lying but did require 'taste' (*vkus*), by which he meant knowing when to speak and when to stop, how to avoid giving offence, how to focus on the essentials, create a friendly atmosphere and get inside another person's soul (s6, 526–7). Like the seemingly more powerful American president, he could get little done if he was not persuasive when addressing the legislature (as he did ten times from 1990 to 1992) or enlisting the public to press their representatives to act on his proposals. Havel also sought partnership with other institutions; his ideal arrangement would have been a tandem with a small, distinguished body to supervise, in the spirit of VONS and Charter 77, the workings of the primary legislative chamber and the cabinet answering to it. Before the Czech–Slovak split, he proposed (in vain) the creation of a 'council of wise men' of thirty members drawn from the two republics' legislatures, with whom he would keep an eye on a separately elected, unicameral federal assembly (s6, 431). He later hoped to team up with the Czech Senate, to which 81 individuals were elected from single-member constituencies, to monitor the Chamber of Deputies, whose 200 members were elected from party lists (s7, 387–8, 660–61).

Those parties were something of a dilemma for Havel. He accepted their importance in a democracy and rejected the allegation that he wanted them to be supplanted by less formal associations or more footloose personalities (s6, 725). He remained unaffiliated but at times communicated his sympathy, first for Civic Forum, then for the small centre-right Civic Democratic Alliance, and finally for the Greens. Masaryk's experience taught that it was risky for a president to create a party of his own, as there was no guarantee that the popularity of the head of state would flow to a group seeking votes. When a faction of Havel's advisers recommended in 1991–2 that he set up a party to prevent the breakup of Czechoslovakia, he demurred in favour of pro-federation rallies, exerting 'taste' at countless high-level talks and proposing stop-gap amendments to stabilize the existing constitution.[11] However, the federal assembly's rejection of most of his amendments and then the decision of the largest Czech and Slovak parties to terminate the union at the end of 1992 proved that without a significant parliamentary bloc Havel's preferred methods were ultimately ineffectual.

Even Hrádeček failed to work its magic when Havel hosted the leaders of the two republics there in November 1991: he laid on his best brandy and goulash and laid out a clear agenda, only to despair as the sides talked at cross-purposes into the wee hours, stymied by a largely symbolic treaty to refound the union.[12]

Havel defended his abstention from party politics as freedom to listen to the public without concern for 'his own electoral base and its momentary moods or the horizon of the next elections' (s7, 318). It also gave him more freedom in performing his primary task, speaking, and his 300 speeches, like his poems and prison letters, developed themes.[13] Arching over them all was the need for moral renewal, which Havel described as a *velké dílo* (s6, 136, 159, 183, 561, 659; s7, 145, 173, 502, 565). *Velké dílo* is the equivalent of magnum opus, a Great Work. Havel used it as a term of art but also of alchemy, taken from the literature he had consulted for *Temptation* and associated with a previous occupant of Prague Castle, the eccentric Habsburg emperor Rudolf II (1552–1612), to whom he compared himself (s8, 618). In some Hermetic traditions, the Great Work was a spiritual process, out of which the alchemist would emerge a purified, superior being. Havel hoped that his country would undergo a comparable conversion to a life of *duch* (mind or spirit), resisting the 'harmful pressures of technical civilization, with its stupefying dictatorship of consumption and omnipresent commercialism' (s6, 75, 102). His mission was to inject into public life

duchovnost [spirituality or intellect], moral responsibility, humaneness, humility and regard for the fact that there is something higher than us, that our conduct is not lost in some black hole of time, but is inscribed somewhere and assessed, that we have no right or reason to believe that we understand everything and can do anything. (s6, 53)

Havel's presidential addresses were picking up where his prison letters had left off, with their call for existential revolution.[14] He would refer often to his time in prison, to bolster his authority and to compare the post-Communist mindset to that of a person after sudden release from captivity (s7, 530). And it was in prison, especially in letter 96 from October 1981, that he had clarified the outlook that would guide his presidency – idealistic but not utopian.[15]

What distinguished the former from the latter became clearer after 1989, when Havel equated utopianism with an ideology like Communism, pursued by 'ugly means' because it was believed to be scientific, and science has no conscience. Unlike a state based on ideology, a state based on *duch* would rehabilitate the person of conscience, responsibility and ideas 'avouched by his own existence' (s6, 544). Ideals represented the 'hand of a compass' showing the way ahead, a horizon towards which societies should be forever striving, a permanent challenge that is never met but that leaves a positive trace (s6, 68–70, 375; s7, 25, 255). The finest summary of his attitude, offered to an audience in Bangkok in 1994, accepted that

> people will never be angels and evil will not vanish from the world. But that does not mean that we are not duty-bound again and again to think about how to make the world better, again and again to articulate certain ideals, set our sights on them and act in their spirit. (s7, 212)

To a Dublin audience in 1996, he put it still more succinctly in the words of the poet Holan's 'First Testament': 'without the pure transcendental/ no construction will be complete' (s7, 619).

President Havel's use of religion was, like Masaryk's, ecumenical; he would refer broadly to 'God' or 'the Lord' but rarely to Jesus, and then only as a historical person.[16] As he told a group of children at

Christmas in 1995, 'I consider myself a believer, but my Lord God is a bit strange, rather hazy, he does not much demand that I pray and such like.'[17] His frequent remarks on nature and the environment harkened back to his pantheism, in seeing the universe as a single infinite meta-organism of which humanity was a special part but not apart (s6, 575). At Davos in February 1992 he paraphrased Edward Lorenz's meteorological theory of the 'butterfly effect' and his grandfather Vácslav's theosophy: 'We are just a special knot of Being, its living atom, or rather a cell that – if it is sufficiently open to itself and its own mystery – is also able to experience and perceive the mystery, will, pain and hope of the world' (s6, 648–9).

Each of Havel's four presidencies was a distinct stage in the Great Work. His short but frenetic first term (December 1989– June 1990) was dedicated to the resumption of historical time and telling the truth: the president would no longer lie to the people and the people should no longer lie to themselves. The country's past and Havel's own were intertwined in many of his first acts and remarks. As commander-in-chief, he advocated the reduction and eventual elimination of the military service he had so disliked, but also vowed never to capitulate if menaced as in 1938 (s6, 95, 131, 339, 347). His first foreign visit was to West Germany, to confront the legacy of Munich and the post-war expulsion of Czechoslovakia's Germans. The first Soviet bloc country he visited as president was the first he had visited as a young man (Poland), followed by a speech in Canada honouring émigrés. He amnestied 80 per cent of the country's 30,000 prisoners, whom he had long regarded as victims of a system that needlessly criminalized misfits and nonconformists. He appointed veterans of Charter 77 and the Kampademy as university rectors, urging them to steer their institutions away from politically biased admission policies and towards the humanities and respect for 'the meaning of life' and everything 'beautifully mysterious' (s6, 20–24). An honorary degree from the university in Olomouc was occasion to reminisce about Josef Ludvík Fischer (s6, 161–4).

Havel's second presidency (July 1990–July 1992) confronted the anxiety that surged once the euphoria of revolution had worn off. Many worried about the spike in inflation and unemployment that would accompany the return to a market economy, while radicals fumed that the old guard was not being dislodged more quickly from the bureaucracy and enterprise management. Havel acknowledged those fears and frustrations and admitted to harbouring them himself, to the point of being almost depressed by the responsibility that came with victory in revolution (s6, 230). On the first anniversary of those events, he drew attention not just to a public mood of dissatisfaction and disappointment, but to the spread of ill will, envy and vanity, asking whether the two nations were capable of good only for several months every few decades (s6, 298). His New Year's television address for 1991 echoed Fromm in its claim that everyone had been 'neuroticized by the burden of freedom' (s6, 315, 322). As in his dissident essays, however, Havel tried to balance critique with encouragement, and in a short book of *Summer Meditations*, rushed out in August 1991 in a print run of 100,000, he offered a positive vision of where he hoped the country would be in ten to fifteen years.[18]

His third presidency, and first just as head of the Czech state (February 1993–February 1998), helped Czechs accept the loss of the union with Slovakia, which he himself slowly came to regard as a good thing, for a nation must first experience standing on its own in order to cooperate well with others (s8, 221). The keyword of this term in office was 'authority', both of the new state (especially of its laws) and of something higher, above man, the absolute horizon that could provide essential values (s7, 430). As war raged in another failed federation, Yugoslavia, and Russia's constitutional crisis turned violent in October 1993, Havel wanted to win an international security guarantee and to foster in Czechs a passionate

Havel in New York in summer 2000, with Saša Vondra.

but not fanatical attachment to their republic. For both ends he used the memory of 1938, reminding the West of its failure to resist evil at Munich and Czechs of Beneš's loss of resolve afterwards.[19]

In his early federal presidency, Havel had followed dissident writing in wanting a new, Europe-wide form of collective security. The intransigence of Western officials, especially in the United States, forced him instead to become an advocate of NATO enlargement (and transformation). Later, he became an ever stronger proponent of the use of force for humanitarian ends, even without a clear mandate from the United Nations, such as during the Kosovo crisis of 1999 (s7, 860, 868; s8, 56). He admitted that this was a precarious position to take, since his own country had been invaded by Germany in 1939 and the USSR in 1968 on the pretext of coming to someone's rescue (Czechoslovakia's German minority and pro-Moscow Communists, respectively). Intervention was legitimate, he stipulated, only if done in good faith to protect a group threatened by a criminal regime and only as a last resort (s8, 207). Havel, however, could offer no objective test to distinguish such situations from cover stories, and his advocacy of NATO strikes on Yugoslavia put him at odds with much of Czech public opinion and the government, as would his endorsement of the American invasion of Iraq in 2003.[20]

On his many trips abroad, Havel spoke of the other authority, 'the renewed authority of the universe' (s7, 292), from which to derive a common denominator of care for the planet. In his relatively little spare time, he read books about human origins and the history of religion, to prepare himself for the unfamiliar cultures he would encounter in Asia and South America. From this literature and the research of a Czech-American psychiatrist, Stanislav Grof, he assumed the existence of a prehistoric, collective unconscious, expressed archetypically in virtually all religions but obscured by historic, local identities. With the emergence of a postmodern, global civilization, one that tended to be secular, cosmopolitan and Westernizing (America symbolized all that was good and bad about it), Havel feared that traditional cultures were seeking safety in ethnically discrete nation-states, the pursuit of which paradoxically exposed them to greater risk of conflict.[21] To make the new global civilization less disturbing and more meaningful, Havel's speeches in São Paulo, Hiroshima and Philadelphia and at Harvard called for a 'codex of human coexistence' using the 'common roots of human spirituality and religiosity' (s7, 483, 635). It need not take the form of a single world religion, nor require the revival of older, organized ones; it would suffice to agree on a spiritually informed order (řád, a Fischer keyword) within which groups could preserve their identities (s7, 544–5). The West could offer the East the openness of democracy, but the East could teach the West about authority in the Confucian tradition, which Havel summarized as 'respect for neighbours, family, certain natural authorities' (s7, 483). Human rights could be universalized if rooted not in Western metaphors of the social contract but in a transpersonal experience of 'the absolute' (s7, 500).

With the Czech state established and its security covered by accession to NATO in 1999, Havel's fourth and final presidency (February 1998–February 2003) turned to the ways in which the central state's power could be delegated down to the local level, out to the non-profit sector and up to the European Union (EU). Although some of his speeches became (in)famous for attacking the utilitarian egoism that he felt had played too large a role in economic policy and in the conduct of the new business class (just as he had disliked it in Thirty-sixer Radim Kopecký's variant of optimism[22]), Havel objected primarily to the 'big-state conservatism' of ostensibly neoliberal politicians who did not want to surrender ministerial power (s7, 744, 853; s8, 147). He pressed the governing parties to meet the EU's exacting membership conditions, since doing so would force them to undertake the necessary next round of reforms and crack down on corruption.

He reassured the nation that even in a globalizing world they retained the power to care for their home, environment, architecture and public spaces (s8, 94–5) and need not see a threat to their identity in pooling sovereignty with other states (he had already said as much to Kopecký in 1953).[23] He in turn spoke to the EU as he had to NATO, urging it to admit new members as a form of historical justice; to make its institutions leaner and more comprehensible; and to develop a sense of belonging that Europeans could combine with their national identities. He generally urged Europe to seek an alternative to consumerism rather than race to overtake America, just as he had once derided socialism's efforts to match Western capitalism (s7, 826–39; s8, 59, 155, 163).

Like his prison letters, his presidential speeches allude to but do not convey the full toll – emotional and physical – of the Great Work on Havel. He had become a global statesman and international public intellectual, making almost 200 official trips outside the country, but at the expense of the literary work he always claimed to prefer. Writing, which he said had never come easily to him, became a chore as he insisted on composing most of his speeches himself, and already by July 1990 he was finding it tedious (s6, 230–32). As in the past, he had Olga by his side, and she quickly became a very popular First Lady through her charity work with children and the disabled, but in 1994 she was diagnosed with cancer, and died on 27 January 1996.

Havel honoured Olga as an 'absolutely irreplaceable and fundamental part' of his soul, but he already had a new companion, the actress Dagmar Veškrnová (b. 1953).[24] He had noticed her shortly before the revolution, when she embodied his desire to reconnect to the world of official culture: she had starred in dozens of films and Dietl's television serials and was a cast member at Prague's prestigious Vinohrady Theatre. He later dated the start of their affair to April 1990, and he married her on 4 January 1997, in the same place (Žižkov town hall) and with as little fanfare as he had Olga. Whereas he had had to justify his first marriage only to his parents, he had to explain his second to the country's media, which insinuated that he had sullied Olga's memory by his haste and choice of spouse, a divorcée celebrity whose every remark, dress and hairdo the press would now be only too happy to pick apart. Although most of Havel's friends gave the couple their blessing, Dagmar rankled several of his closest aides, who worried that she encouraged him to be less circumspect.[25]

Even if Dagmar was an awkward fit with the ways of the Castle, the charge that she unmoored Havel is unfounded. Havel had always acted on flights of fancy and prided himself on an idealistic amateurism, such as his insistence on receiving the Dalai Lama in 1990 without regard for the diplomatic fallout (he never visited China) or turning up unannounced to startle the legislature into action.[26] If he did become more rash or delusional in his final presidential term, convening forum after forum of the great and the good to save the world, it was in reaction to several life-threatening illnesses (a lung tumour in 1996 and an intestinal perforation in 1998). Decades of heavy smoking, which he was forced to quit in 1996, and the bouts of pneumonia in prison put him in constant danger of respiratory infection, and after 2000 he had attacks of cardiac arrhythmia. Always quick to pop pills, he was on a cocktail of medications throughout the presidential years, including some to pep him up in the morning and others to put him to sleep at night.[27] In all likelihood, his sudden marriage to Dagmar, whose insistence on better medical care saved his life twice, was itself a reaction to brushes with death.

In February 1990 Havel had vowed that he would step down if it ever seemed that he was not up to the task (s6, 79). Strictly speaking, that moment did not come: despite the increasingly frequent hospitalizations, he was never as incapacitated as Masaryk became in his fourth term, or as Svoboda when Husák ousted him in 1975. But with hindsight it could be argued that

Havel and Dagmar (Dáša) Veškrnová at Lány, May 1998.

President Havel, shortly after re-election in 1998.

he did himself a disservice by pursuing re-election in 1998. His candidacy faced stronger opposition in the legislature than ever before from the Communists (who had 10 per cent of the seats) and the far-right Republicans, who so vilified him that Dagmar, watching from the back of the Castle's Spanish Hall, protested with a piercing whistle. It took two rounds to get him elected, and then only with the bare minimum of votes required.[28] By autumn 1999, he was feeling as overstretched as he had as the chief dissident in the 1980s, and privately said so in splenetic memos to staff.[29] He simultaneously signalled his unhappiness to the public through remarks about the martyred tenth-century St Vojtěch (Adalbert), 'a great dreamer, today we would say an idealist', 'a challenge, an appeal, a reproach, an inspiration' who disturbed pragmatic realists and ended up leaving his homeland in disgust (s8, 11–16, 22). As Havel approached 4 January 2000, the date of his childhood fantasy about the *Dobrovka* goodness factory (see Chapter One), he resembled not so much Professor Václav Havel the wildly popular explorer and entrepreneur as Doctor Leopold Kopřiva of *Largo desolato*, playing his part 'mechanically and outwardly' so that he can believe he is still the person to whom that part once rightly belonged (s2, 711–12).

On his own standard, Havel was not to be pitied, just as he had refused to pity Mikhail Gorbachev when he witnessed him being mobbed on a Prague street in 1987. Havel had imagined the Soviet leader's long day, an unceasing stream of people whose faces, names and needs he was expected to remember, for whom he always had to have ready a cheery, witty but uncontroversial remark. Havel had restrained his sympathy and reminded himself that Gorbachev had 'what he wanted. He had known, after all, what awaited him' (s4, 962). As for himself, Havel had sensed in 1985 that if Czechoslovakia did return to normal, open politics, he could not expect to be its 'driving motor' (s4, 599); had he wanted to be it, he would have had to lead a large party and become prime minister. And he admitted that as president he fixated unduly on the prurient tabloids and the odd jab from a pundit or irreverent official, rather than on the polls that showed him to be enjoying steadily high approval and trust ratings (70 per cent had wanted him to seek another term in 1998).[30]

Those surveys did turn up one weakness in Havel's standing: although large majorities each time reported satisfaction with how he represented the country abroad and performed his duties, an equally large majority (around two-thirds) complained that during his last term he was not 'in contact with citizens' and 'did not know their problems'.[31] To some degree this impression was to be expected, given Havel's long-standing sense of remoteness from ordinary folk, but it had not been so evident in his earlier presidencies; before his first election he conducted a very successful get-acquainted tour, especially of working-class areas, and in his first month in office he received 30,000 letters from citizens. His initial fear was that he would become the subject of a kitschy cult, and he deliberately took a few controversial steps, such as the prisoner amnesty, to burst the bubble.[32]

The basis of his later reputation for detachment was the restitution of the nationalized property – the Lucerna and Barrandov Terraces – that had caused the Havel family's social unease in the first place. Neither Havel nor Ivan was interested in managing their equal shares in the Lucerna. Ivan transferred his to his new wife, also called Dagmar, while Havel, on the advice of Marián Čalfa, the former prime minister, in whom Havel placed inordinate trust, sold his stake in February 1997 to an industrial conglomerate, Chemapol, for 200 million crowns (at the time, $7 million or £4 million). Despite giving half of his proceeds to charity, Havel could never dispel the whiff of hypocrisy in doing business with a firm that symbolized everything he found objectionable in contemporary capitalism. The sale also infuriated his sister-in-law, who sued to stop it on the claim that she had the right of first refusal; she lost in court, but acquired the share after the spectacularly mismanaged Chemapol went into bankruptcy.[33] Although she had to continue to fend off Chemapol's creditors, in her hands Lucerna's fate was far happier than that of the derelict Terraces. Havel followed Ivan's example and gave his share to his wife, who bought out Ivan's Dagmar and then sold the controlling interest in 2003 to a group of investors. A decade later, their grand plans remained on paper, and the Terraces languished as a haven for squatters and the homeless.

As a wealthy man, Havel knew that he would not want for a home when his presidency ended and he lost the right to the Castle and to the country seat, Lány, where he had spent half of his last year in office.[34] With Olga he had already bought a villa in an affluent street, Dělostřelecká, near the Castle, and with Dagmar a villa on the Algarve coast of Portugal, where the sea air eased his lungs. And there was always Hrádeček. The challenge would instead be to create a new home in the wider sense of *domov*, since previous presidents had tended to die in office or vanish upon leaving it, so there was no precedent of one remaining publicly active. Havel's Great Work, like alchemy, was an inherently unfinishable project, and he fully intended to continue in it while struggling to sum up the meaning of his life.

7

Exiting (2003–11)

– Darling, what do you think, is the world all bad?
– I don't think so. Come, let us be going.
Václav Havel, 'On the Observation Tower' (s1, 173)

Everything Havel did and wrote in the last decade of his life was, he said, in some way conclusory, an attempt to impart the lessons of a life lived in the open but whose meaning could be lost in an age of deafening informational noise (s8, 8, 112, 183). He was impeded in this already difficult task by two things. The first was his familiarity at home and his legend abroad as a one-time dissident, prisoner and leader of a peaceful revolution. This status paradoxically made it more difficult for him to get heard with the ability to shock that he had enjoyed, for example, as a youth at the Dobříš writers' conference in 1956. Freed from the presidency's handcuffs of 'taste', he could be ever blunter in reproaching corporate executives and state officials for destroying the fabric of communities and nature in the name of efficiency and profit; to his horror, such audiences did not boo or walk out but clapped and cheered, venerating the icon of the man who had fought Communism in the fast-receding past (s8, 273–83, 339–40).

The second, still greater obstacle was Šafařík's reminder in *Seven Letters to Melin* that nature obliges a heretic never to become pope, by which he meant an external enforcer of morals. Instead, he must inspire others to become equal avouchers of their own truths, beings as internally free as he is.[1] This is easier said than done if that heretic believes, as Havel did, that the very medium of inspiring and avouching, language, 'can never capture precisely what it wants to capture . . . can never grasp something as continuous as reality, experience, or our souls'. This gap between language and meaning is good in that it has pushed humanity through the ages into a creative struggle for self-expression and 'it is in this struggle that man becomes himself.' But it means that 'man will carry the complete truth about himself to the grave', knowable only to the 'memory of Being' (s8, 693).

That observation came near the end of one of Havel's attempts to sum up his experience as revolutionary and president, *Please Be Brief* (2006).[2] The book's immediate purpose was the same as that of *Questioning from Afar* had been twenty years earlier – to set out his version of events and roundly refute less friendly ones – and he enlisted the same journalist, Karel Hvížd'ala, to reprise the role of sympathetic interviewer. Unlike their previous conversation, however, this one was sandwiched between excerpts of memos to the presidential staff and entries from a diary he had kept in 2005 while in residence at the Library of Congress in Washington, DC, then as a guest of the Polish president, and finally at Hrádeček. The result was a collage, 'one that has its own architecture, one that unfolds and interweaves themes and motifs and time periods'.[3] Havel used this format in part because he had neither the stamina nor the desire to write the traditional monologue of an elder statesman. He also believed that a collage, like his plays, might tease out the hidden structures whereby 'anything from one period points to something from the preceding or ensuing period; everything is tied together in all sorts of ways' (s8, 621). The difference between *Questioning from Afar* and *Please Be Brief* can be encapsulated in Šafařík's's distinction between *paměť* (memoir) and *vzpomínka* (remembrance, reminiscence): the former is a document, a rational attempt to reconstruct the past, while the latter is like a poem, coming from the heart 'in that critical, liminal, concluding stage of life, when we feel that we are leaving and will not return again'.[4]

Even before the end of his presidency, Havel and Dagmar had begun to prepare for life without the Castle's secretariat and venues. Like many eminent European politicians, they followed the American example of creating a presidential library to house papers and display artefacts telling a life's story. The Václav Havel Library, however, became something very different from the typical American institution. The latter serves mainly as an outpost of the national archives, a museum, and ultimately a mausoleum and place of pilgrimage; Havel envisioned his library as something far more vibrant, a 'thoroughly independent centre [*ohnisko*] of learning' and a 'hotspot [*ohnisko*] of critical thinking' (s8, 297–8). It would be a den wherein and whereby others would continue in the Great Work, using a packed calendar of events, Internet presence and a stream of publications to remind the country of its past but also to debate its present. The library was split between two sites in Prague until 2014, when it moved into the former headquarters of the postal service in Ostrovní Street. Other islands in the Havel archipelago included a philanthropic foundation that he established with Dagmar and an ecumenical spiritual centre, Prague Crossroads, in a converted Gothic church a short walk from the Theatre on the Balustrade.[5]

But what was most expected from Havel was a new play, one that would utilize his Castle experience. He had already been trying to write plays with a political subject in the brief interval between *Asanace* (1987) and the revolution in 1989. One effort came to fruition, thanks to a commission from an experimental theatre group, the Theatre on a String, to contribute (without attribution) to a show in October 1988 marking the seventieth anniversary of Czechoslovakia's founding.[6] A 'historical meditation' in five short acts, *Tomorrow We'll Start it Up!* is set on the eve of independence and focuses on Alois Rašín, the friend of Havel's grandfather Vácslav who would become finance minister and for whom the embankment on which Number 78 stood would be renamed, yet again, in 1990. On one level, the play was intended to revive awareness of a man who had gone to prison (in Bory, like Havel) for his cause, was 51 years old in 1918 (the same age as Havel when he wrote the play) and was then erased from an ungrateful public's memory. It was also a tribute to Rašín's wife (his 'important and faithful support', s2, 971) and to the conspiratorial methods used against Habsburg rule, which in the play bear an uncanny resemblance to those used by dissidents under socialism. Deeper still, the play grappled with the challenge of ascertaining the relative importance of those methods and of dedicated individuals in determining the course of history compared to the spontaneous effect of random strangers, personified in the play by a hitherto conformist greengrocer who whips up a patriotic crowd on Wenceslas Square. Havel was working through theoretical questions that would become practical concerns a year later, and the play suggests that a happy balance can and must be struck between leaders and masses. A paragon of sobriety and foresight, the play's Rašín already recognizes the hard work lying ahead to build and protect the new state, enliven a plundered, work-shy society, combine freedom with responsibility, and ensure influence for revolutionary leaders such as himself whose party will not be a big vote-winner. It closes with Rašín's dream of events to come in the form of an acoustic collage, like the one Havel compiled for the state's fiftieth anniversary in 1968.

Tomorrow was a study in political beginnings, but Havel was also working at the time on a play about endings. Grandees of the Communist apparatus were already falling before the cataclysm of 1989. Although he remained president, Gustáv Husák had been forced by his comrades to relinquish the more important post of general secretary in December 1987, and Havel's notes refer to 'Husák's fall' as source material.[7] But Havel was also thinking about his own departure from the role of chief dissident, shifting the burden onto the younger men he had groomed so that he could focus on breaking back into theatre. Such situations are exacting tests of an identity: if someone has been playing a role, especially one with great responsibility and for a long time, what dangers arise when that role ends? Is anyone truly indispensable, or is everyone fundamentally replaceable?

In drama, those questions are associated with Shakespeare's *King Lear*, in which a man's persona collapses when he abdicates his throne and divides his kingdom. Like many classics, it had entered Havel's consciousness at an early age, when he was 'strongly affected' by Peter Brook's famous production in 1964.[8] In the late 1980s, Lear was in the air as Faust had been a few years before. Courtesy of a friend's translation, Havel had access to a new play by Gaston Salvatore, a Chilean in exile in West Germany, which turned the dialogue between the king and his fool into one between Joseph Stalin and an actor who has been playing Lear.[9] Shakespeare also inspired Josef Topol, with whom Havel had long been in friendly competition, for *The Voices of Birds*, the first new play Topol could get staged, in June 1989, after decades on the blacklist. Topol's play takes place almost entirely in the garden of the villa of an ageing actor, who has collapsed while playing Lear. He is cared for by his stern yet devoted housekeeper, Anna, and his gardener Bert (Lear's Fool). He wrangles with two former lovers and the estranged sons he fathered by them, and embarks on a new affair with a young student, Yveta, who wants to write his biography. His needs are met, he is even loved, yet he craves the respect that he has lost. Near the end he is told that the authorities intend to raze his villa as part of a grand redevelopment, and he ends up in a mental asylum with Anna and Bert.[10]

Havel read and then saw Topol's play, and liked the perform-ances, especially of the actress who played the student Yveta, a certain Dagmar Veškrnová, of whom he said to a journalist in

August 1989 that she 'seemed to me to be good, although I don't know what kind of a person she is'.[11] Havel also liked the first two-thirds of Topol's text. The last third, however, disappointed him, as he felt it descended into a forced explication of each character's history and dramatic significance, rather than letting them emerge surreptitiously as they would in Chekhov or Ibsen.

What to do in the last third was also bedevilling Havel's own effort at a play based on Lear, with elements of Chekhov, Beckett and Pinter. The first outline and draft of three of five projected acts are undated, so we do not know how much he had composed before encountering *The Voices of Birds*, but the similarities are striking (Havel claimed in 1989 that he and Topol agreed to pretend that they had planned the coincidence[12]). The initial outline describes the protagonist, Vilém (William) Lír, as a politician around 55 (thus, close to Havel in age), elegant, mildly vain and accustomed to publicity. He is taking his recent loss of power badly but trying not to let it show and, like Dubček after 1969, is under the illusion that he will soon be called back. He has a court consisting of three women: Zdena, his older sister, who tries to keep him grounded and like Lear's daughter Cordelia (and Topol's Anna) will stand by him to the end; Alice, his companion (*družka*), an intelligent coquette of forty-ish who inadvertently undermines Lír's dignity; and his daughter Zuzana, a somewhat punky, apolitical free spirit. Lír will be visited by his neighbour, Knobloch, who will be the conduit for increasingly bad news from the outside world, and by a journalist and photographer who will throw his court into bedlam. All the action was to take place in the garden or lounge of Lír's villa, in a country that is the anywhere-land of *The Conspirators* and *Mountain Hotel*.[13]

In the first draft, Act I introduces the cast, with Lír now called Ilja Rieger, a jarring compound with Russian and patriotic Czech connotations.[14] Their persiflage in the garden thinly veils the tension between Zdena and Alice, made only worse by Knobloch's news that Rieger is under investigation for abuse of power. In Act ii, the journalist (Jack) and photographer (Bob) arrive, and allow Rieger to speak at length about his supposed ideals, couched in the 'dialectical metaphysics' that Havel lampooned in the 1960s; like Huml's treatise on values in *The Increased Difficulty of Concentration*, Rieger's programme seems faultlessly humane, democratic and moderate, but has a hollow ring.[15] (One of Havel's translators, Paul Wilson, argues convincingly that Rieger originated as a personification of Gorbachev's halfway democratization.[16]) Act iii moves inside, as Jack and Rieger try to have a serious discussion, but they are constantly interrupted by the other characters' inanities, and Rieger invites the visitors to stay the night. At this point the play becomes a depiction of life at Hrádeček in the late 1980s, with the Olga figure Zdena complaining that Rieger (read: Havel) is drinking too much, is too keen to throw a party without first consulting her, and tomorrow will be in a foul funk that she will have to alleviate. Alice (read: Jitka Vodňanská) reveals to Jack that Rieger is reluctant to acknowledge publicly that she has been his lover for seven years because he cannot free himself from the (s)mothering Zdena, who will not allow Alice even to rinse a cup. Both women threaten to leave, but Rieger insists that both stay. As the act ends, Alice and Jack embrace and flee into the garden.

That was as far as Havel got. His schematic notes for Acts iv and v anticipated a big row between Rieger and Alice, whereupon she would leave with the photographer, Bob; Zuzana would belittle her father for his refusal to accept the end of his career and for his neglect (Zdena raised her after Rieger's wife, like Stalin's, committed suicide); and Knobloch would confess that he had signed an anti-Rieger petition to protect his son's place at university. Rieger, finally face-to-face with reality as a storm rages, would be reduced to quoting Beckett as Zdena, the only character staying by his side, 'bravely and unsentimentally' wipes the spittle from his lips. The play would thus have ended with the crisis of identity that Shakespeare's *Lear* already reaches by the start of its third act.

The play was left unfinished not because Havel was diverted into politics in November 1989, but because he had already lost interest several months before. While in prison he was still expecting to complete it upon his release, but by August he was telling a journalist that the themes that drew him to the subject had 'lost their liveliness' and for 'private reasons' he now felt repelled.[17] This may have been an oblique admission that the circumstances at Hrádeček had changed, if indeed he had ended his affair with Vodňanská and no longer had the masochistic need to depict the ménage as he had in *Largo desolato*. He nevertheless assured the journalist of his determination to find a way back into theatre without resorting to the 'workmanlike' melodrama that Dietl had churned out until his death in 1985.[18]

It may have been the approach of the end of his presidency, or the sight of his friend Jan Tříska, back from America in 2002 to play Lear at the Castle's Shakespeare festival, that moved Havel to fish out the old notes. It would take five years for him to revise the play, polishing the final draft during another sojourn in the United States in 2006–7. He finally gave it a title: *Odcházení*, which is usually translated as *Leaving* but could also be *Exiting*, since it is the Czech verb used in stage directions to send a character off.

Although outwardly reworked like his early plays had been, *Leaving* preserves so much of the first attempt that it is not apparent that in the intervening years the author had had his own experience of high office. Strikingly, of all the characters it was the central figure, now named Vilém Rieger, who changed the least. This continuity suggests that the play, like most plays about politicians, uses him only as a vehicle for a bigger theme, in this case the undue reliance on a role, on the affirmation of others and on the delusion of one's indispensability rather than on an avouched truth as the bedrock of identity. Havel could not make politics itself the true subject because politics as he understood it in his essays and speeches was 'applied morality', whereas his plays depicted worlds without values.

The other characters changed somewhat more. Alice became Irena, Rieger's long-term girlfriend, who still indulges his bombastic delusions, infantilizes him and is hurt by his reluctance to parade her in public. She eventually leaves him, but only in the company of her lady-in-waiting, Monika, and not with Jack or Bob, who are now portrayed as simpleton hacks. (This was Havel's way of getting back at the scandal sheets that had plagued him, as was the title of *Please Be Brief*, an infuriating request he often heard from interviewers who wanted facile answers to big questions.) The Olga-like Zdena was much reduced and turned into Rieger's mother, known only as Grandma – one of the many allusions to a canonical Czech novel, Božena Němcová's *Babička* (1855), that run through the play and especially the later film adaptation. On its surface, *Babička* is a nostalgic tale of harmony between people and nature, between generations and between nobles and commoners. But even in Němcová's Biedermeier arcadia, which Rieger's court at first seems to resemble, there are serpents, such as the 'dark chasseur' who ruins a girl with the 'diabolical power' of his charm.[19] Havel had originally planned to model Bob the photographer on that character but then opted to bring in the eponymous Grandma, a touch as ridiculous as naming the *Garden Party*'s Pludeks for Oldřich and Božena of yore.

Havel kept Zuzana as Rieger's daughter but made her more like Lear's quietly loyal Cordelia, and added a second, Vlasta, comparable to Lear's ungrateful, scheming Regan and Goneril. Also added was a character like Yveta in Topol's *Voices of Birds*, a keen student, Bea, who wants to write Rieger's biography; unlike the Gretchen characters of Havel's earlier plays, she is a necrophile who is attracted to powerful men and eager to let Rieger have his way with her. Knobloch is now the groundskeeper who, like Bert in *The Voices of Birds*, speaks the unvarnished truth.

The finished play takes place entirely in the open, like *Mountain Hotel* and *The Voices of Birds*, with the villa as a backdrop facade. The biggest plot change arose not from the use of *Lear* but of a Chekhov play: whereas the first sketch had traces of *Three Sisters*, *Leaving* drew on *The Cherry Orchard*, in which a Russian family blithely ignores the financial woes and social upheaval that will cause them to lose their estate. Borrowing from that plot gave Havel the wherewithal to fill in the acts he could not write in 1989. Rieger's villa, we now learn, belongs to the state, and he assumes he can stay there, just as Masaryk was allowed to live out his last years at Lány and Husák remained in the Castle after losing the top job in the Communist Party. However, Vlastík Klein, Rieger's one-time deputy on the fast track to power, plans to evict him and carry out a post-Communist *asanace*, turning the villa into a shopping centre, casino and sex club. To ensure his quiescence, Rieger is blackmailed, interrogated and then offered the post of junior adviser to an adviser to Klein. As in the first draft, Rieger suffers a breakdown during a storm, but now does so in Act IV, giving him time to recover. Unlike Lear, he does not emerge from madness into clarity, but succumbs to a new delusion, accepting Klein's humiliating offer in the kind of rationalizing monologue with which Havel's flawed men usually end his plays.

The publication of *Leaving* in 2007 spurred an immediate rush to guess the real-life inspiration for Klein. Such speculation missed the character's purpose, which was to be another incarnation of the type first represented by Hugo Pludek in *The Garden Party* and Baláš in *The Memorandum* – a thief of others' catchphrases, machinator, liquidator of the nation's traditions and culture as well as the villa and garden that embody them.[20] But it was tantalizing that the character shared initials with Václav Klaus, for if anyone was the bane of Havel's presidency, it was he. Klaus was an economist who, like Staněk in *Protest*, had loathed the Communist system but was careful to protect his access to satisfying work. A natural politician, he became leader of Civic Forum's largest spin-off, the centre-right Civic Democratic Party, served as the Czech prime minister from 1992–7, and followed Havel as president in 2003. Havel was actually very supportive of the economic reforms that Klaus oversaw, and objected primarily (some would say belatedly) to their 'halfway-ness', the state left too strong where it should have been shrunk and vice versa.[21] Although the two men disagreed publicly on the non-profit sector, the EU, humanitarian intervention and the nation's past,[22] it was their more private difference in manner that caused friction: Klaus was a master of low-intensity bullying, which frazzled Havel's nerves.

There are a few moments in *Leaving*, such as when Klein brandishes a collection of speeches titled *Democracy, Freedom, the Market and Me*, that indeed suggest Klaus, a man to whom the adjective 'modest' would never be applied. But Klein, especially in the film version directed by Havel, is crass, louche and venal – also adjectives that would not be applied to Klaus. The very name Klein

Havel on the set of *Leaving*.

('small' in German) hints that he is a composite of other, younger politicians, such as Vlastimil Tlustý (whose surname means 'fat') and Stanislav Gross (whose surname in German is the opposite of *klein*). Tlustý, the leader of the parliamentary faction of Klaus's party, allegedly approached Havel before he left the presidency to offer a generous pension in return for Havel's endorsement of Klaus as his successor, and there is a moment in *Leaving* when Klein offers a similar quid pro quo.[23] Stanislav Gross, like Klein, had a meteoric rise (through the Czech Social Democratic Party), like Klein became deputy prime minister (during Havel's last year in the Castle) and was one of the few politicians who could surpass Havel in approval ratings. At the age of 34 he became prime minister, but he soon fell from power in a property scandal that involved a high-end flat in Barrandov and the proprietor of a brothel.

If Havel completed *Leaving* primarily to discharge an obligation to write a new play, it at least gave him the opportunity to fulfil a lifelong ambition: to make a film. Before his military service Havel's greatest wish had been to enter the film academy in order to become a director or screenwriter, but he had been rejected for the same reason he was later refused entry to the theatre academy (his class origin). Many of his earliest essays concerned film, including a study of the problem of adapting Shakespeare for the screen (s3, 150–56). His archive was full of never-realized scripts, one of which he was developing with Miloš Forman about the 1938 Munich crisis. At first he planned only to write a screenplay of *Leaving* and entrust it to someone else to direct, but changed his mind as he had been very unhappy with a film of *Beggar's Opera* made without his involvement in 1990.[24] He also had strong opinions about casting, starting with his wife Dagmar in the role of Irena. The part of Rieger, who on stage had been played by Tříska, went to the talented but less Lear-like Josef Abrhám. Filming took place in summer 2010 at the Villa Čerych in Česká Skalice, a town 25 kilometres from Hrádeček and intimately associated with Němcová's *Babička*.

The film stuck close to the play, with one noticeable difference. The play contains many pauses in the dialogue and spells of empty stage, moments Havel relished for 'their own special content' and 'message' (s8, 746). It also has sixteen points when the characters freeze and the author comments on his writing process. Cut off from the theatre for so long, Havel tortured himself in anticipating the analyses and criticisms that would greet a new play and he pre-emptively built them into the text (the diary entries in *Please Be Brief* had the same function). When learning about commercial moviemaking, however, Havel discovered that he would have to trim the running time or distributors would baulk, so he cut out the pauses and disembodied authorial voice.[25] Those deletions hastened the pace: the film of *Leaving* is a delirium of short takes, *The Cherry Orchard* on phenmetrazine.

The reception of the movie of *Leaving* was lukewarm: whereas the theatre production directed by Alfréd Radok's son David had played to full houses most nights, the film did poorly at the box office and awards ceremonies.[26] Part of the problem lay in the wider public's expectation that it would be treated to an insider's exposé of Czech politics; instead, it got a postmodern pastiche of gags and grotesques with whole passages from Shakespeare and Chekhov spliced in. Havel defended his technique as befitting the spirit of the age, with its 'fragmentation and equal worth of all sources, its non-hierarchifying'.[27] For conventional dramatic effect, however, the intertextuality of Gaston Salvatore's play is more potent, since the moments when Stalin or the actor quotes from *Lear* work organically towards a predictable but still devastating conclusion. Havel did not write orthodox Aristotelian tragedy, so *Leaving* does not end in a way that evokes pity, horror or guilty glee. When Rieger, Zuzana and Grandma depart from the villa – in the film, aboard an overloaded Wild West wagon driven by Pavel Landovský – the viewer feels only indifference, contempt or relief.

Havel at the premiere of *Leaving* in March 2011, with his wife Dagmar on his left and Josef Abrhám, who played Rieger, on his right.

Another problem of reception lay in the timing. The play and film appeared just before and just after the twentieth anniversary of the 1989 revolution, and the Czech public was in the mood for stories, preferably comforting, about its recent experience. On television, the most popular show at the time was *Vyprávěj* (Tell Us about It), a Dietl-style serial that tracked an extended family from 1964 to 2005. But Havel would never write a soap opera or saga, just as he did not directly satirize Czech politics in the manner of younger dramatists, such as Iva Klestilová and Roman Sikora. Havel admitted that he was not acquainted with their work, and they in turn tended not to mention him as a role model.[28]

After finishing the film of *Leaving*, Havel planned to write one more full-length play, *Sanatorium*, using hospital patients as archetypal figures of *commedia dell'arte*. It would have been much like his *Mountain Hotel* and likely to appeal only to very discriminating theatregoers.[29] What Havel might have done that would have been popular while staying faithful to his poetics would have been to revisit Vaněk. If there truly was a missed opportunity

The coach on which Rieger departs in the film of *Leaving*.

in his final efforts, it was not *Leaving*, but *Five Aunts*, written in
2010 for the same troupe that had commissioned *Tomorrow We'll
Start it Up!* It was a mini-sequel to *Vernissage*, with Vaněk again
the guest of Michal and Věra, catching up on their lives since
the revolution. A healthier, restored Havel could have used their
reunion to speak about the present as the Vaněk trilogy had about
'self-totalitarianism' in the 1970s, but it came too late: *Five Aunts*
was just a three-page drollery, a parting gift to old friends.[30]

One of the last diary entries in *Please Be Brief* recalled Josef
Šafařík's stubborn refusal to finish an essay that he had been
working on since the mid-1960s, to the point where it had
ballooned to more than 600 pages with no chapter breaks. The
1989 revolution made its publication possible, so he finally agreed
to let it go; on the day the first printed copy reached him, Havel
claimed, Šafařík died: 'Clearly, at the moment of finishing his life's
work, his life lost its meaning' (s8, 682).[31] A somewhat similar
determination could be ascribed to Havel: he fought off round
after round of potentially fatal illness in order to see his dream of

making a film come true, and after its premiere at the Lucerna in March 2011 – which he was barely well enough to attend – he went into rapid decline. As his heart, lungs and appetite gave out, he prepared himself in spirit, arranging final meetings with the Dalai Lama and the Archbishop of Prague, who had been imprisoned with him thirty years earlier. He also made sure to see Terrence Malick's film *The Tree of Life*, a transcendent vision of the cosmos that would have appealed to the pantheistic young Havel, if not to his older self. He was cared for in his final months by nuns seconded from the hospital below Petřín Hill where he had convalesced after prison in 1983.[32] But it may have been the poetry of his youth that gave him the simplest comfort, as he took to paraphrasing a Jiří Wolker poem: 'Death I do not fear, death is not evil, death is just a part of hard life/ what is terrible, what is evil, is dying'.[33]

And it was that poetry, not the tributes paid to him from around the world after his death at Hrádeček on 18 December 2011 or at the grandiose state funeral five days later, that provided the most fitting eulogy. Havel had embedded in *Leaving* references to 'The Marvellous Magician', the epic by Vitězslav Nezval with which he had concluded his own obituary for the great poet in 1958:

And I remained, standing over my work
Like a machinist over a boiler in which simmering oil is rising
And when the hand on the water gauge had stopped
The sudden scream of the siren sounded
And exiting between the smocks of iron people
I finished my poem.[34]

References

Introduction

1 David Danaher, *Reading Václav Havel* (Toronto, 2015), pp. 17–55.

2 Hazard Adams, *The Offense of Poetry* (Seattle, WA, 2007), pp. 4–13.

3 F. X. Šalda, quoted in Alexej Kusák, *Kultura a politika v Československu 1945–1956* (Prague, 1998), p. 20.

4 Danaher, *Reading Václav Havel*, p. 96.

5 Václav Havel and Vilém Prečan, *Korespondence (1983–1989)* (Prague, 2011), p. 652; Ladislav Hejdánek, *Havel je uhlík: Filosof a politická odpovědnost* (Prague, 2009), pp. 57–61.

6 Danaher, *Reading Václav Havel*, pp. 118–19, 181–7; Aviezer Tucker, *The Philosophy and Politics of Czech Dissidence from Patočka to Havel* (Pittsburgh, PA, 2000), pp. 253–6.

7 Vladimír Just, 'Příspěvek k jazyku experanto aneb Dramatické neosoby Václava Havla', *Divadelní revue*, XV/3 (2004), pp. 3–13.

8 James F. Pontuso, *Václav Havel: Civic Responsibility in the Postmodern Age* (Lanham, MD, 2004), p. 73, 113.

9 Robert B. Pynsent, 'The Work of Václav Havel', *Slavonic and East European Review*, LXXIII/2 (1995), p. 272.

10 Daniel Kaiser, *Disident: Václav Havel, 1936–1989* (Prague and Litomyšl, 2009), p. 200.

11 Thomas Ort, *Art and Life in Modernist Prague: Karel Čapek and his Generation, 1911–1938* (Basingstoke, 2013), pp. 3–5, 11–13, 121–9.

12 Oleg Sus, 'Stesk po koncepci', *Literární noviny*, XIV/46 (1965), p. 4.

13 Kusák, *Kultura a politika v Československu*, pp. 21–3.

14 Jaroslav Dietl, *Nehoda. Ministerská komedie* (Prague, 1964), p. 76.
    Dietl's career is recounted in Paulina Bren, *The Greengrocer and
    His TV: The Culture of Communism after the 1968 Prague Spring*
    (Ithaca, NY, 2010).

15 Tomáš Koloc, 'Jaroslav Dietl jako Jára Cimrman', www.blisty.cz,
    27 August 2010.

16 Martin Porubjak, 'Havel do tretice', *Kultúrny život*, XXIII/17 (1968), p. 8.
    The play was *The Increased Difficulty of Concentration* (1968).

1 'Every Soul is a Certain Architecture' (1936–52)

1   Ivan M. Havel, *Dopisy od Olgy* (Prague, 2010), p. 50.

2   Milan Kašpar and Alena Michálková, 'Dvě výročí stavitele Vácslava
    Havla', *Stavebnictví a interiér*, XII/10 (2011), pp. 58–60.

3   Rostislav Švácha, *Od moderny k funkcionalismu* (Prague, 1995),
    pp. 60–62; Elizabeth Clegg, *Art, Design and Architecture in Central
    Europe, 1890–1920* (New Haven, CT, 2006), pp. 37–8.

4   Christopher Long, personal communication, 8 January 2015. On
    the mixing of styles at the time, see Ákos Moravánszky, *Competing
    Visions: Aesthetic Invention and Social Imagination in Central European
    Architecture, 1867–1918* (Cambridge, MA, 1998), p. 112.

5   V. M. Havel, *Mé vzpomínky* (Prague, 1993), p. 37.

6   Ibid., pp. 270–71.

7   Dave Weinstein, 'Joseph A. Leonard: Suburbs in the City',
    www.sfgate.com, 10 April 2004.

8   Švácha, *Od modérny k funkcionalismu*, pp. 442, 445; Zdeněk Lukeš,
    *Praha moderní II: Velký průvodce po architektuře 1900–1950. Levý břeh
    Vltavy* (Prague and Litomyšl, 2013), pp. 119–30.

9   'Vánoční setkání prezidenta republiky Václava Havla s dětmi,
    Purkrabství Pražského hradu 15. prosince 1995', in the Archive
    of the Václav Havel Library, Prague (hereafter, AKVH), item 17242.

10 Jiří Kuběna, *Paměť básníka* (Brno, 2006), p. 274.

11 Ivan M. Havel, 'Didasko – učím', in *Didasko – učím: Naučné obrazky
    Boženy Havlové* (Prague, 2003), p. 7.

12 Krystyna Wanatowicová, *Miloš Havel: český filmový magnát* (Prague,
    2013), p. 387.

Pavel Kosatík, 'Člověk má dělat to, nač má sílu': Život Olgy Havlové (Prague, 2008), p. 68.

Kimberly Elman Zarecor, Manufacturing a Socialist Modernity: Housing in Czechoslovakia, 1945–1960 (Pittsburgh, PA, 2011), p. 231. See also Annett Steinführer, 'Stadt und Utopie: Das Experiment Zlín 1920–1938', Bohemia, XLIII/1 (2002), pp. 33–73, and Zachary Doleshal, 'Life and Death in the Kingdom of Shoes: Zlín, Baťa, and Czechoslovakia, 1923–1941', PhD thesis, University of Texas, 2012.

Michael Zantovsky, Havel: A Life (New York, 2014), p. 27.

Martin C. Putna, Václav Havel: Duchovní portrét v rámu České kultury 20. století (Prague, 2011), pp. 27–42.

Vácslav Havel (Atom), Kniha života (Prague, 2011), p. 37; V. M. Havel, Mé vzpomínky, p. 24.

T. G. Masaryk, Cesta demokracie I. Projevy – články – rozhovory 1918–1920 (Prague, 2003), p. 233.

William M. Johnston, The Austrian Mind: An Intellectual and Social History, 1848–1938 (Berkeley, CA, 1972), p. 277. See also Robert B. Pynsent, Questions of Identity: Czech and Slovak Ideas of Nationality and Personality (Budapest, 1994), p. 5.

Jana Čehurová, Čeští svobodní zednáři ve XX. století (Prague, 2002), pp. 115–18, 311–12, 415; Putna, Václav Havel, pp. 60–62.

Wanatowicová, Miloš Havel, pp. 50–51.

Peter Heumos, 'Konfliktregulung und soziale Integration: Zur Struktur der Ersten Tschechoslowakischen Republik', Bohemia, XXX/1 (1989), pp. 52–70.

Peter Bugge, 'Czech Democracy, 1918–1938: Paragon or Parody?', Bohemia, XLVII/1 (2006–7), pp. 3–28; Andrea Orzoff, The Battle for the Castle: The Myth of Czechoslovakia in Europe, 1914–1948 (Oxford, 2009).

Wanatowicová, Miloš Havel, pp. 123–4; Ivan Jakubec, 'Ekonomické pozadí podnikání bratrů Havlových ve třicátých letech 20. století', Iluminace, XVIII (2006), pp. 155–68.

Karel Čapek, 'Ideální Velká Praha', Národní listy, 16 April 1919, p. 2.

Josef Ludvík Fischer, Listy o druhých a o sobě (Prague, 2005), p. 247.

Josef Ludvík Fischer, Výbor z díla, vol. I (Prague, 2007), pp. 411, 420, 679–86.

Ibid., p. 699; J. L. Fischer, Krise demokracie (Prague, 2005), p. 304.

Fischer, Výbor z díla, vol. I, p. 669.

30 V. M. Havel, 'Před nástupem mladých', in *Mé vzpomínky*, pp. 229–47; John Keane, *Václav Havel* (London, 1999), pp. 32–3.

31 V. M. Havel, 'Barrandovská skupina', in *Mé vzpomínky*, pp. 247–60.

32 Vavrečka's radio message of 21 September 1938 is reprinted in Hubert Ripka, *Munich: Before and After* (New York, 1969), pp. 107–8, and that of 30 September can be heard on track 33 of the CD accompanying David Vaughan, *Battle for the Airwaves: Radio and the 1938 Munich Crisis* (Prague, 2008).

33 Vlastimil Klíma, *1938: Měli jsme kapitulovat?* (Prague, 2012); Fischer, *Listy o druhých a o sobě*, pp. 381–5.

34 Libor Vodička, *Vyjádřit hrou: Podobenství a (sebe)stylizace v dramatu Václava Havla* (Prague, 2013), p. 73.

35 Wanatowicová, *Miloš Havel*, pp. 28–30, 71–3.

36 Ibid., pp. 133–259; see also Peter Demetz, *Prague in Danger* (New York, 2008), pp. 194–207; and Keane, *Václav Havel*, pp. 58–60. On Nazi racial intentions, see Vojtech Mastny, *The Czechs under Nazi Rule* (New York, 1971), pp. 123–39, and Chad Bryant, *Prague in Black: Nazi Rule and Czech Nationalism* (Cambridge, MA, 2007), pp. 114–38.

37 Wanatowicová, *Miloš Havel*, pp. 362–481.

38 Benjamin Frommer, *National Cleansing: Retribution against Nazi Collaborators in Postwar Czechoslovakia* (Cambridge, 2005), pp. 300, 337.

39 Daniel Kaiser, *Disident: Václav Havel, 1936–1989* (Prague and Litomyšl, 2009), p. 32; Keane, *Václav Havel*, pp. 86–8.

40 Kaiser, *Disident*, p. 28.

41 Putna, *Václav Havel*, pp. 63–4; Havlová, *Didasko – učím*, p. 76.

42 A. J. Liehm, *The Politics of Culture* (New York, 1973), p. 378.

43 Havel's letter to Radim Kopecký, 17 December 1952, AKVH, item 1779.

44 Václav Havel and František Janouch, *Korespondence 1978–2001* (Prague, 2007), p. 97.

45 Kaiser, *Disident*, p. 32.

46 'Lyrika', a poem Havel included in a letter to Jiří Paukert on 27 February 1955, AKVH, item 1549.

47 Pavel Kosatík, *'Ústně více': Šestatřicátníci* (Brno, 2006), pp. 75–7.

48 Ibid., p. 78.

49 Fischer, *Listy o druhých a o sobě*, pp. 128, 155, 608; David Addyman and Matthew Feldman, 'Samuel Beckett, Wilhelm Windelband, and the

Interwar "Philosophy Notes"', *Modernism/Modernity*, xviii/4 (2011), pp. 755–70.

50 Fischer, *Výbor z díla*, vol. i, p. 155.

51 David Drozd, 'Dobové kontexty *Sedmi listů Melinovi* Josefa Šafaříka', *Estetika*, xlii/2–3 (2006), pp. 149–87 (at p. 149).

52 Josef Šafařík, *Sedm listů Melinovi* (Brno, 1993), pp. 190, 193, 230.

53 Ibid., p. 175.

54 Ibid., p. 217.

55 Ibid., p. 213.

56 Ibid., p. 216. In this respect, Šafařík was probably borrowing from a leading Czech philosopher of the preceding generation (and V. M. Havel's teacher), Emanuel Rádl; see Zuzana Škorpíková, *Rádlovo pojetí pravdy* (Prague, 2003), pp. 24, 30, 69–70.

57 Šafařík, *Sedm listů Melinovi*, p. 221.

58 Ibid., pp. 128–30, 154–65, 229–30. On Šafařík's debt to Nietzsche, see Drozd, 'Dobové kontexty *Sedmi listů Melinovi*', p. 158.

2 Poetry's False Start (1952–7)

1 Krystyna Wanatowicová, *Miloš Havel: Český filmový magnát* (Prague, 2013), pp. 253–4, 349, 364, 378.

2 Havel's letter to Jiří Paukert, 4 October 1953, in the Archive of the Václav Havel Library, Prague (hereafter, akvh), item 1517.

3 Josef Ludvík Fischer, *Listy o druhých a o sobě* (Prague, 2005), p. 326.

4 Ladislav Štoll, 'Třicet let bojů za českou socialistickou poezii', in Ústav pro českou literaturu av čr, *Z dějin českého myšlení o literatuře 2: 1948–1958* (Prague, 2002), p. 19.

5 Vladimír Novotný, 'Poslední veliký špatný básník český?', in Jiří Wolker, *Dnešek je jistě nesmírný zázrak* (Prague, 2006), pp. 16–19; Ben F. Stoltzfus, 'Unanimism Revisited', *Modern Language Quarterly*, xxi/3 (1960), pp. 239–45.

6 Havel to Jiří Paukert, 8 March 1953, akvh, item 1515.

7 Pedagogickopsychologická charakteristika ods. Havel Václav, z.č. 9658 (15 January 1980), akvh, item 18114; Michael Zantovsky, *Havel: A Life* (New York, 2014), p. 231.

8   V. M. Havel, *Mé vzpomínky* (Prague, 1993), p. 114; Daniel Kaiser, *Disident. Václav Havel 1936–1989* (Prague and Litomyšl, 2009), p. 15.

9   A. J. Liehm, *The Politics of Culture* (New York, 1973), p. 378.

10 Ibid., p. 379.

11 Viktor Shklovsky, *O teorii prozy* (Moscow, 1929), pp. 11–17; a Czech translation had been published in 1933 and reissued in 1948. See also David Danaher, *Reading Václav Havel* (Toronto, 2015), p. 23.

12 Martin C. Putna, *Václav Havel. Duchovní portrét v rámu české kultury 20. století* (Prague, 2011), pp. 75–93; John Keane, *Václav Havel* (London, 1999), pp. 101–8; Zantovsky, *Havel*, pp. 33–41.

13 Havel to Kopecký, 17 December 1952, AKVH, item 1779.

14 Pavel Kosatík, 'Ústně více'. *Šestatřicátníci* (Brno, 2006), p. 27.

15 Václav Havel, 'Optimalismus a humanismus', in *Rozhovory '36. Stříbrný vítr. Výběr z tvorby Šestatřicátníků*, ed. Martin C. Putna and Jan Hron (Prague, 2010), pp. 18–25.

16 Havel to Kopecký, 17 December 1952, AKVH, item 1779.

17 Havel to Kopecký, 27 March 1953, AKVH, item 1783.

18 Jiří Kuběna [Paukert's nom de plume], *Krásný rytíř na vysoké skále* (Zlín, 2011).

19 Kosatík, 'Ústně více', p. 42.

20 Jiří Kuběna, *Paměť básníka* (Brno, 2006), p. 115.

21 The Hegel lectures were excerpted in *Filosofie, umění a náboženství a jejich vztah k mravnosti a státu*, trans. František Fajfr (Prague, 1943). Havel mentions this collection in a letter to Kopecký from 17 December 1952, AKVH, item 1779.

22 Pitirim A. Sorokin, *The Crisis of Our Age: The Social and Cultural Outlook* (New York, 1942), p. 317. In Czech as *Krise našeho věku*, trans. František Dědek (Prague, 1948). Havel cited Sorokin's book at length in a letter to Paukert on 22 November 1953, AKVH, item 1521.

23 Raymond Keith Williamson, *Introduction to Hegel's Philosophy of Religion* (Albany, NY, 1984), p. 244. Havel admitted this problem in a letter to Kopecký on 27 March 1953, AKVH, item 1783.

24 Jiří Paukert, 'Pod tíhou dozrávajících plodů', in *Rozhovory '36*, ed. Putna and Hron, p. 58.

25 Libor Vodička, *Vyjádřit hrou: Podobenství a (sebe) stylizace v dramatu Václava Havla* (Prague, 2013), p. 19.

26 Ibid., p. 15.

27 Kosatík, *'Ústně více'*, p. 50.

28 Ibid., pp. 44–5, 68.

29 Quoted in Marek Suk, '"Jsem člověk, který se těžko podvoluje": Proces s Jiřím Kolářem v roce 1953', *Česká literatura*, LXI/4 (2013), pp. 547–58 (at p. 552).

30 Xavier Galmiche, *Vladimír Holan, bibliotékář Boha*, trans. Lucie Koryntová (Prague, 2012), pp. 36–61.

31 Havel to Paukert, 8 March 1954, AKVH, item 1528.

32 Galmiche, *Vladimír Holan*, pp. 114–21.

33 Kosatík, *'Ústně více'*, p. 70; Paukert, *Paměť básníka*, pp. 160–64.

34 Anna Freimanová, ed., *Síla věcnosti Olgy Havlové* (Prague, 2013), pp. 24, 155.

35 Timothy Garton Ash, 'On Olga Havel (1933–1996)', *New York Review of Books*, XLIII/5 (21 March 1996), p. 32.

36 Pavel Kosatík, *'Člověk má dělat to, nač má sílu'. Život Olgy Havlové* (Prague, 2008), pp. 54–5; Zantovsky, *Havel*, pp. 52–6.

37 Kosatík, *'Ústně více'*, pp. 48, 50–51.

38 Freimanová, ed., *Síla věcnosti Olgy Havlové*, p. 13.

39 *Literární noviny*, V/19 (29 April 1956), p. 9.

40 Walt Whitman, *Leaves of Grass: The First (1855) Edition* (Harmondsworth, 1986), p. 24.

41 See also Kosatík, *'Ústně více'*, pp. 69, 180. Some would argue that by the 1950s Seifert's best work was behind him and he was producing 'sentimental drivel'; see the letter to the editor of *The Times* of London from Karel Brušák, R. B. Pynsent and David Short, 20 October 1984, p. 9.

42 Havel to Paukert, 8 June 1955, AKVH, item 1552.

43 Kosatík, *'Ústně více'*, p. 167.

44 Ibid., p. 158; Havel to Paukert, 24 November 1956, AKVH, item 1583.

45 Paul I. Trensky, 'The *Květen* Generation in Perspective', *Slavic and East European Journal*, XVII/4 (1973), pp. 414–26 (at p. 416).

46 Havel to Paukert, 4 November 1956, AKVH, item 1581.

47 Kosatík, *'Ústně více'*, p. 157.

48 Jan Zábrana, *Celý život: Výbor z deníků 1948/1984* (Prague, 2001), p. 977.

49 Kosatík, *'Ústně více'*, p. 175.

50 Liehm, *The Politics of Culture*, pp. 388–9.

51 Kosatík, *'Ústně více'*, p. 152.

3 Into Theatre and *Političnost* (1957–69)

1 Havel to Paukert, 25 September 1957, in the Archive of the Václav Havel Library, Prague (hereafter AKVH), item 1611; Michael Zantovsky, *Havel: A Life* (New York, 2014), p. 45.

2 Pavel Landovský, quoted in Eda Kriseová, *Václav Havel*, 2nd edn (Prague, 2014), p. 39.

3 Jan Císař, *Přehled dějin českého divadla* (Prague, 2006), p. 175; V. M. Havel, *Mé vzpomínky* (Prague, 1993), pp. 17, 55, 62, 111. V. M. also befriended Kvapil through the Masons, for whom Kvapil devised initiation rituals.

4 According to the documentary film *Ivan Havel: Pozdní sběr*, on Česká Televize 2 (13 October 2013), at minute 24; Carol Rocamora, *Acts of Courage: Václav Havel's Life in the Theater* (Hanover, NH, 2005), p. 59.

5 Pavel Kohout, *Prahry* (Prague, 2010), pp. 103–9.

6 Ibid., p. 73.

7 For competing interpretations, see John Keane, *Václav Havel* (London, 1999), pp. 145–8; Rocamora, *Acts of Courage*, p. 23; and Zantovsky, *Havel*, p. 47.

8 Jiří Žák, *Hovory s V. H.* (Prague, 2012), p. 23.

9 Kosatík, 'Ústně více'. *Šestatřicátníci* (Brno, 2006), p. 202.

10 Ibid., p. 203.

11 Jarka M. Burian, 'The Liberated Theatre of Voskovec and Werich', *Educational Theatre Journal*, XXIX/2 (1977), pp. 153–77 (at p. 153).

12 Krystyna Wanatowicová, *Miloš Havel: Český filmový magnát* (Prague, 2013), pp. 35–6, 378, 421–2.

13 Jindřich Černý, *Osudy českého divadla po druhé světové válce* (Prague, 2007), pp. 375–6.

14 *Rudé právo*, 12 June 1954, p. 6.

15 František Buriánek, 'Po konferenci o satiře', *Literární noviny*, III/46 (1954), p. 1.

16 Vladimír Just, *Werichovo Divadlo ABC* (Prague, 2013), pp. 22–6, 72.

17 Ibid., p. 7.

18 Donald G. Daviau and Harvey I. Dunkle, 'Friedrich Dürrenmatt's *Der Besuch der alten Dame*: A Parable of Western Society in Transition', *Modern Language Quarterly*, XXXV/3 (1974), pp. 302–16 (at p. 305).

19 Havel to Paukert, 21 May 1958, AKVH, item 1620.

20 Paul Trensky, *Czech Drama since World War II* (New York, 1978), pp. 26–30.

21 Otakar Blanda, 'Vzpoura mladí', in Josef Topol, *Jejich den* (Prague, 1962), p. 98.

22 Topol, *Jejich den*, p. 7.

23 Steinberg made such a lasting impression that as president Havel sought him out for dinner in 1991; see Deirdre Bair, *Saul Steinberg* (New York, 2012), p. 532.

24 Pavel Janoušek, *Ivan Vyskočil a jeho neliteratura* (Brno, 2009), p. 39.

25 Ibid., p. 95.

26 Václav Havel, *Motomorfózy* (Prague, 2011), pp. 11–35.

27 Ibid., pp. 41–55.

28 Lenka Jungmannová, 'Havlovy první profesionální dramatické texty', ibid., p. 62.

29 Lenka Jungmannová, 'Jak to vlastně bylo? Geneze Zahradní slavnosti (1960–1963)', in *Zahradní slavnost: Klíčová událost moderního českého divadla*, ed. Lenka Jungmannová (Prague, 2015), p. 13.

30 Zantovsky, *Havel*, p. 67.

31 All references are to the 1961 draft of *Jeho den. Komedie o třech jednáních a jedné mezihře* in the Havel Library, AKVH, item 17614.

32 Daria Ullrichová, 'Pohádka, horor a národní mýtus', in Václav Havel, *Zahradní slavnost* (Prague, 2013), pp. 22–5; Černý, *Osudy českého divadla*, p. 365; Veronika Ambros, 'Fictional World and Dramatic Text: Vaclav Havel's Descent and Ascent', *Style*, XXV/2 (1991), pp. 310–19.

33 On Topol and the Kunderas, see Trensky, *Czech Drama*, pp. 49–56, 73–9, 90–94.

34 Eva Uhlířová, 'České antidrama', in *Čtení o Václavu Havlovi*, ed. Michal Špirit (Prague, 2013), p. 17.

35 Lenka Jungmannová, 'Zrození *Zahradní slavnosti* z Havlových literárních počátků', *Divadelní revue*, XXII/3 (2011), pp. 7–29 (at p. 8); Jan Čulík, 'Václav Havel', in *The Dictionary of Literary Biography*, ed. Steven Serafin (Detroit, MI, 2001), vol. CCXXXII, p. 117.

36 Michelle Woods, 'Václav Havel and the Expedient Politics of Translation', *NTQ*, XXVI/1 (2010), pp. 3–15.

37 Daniel Kaiser, *Disident. Václav Havel, 1936–1989* (Prague and Litomyšl, 2009), pp. 54–5.

38   The letter is reprinted in Anna Freimanová, ed., *Síla věcnosti Olgy Havlové* (Prague, 2013), pp. 9–14.

39   Ibid., p. 11.

40   Pavel Kosatík, *'Člověk má dělat to, nač má sílu': Život Olgy Havlové* (Prague, 2008), pp. 95–6; Zantovsky, *Havel*, pp. 54–5.

41   J. R. Pick, 'Romeo a Julie', *Plamen*, VI/4 (1965), p. 28.

42   David Danaher, *Reading Václav Havel* (Toronto, 2015), pp. 32–7, 218–22.

43   A. J. Liehm, *The Politics of Culture* (New York, 1973), p. 383.

44   Jungmannová, 'Zrození *Zahradní slavnosti*', p. 23, n. 84. The handwritten draft is archived at the Havel Library, item 38179.

45   Jude R. Meche, 'Female Victims and the Male Protagonist in Václav Havel's Drama', *Modern Drama*, XL/4 (1997), pp. 468–76.

46   Jeanette R. Malin, *Verbal Violence in Contemporary Drama: From Handke to Shepard* (Cambridge, 1992), p. 87.

47   Jungmannová, 'Zrození *Zahradní slavnosti*', p. 25; Zantovsky, *Havel*, pp. 93–5.

48   Ladislav Hejdánek, *Havel je uhlík: Filosof a politická odpovědnost* (Prague, 2009), p. 37.

49   See the survey of 33 critics in *Divadlo*, XVII/9 (1966), pp. 5–8, in which only four listed *The Memorandum* as the best new play of the 1965–6 season.

50   Libor Vodička, *Vyjádřit hrou: Podobenství a (sebe)stylizace v dramatu Václava Havla* (Prague, 2013), p. 197, n. 124. The fraught relations between Vácslav Havel and his 'paranoid' brother-in-law Richard Baláš, who managed the Lucerna cinema, are mentioned in Ivan M. Havel, *Dopisy od Olgy* (Prague, 2010), p. 35.

51   Kaiser, *Disident*, p. 55.

52   Karel Kaplan, *'Všechno jste prohrali!'* (Prague, 1997), pp. 36–52; Emanuel Mandler, *Škodolibé úsměvy svobody z let 1955 až 1992* (Prague, 2005), pp. 50–56.

53   Jiří Šotola, 'Výměna názorů tak vůbec', *Literární noviny*, XIV/36 (1965), p. 4.

54   Liehm, *The Politics of Culture*, pp. 375–6.

55   According to an Information Report of the CIA, dated 19 July 1966, released through FOIPA request FBI 1330660-000.

56   Kaiser, *Disident*, p. 61; Pavel Žáček, 'Akce 'Tomis III' a ideologická diverze: Václav Havel v dokumentech Státní bezpečnosti, 1965–1968', *Paměť a dějiny*, VI/1 (2012), pp. 70–83.

57 Žáček, 'Akce "Tomis III" a ideologická diverze', master's thesis, pp. 79, 82.

58 Jan Hron, *Korespondence Václava Havla*, dissertation, Univerzita Karlova, Prague (2008), p. 52.

59 Kieran Williams, *The Prague Spring and its Aftermath* (Cambridge, 1997), p. 213; Kaplan, 'Všechno jste prohráli!', pp. 55–7, 97–101, 129–31.

60 Liehm, *The Politics of Culture*, p. 386. Several of their plays had appeared in a collection of translations, *Absurdní anglické divadlo* (Prague, 1966).

61 Josef Šafařík, *Noční můra: Kurs pro utopisty* (Vranov nad Dyjí, 1993); David Drozd, 'Setkání myslitele a dramatika – hry Václava Havla očima Josefa Šafaříka', *RozRazil*, I/8 (2006), pp. 59–69 (at p. 65).

62 Josef Šafařík, *Hrady skutečné a povětrné* (Prague, 2008), p. 24.

63 Herta Schmidová, *Struktury a funkce: Výbor ze studií 1989–2009* (Prague, 2011), p. 362; Hron, *Korespondence Václava Havla*, p. 58.

64 *Dílo Jiřího Koláře* (Prague, 1992), vol. I, pp. 467–75.

65 John Carpenter, 'Jiří Kolář: Visual Poetry and Verbal Art', *Cross Currents*, VIII (1989), pp. 209–28 (at p. 218); Jiří Kolář, 'Snad nic, snad něco', in *Slovo, písmo, akce, hlas*, ed. Josef Hiršal and Bohumila Grögerová (Prague, 1967), p. 182.

66 Quoted in Carpenter, 'Jiří Kolář', p. 221.

67 Havel cited Robbe-Grillet's *Jealousy* as an influence in a letter to Šafařík (Hron, *Korespondence Václava Havla*, p. 58). Earlier, Havel had been impressed by the 'technology' of Robbe-Grillet's *Erasers* (*Literární noviny*, XIII/51–2 [1964], p. 14).

68 Václav Havel, *Eduard* (Prague, 1996), pp. 11–12.

69 Šafařík's 'O rubatu čili vyznání' (*Hrady skutečné a povětrné*, pp. 55–88) appeared in an anthology Havel edited, *Podoby II* (Prague, 1969).

70 Zantovsky, *Havel*, p. 106.

71 Rocamora (*Acts of Courage*, pp. 67–8) reprints Havel's notes on troubleshooting at the Balustrade in 1965.

72 Kaiser, *Disident*, p. 50; Pavel Juráček, *Deník (1959–1974)* (Prague, 2003), p. 518 (diary entry for 16 April 1967).

73 Michael Quinn, 'Delirious Subjectivity: Four Scenes from Havel', in *Critical Essays on Vaclav Havel*, ed. Marketa Goetz-Stankiewicz and Phyllis Carey (New York, 1999), pp. 209–23.

74 Freimanová, *Síla věcnosti*, p. 12.

75 Juráček, *Deník*, p. 503.

76 Kaplan, *'Všechno jste prohrali!'*, p. 131. The slow evolution of Communist writers is documented in Marci Shore, 'Engineering in the Age of Innocence: A Genealogy of Discourse Inside the Czechoslovak Writers' Union, 1949–67', *East European Politics and Societies*, xii/3 (1998), pp. 397–441.

77 Zantovsky, *Havel*, pp. 109–11. On Papp in particular, see Rocamora, *Acts of Courage*, pp. 88–94.

78 Kaiser, *Dissident*, pp. 69–73.

79 Quoted in Hubert Ripka, *Munich: Before and After* (New York, 1969), p. 108.

80 Havel to Meda Mládková, 2 October 1968, akvh, item 39670.

81 Jarmila Cysařová, '"... stát tvrdošíjně na svém ..."': Neznámý projev Václava Havla z listopadu 1968', *Soudobé dějiny*, viii/1 (2001), pp. 166–82 (at p. 174).

82 Jan Kolář, 'Na vnitřní rezistenci je vždycky čas', *Akademický časopis*, xv/12 (1969), p. 2.

83 akvh, item 33887. Footage of Havel's appearance on 21 January 1969 can be viewed in Kristina Vlachová's film *Poselství Jana Palacha* (2008).

84 Vilém Faltýnek, 'Havlova rozhlasová koláž, která měla být zničena', www.radio.cz, 23 August 2008. See also Danaher, *Reading Václav Havel*, p. 65.

85 Václav Havel, Jaroslav Střítecký and Milan Uhde, 'Trialog o radikalismu', *Host do domu*, xvi/6 (1969), pp. 32–6. See also Charles Sabatos, 'Criticism and Destiny: Kundera and Havel on the Legacy of 1968', *Europe-Asia Studies*, lx/10 (2008), pp. 1827–45, and Tim West, 'Destiny as Alibi: Milan Kundera, Václav Havel and the "Czech Question" after 1968', *Slavonic and East European Review*, lxxxvii/3 (2009), pp. 401–28.

86 According to the letter of William P. Gormbley to Havel informing him of the grant (number 06990026) on 15 November 1968, in the Rockefeller Archive Center, Sleepy Hollow, New York, reel 5652. Havel had already decided before the invasion that he would not take up the Iowa fellowship, because he did not want to be out of the country for so long; see his letter to Meda Mládková from 4 August 1968, akvh, item 39661.

87 Havel's letter to Judith Symington of the Ford Foundation, 6 June 1969, Rockefeller Archive Center, reel 5652.

88 Freimanová, *Síla věcnosti*, p. 29.

4 To Hrádeček and Dissent (1970–79)

1 Daniel Kaiser, *Disident. Václav Havel 1936–1989* (Prague and Litomyšl, 2009), pp. 82, 87.

2 Pavel Kosatík, *'Člověk má dělat to, nač má sílu'. Život Olgy Havlové* (Prague, 2008), pp. 99–101; John Keane, *Václav Havel* (London, 1999), p. 187.

3 Pavel Juráček, *Deník (1959–1974)* (Prague, 2003), p. 672.

4 Irving Wardle, 'The Czech Dream', *The Times*, 29 November 1969, p. 21.

5 Jiří Kuběna, *Paměť básníka* (Brno, 2006), p. 342.

6 Havel to Meda Mládková, 16 March 1969, Archive of the Václav Havel Library, Prague (hereafter, AKVH), item 39668.

7 Carol Rocamora, *Acts of Courage: Václav Havel's Life in the Theatre* (Hanover, NH, 2005), p. 95.

8 Jindřich Černý, 'Mechanismus života a hry', in *Čtení o Václavu Havlovi*, ed. Michal Špirit (Prague, 2013), p. 46.

9 Paul Trensky, *Czech Drama since World War II* (New York, 1978), pp. 15, 24.

10 Erich Fromm, *The Heart of Man: Its Genius for Good and Evil* (New York, 1964), p. 57.

11 Ibid., p. 40.

12 Kenneth Tynan, *Letters* (New York, 1994), pp. 475–7, 486, 491–2; Michelle Woods, 'Václav Havel and the Expedient Politics of Translation', *NTQ*, XXVI/1 (2010), pp. 3–15 (at pp. 11–13).

13 Trensky, *Czech Drama*, p. 184. Havel warmed to the play only after seeing a production of it in New York in 2006.

14 Ibid., p. 185; Ivan M. Jirous, 'Horský hoteliér Havel', in *Čtení o Václavu Havlovi*, ed. Špirit, p. 49.

15 A. J. Liehm, *The Politics of Culture* (New York, 1973), p. 386; the literary favourites were one of his answers to Marcel Proust's 33 questions, put to him by Czechoslovak Radio in February 1967: AKVH, item 9112.

16 The play's structure is laid out in Uwe Böker, 'John Gays *The Beggar's Opera* und Vaclav Havels *Zebrácká* [*sic*] *opera* (1975)', in *John Gay's 'The Beggar's Opera', 1728–2004: Adaptations and Re-writings*, ed. Uwe Böker, Ines Detmers and Anna-Christina Giovanopoulos (Amsterdam, 2006), pp. 219–41.

17 Peter Steiner, 'Introduction', in Václav Havel, *The Beggar's Opera*, trans. Paul Wilson (Ithaca, NY, 2001), pp. xiii–xiv. See also Keane, *Václav Havel*, pp. 237–8.

18 Jan Hron, *Korespondence Václava Havla*, master's thesis, Univerzita Karlova, Prague (2008), p. 68.

19 Kosatík, '*Člověk má děat to, nač má sílu*', p. 127; Rocamora, *Acts of Courage*, pp. 125–33.

20 'Wenige Schritte', *Der Spiegel*, XXIX/46 (1975), p. 213.

21 Kaiser, *Disident*, p. 102.

22 Ibid., pp. 93–6.

23 Lenka Jungmannová, 'Paradoxy s Vaňkem', in *V hlavní roli Ferdinand Vaněk*, ed. Lenka Jungmannová (Prague, 2006), p. 389; Michael Zantovsky, *Havel: A Life* (New York, 2014), pp. 142–3.

24 The connection between the two plays was made clear when they were performed back-to-back at the Vinohrady Theatre in 2000. See Zdeněk A. Tichý, 'Havlovy aktovky: trpký obraz jalových rituálů', *Mladá fronta Dnes*, 12 February 2000, p. 21.

25 Alfred Thomas, review of *The Vaněk Plays*, in *Slavic Review*, LI/2 (1992), pp. 348–51 (at p. 349). Havel's *Guardian Angel* was written in 1963 but not broadcast on Czechoslovak Radio until 18 June 1968.

26 Kaiser, *Disident*, pp. 86–7. Kundera gives his fictionalized version of these events in part five, chapter 13 of his 1984 novel, *The Unbearable Lightness of Being*.

27 Andrei Yurchak, *Everything was Forever, Until it was No More: The Last Soviet Generation* (Princeton, NJ, 2006), pp. 77–157.

28 In the four years after the suspension of the subversion trial in October 1970, Havel was mentioned briefly only four times in *The Times* of London (most recently on 16 November 1973), three times in the *New York Times* (most recently on 29 January 1973) and twice in *Der Spiegel* (on 26 February 1973 and 18 February 1974).

29 Milan Otáhal, *Opoziční proudy v české společnosti 1969–1989* (Prague, 2011), pp. 106–9; Jonathan Bolton, *Worlds of Dissent: Charter 77, The Plastic People of the Universe, and Czech Culture under Communism* (Cambridge, MA, 2012), pp. 202–5; Jiří Suk, *Politika jako absurdní drama: Václav Havel v letech 1975–1989* (Prague and Litomyšl, 2013), p. 28.

30 The telegram from 10 January 1969 is in AKVH, item 39590.

31 Branislav Kinčok, 'Vyšetrovanec číslo 1940: Gustáv Husák vo vyšetrovacej väzbe Štátnej bezpečnosti (1951–1954)', *Pamäť národa*, IX/4 (2013), pp. 17–39.

32 Kaiser, *Disident*, p. 96.

33 Otáhal, *Opoziční proudy v české společnosti*, pp. 96–7, 116; Zantovsky, *Havel*, pp. 152–4.

34 Havel had already wanted to include contributions by Němec and Bondy in an anthology he was compiling well before Jirous contacted him; see Havel's letter to Jan Lopatka, 19 August 1975, AKVH, item 4331.

35 Josef Šafařík, *Sedm listů Melinovi* (Brno, 1993), p. 210.

36 Bolton, *Worlds of Dissent*, pp. 134–9.

37 Ivan Martin Jirous, *Pravdivý příběh Plastic People* (Prague, 2008), p. 21. Havel later offered a view along these lines in private correspondence with an émigré historian; see Václav Havel and Vilém Prečan, *Korespondence (1983–1989)* (Prague, 2011), pp. 105–6.

38 Suk, *Politika jako absurdní drama*, pp. 42–3.

39 Petr Blažek and Vladimír Bosák, 'Akce "Bojanovice" – 11. listopad 1976', *Paměť a dějiny*, I/1 (2007), pp. 120–33 (inset at p. 124).

40 Bolton, *Worlds of Dissent*, pp. 142–3.

41 Kaiser, *Disident*, pp. 111–14.

42 Havel took the image of rear-door escape from Šafařík's recent 'Mephisto Monologue' (*Hrady skutečné a povětrné* [Prague, 2008], p. 203), published in an anthology Havel had edited.

43 Blanka Císařovská, Milan Drapala, Vilém Prečan and Jiří Vančura, *Charta 77 očima současníků: Po dvaceti letech* (Brno, 1997), p. 92.

44 Ibid., pp. 93, 169; Suk, *Politika jako absurdní drama*, p. 50.

45 Bolton, *Worlds of Dissent*, p. 155.

46 'Čím je a čím není Charta 77' and 'Co můžeme očekávat od Charty 77', in Jan Patočka, *Češi I* (Prague, 2006), pp. 428–30, 440–44.

47 Bolton (*Worlds of Dissent*, pp. 159–60) deftly distinguishes the facts of Patočka's death from the more dramatic versions that soon circulated, and Putna (*Václav Havel*, pp. 150–53) qualifies Patočka's impact on Havel.

48 Michael Gubser, *The Far Reaches: Phenomenology, Ethics, and Social Renewal in Central Europe* (Stanford, CA, 2014), p. 171.

49 Jindřich Chalupecký, 'Potřeba bdělosti', *Paraf*, II/4 (1986), pp. 4–20 (at p. 9). See also Edward F. Findlay, 'Classical Ethics and Postmodern

Critique: Political Philosophy in Václav Havel and Jan Patocka',
Review of Politics, LXI/3 (1999), pp. 403–38 (at pp. 421–2).

50 Pavel Kosatík, *'Ústně více'. Šestatřicátnici* (Brno, 2006), pp. 282–4.

51 Kuběna, *Paměť básníka*, p. 356.

52 Zantovsky, *Havel*, pp. 174–5.

53 Kaiser, *Disident*, pp. 125–7.

54 Quoted in Suk, *Politika jako absurdní drama*, p. 97.

55 Kaiser, *Disident*, pp. 128–34.

56 Viktor Karlík and Terezie Pokorná, eds, *Anticharta* (Prague, 2002); Suk, *Politika jako absurdní drama*, pp. 63–83; Mary Heimann, *Czechoslovakia: The State that Failed* (New Haven, CT, 2009), p. 288.

57 Kaiser, *Disident*, p. 135.

58 Suk, *Politika jako absurdní drama*, p. 104.

59 Ibid., pp. 106, 116.

60 Elzbieta Matynia, ed., *An Uncanny Era: Conversations between Václav Havel and Adam Michnik* (New Haven, CT, 2014), pp. 7–8, 23–7.

61 Havel was so taken by Sviták's writings that he tried to stage a theatrical rendition in 1963–4 and a public reading in 1967; in 1968 they co-founded a society of non-Party intellectuals. In the 1980s Havel fell out with Sviták, who had gone into American exile.

62 The Heidegger translation appeared underground in 1978, with Havel as the signatory publisher.

63 Peter Steiner, 'Moc obrazu: vizuální poezie Václava Havla', *Estetika*, XLIV/1–4 (2007), pp. 107–24.

64 David Danaher, *Reading Václav Havel* (Toronto, 2015), pp. 41, 228, n. 25; David Danaher, 'Ideology as Metaphor, Narrative, and Performance in the Writings of Václav Havel', *Slovo a smysl*, XII (2015), pp. 115–27.

65 Simon Tormey, *Making Sense of Tyranny: Interpretations of Totalitarianism* (Manchester, 1995), p. 143.

66 Bolton, *Worlds of Dissent*, pp. 226–7; Delia Popescu, *Political Action in Václav Havel's Thought* (Lanham, MD, 2012), p. 115; Kaiser, *Disident*, p. 94.

67 Those debates are recounted in Bolton, *Worlds of Dissent*; Barbara Falk, *The Dilemmas of Dissidence in East-central Europe* (Budapest and New York, 2003); and Aviezer Tucker, *The Philosophy and Politics of Czech Dissidence from Patočka to Havel* (Pittsburgh, PA, 2000), pp. 115–34.

68 Pavel Gregor, 'Vyšetřování akce ASANACE', *Securitas imperii 13* (Prague, 2006), p. 174.

69 Petr Blažek and Jaroslav Pažout, *Nejcitlivější místo režimu: Výbor na obranu nespravidlivě stíhaných (VONS) pohledem svých členů* (Prague, 2008), pp. 7–20, 114.

70 Petr Blažek and Tomáš Bursík, *Pražský proces 1979: Vyšetřováni, soud a vězení členů Výboru na obranu nespravedlivě stíhaných* (Prague, 2010), pp. 110–11.

71 S5, pp. 250–51, 724; Blažek and Pažout, *Nejcitlivější místo režimu*, p. 28. Footage of Havel's enthusiastic, if ungainly, drumming appears at the beginning of Andrea Sedláčková's documentary film *Život podle Václava Havla* (2014).

72 Zdeněk Pokorný, *Václav Havel a ženy* (Plzeň, 1999), p. 128; Irena Jirků, 'Ve znamení Kohouta', *Mladá fronta Dnes*, 10 September 1998, Magazín pp. 22–4.

73 Suk, *Politika jako absurdní drama*, p. 132; Blažek and Bursík, *Pražský proces 1979*, p. 390.

5 From Trial to Castle (1979–89)

1 Martin Procházka, 'Prisoner's Predicament: Public Privacy in Havel's Letters to Olga', *Representations*, 43 (Summer 1993), pp. 126–54.

2 On the challenge of locating Havel's prison letters in terms of genre, see Reinhard Ibler, 'Zur Typologie und kulturellen Funktion von Václav Havels "Dopisy Olze" (Briefe an Olga)', *Zeitschrift für Slawistik*, LIII/3 (2008), pp. 259–70.

3 David Danaher, *Reading Václav Havel* (Toronto, 2015), pp. 47–8.

4 Letter 4, from 8 July 1979 (unpublished section), Archive of the Václav Havel Library, Prague (hereafter, AKVH), item 2827.

5 Letter 6, from 28 July 1979, AKVH, item 2829.

6 Daniel Kaiser, *Disident. Václav Havel, 1936–1989* (Prague and Litomyšl, 2009), pp. 165–9; Carol Rocamora, *Acts of Courage: Václav Havel's Life in the Theatre* (Hanover, NH, 2005), pp. 175–6.

7 Evaluation of Havel by Cpt Miroslav Kadlčák, 17 July 1981, AKVH, item 18061, and Havel's 're-education' file, AKVH, item 18036.

8 Jiří Suk, *Politika jako absurdní drama: Václav Havel v letech 1975–1989* (Prague and Litomyšl, 2013), pp. 170–71; Kaiser, *Disident*, pp. 170–72;

Paul Wilson, 'Introduction', in Václav Havel, *Letters to Olga* (New York, 1989), p. 6.

9   Suk, *Politika jako absurdní drama*, pp. 166–7; Petr Blažek and Tomáš Bursík, *Pražský proces 1979: Vyšetřování, soud a vězení členů Výboru na obranu nespravedlivě stíhaných* (Prague, 2010), pp. 348, 352, 355, 358–9, 361–2.

10 See also Havel's unpublished prison letter 88, 9 August 1981, AKVH, item 2910.

11 Daniel Kroupa, *Dějiny Kampademie* (Prague, 2010). See also Barbara Day, *The Velvet Philosophers* (London, 1999), pp. 21–3, and Martin C. Putna, *Václav Havel. Duchovní portrét v rámu české kultury 20. století* (Prague, 2011), pp. 194–221.

12 Havel to Paukert, 22 November 1953, AKVH, item 1521.

13 Letter 159, from 18 December 1982, AKVH, item 2978. See also Robert B. Pynsent, *Questions of Identity: Czech and Slovak Ideas of Nationality and Personality* (Budapest, 1994), p. 42.

14 See in particular letter 161, from 1 January 1983, AKVH, item 2981.

15 Letter no. 132, from 12 June 1982 (unpublished section), AKVH, item 2953.

16 Ivan M. Havel, *Dopisy od Olgy* (Prague, 2010), pp. 193–7, 212–27. The essay was originally published as 'Sans identité' in Emmanuel Lévinas, *Humanisme de l'autre homme* (Montpellier, 1972). An English translation, 'Without Identity', appears in *Humanism of the Other*, trans. Nidra Poller (Champaign, IL, 2003), pp. 58–70. See also Day, *The Velvet Philosophers*, pp. 137–8.

17 Havel's adaptation of Levinas's essay is analysed in Procházka, 'Prisoner's Predicament', pp. 140–42, and Martin J. Matuštík, 'Havel and Habermas on Identity and Revolution', *Praxis International*, X/3–4 (1990–91), pp. 261–77 (at pp. 269–71).

18 Jan Patočka, 'Kacířské eseje o filosofii dějin', in Patočka, *Péče o duši III* (Prague, 2002), p. 18.

19 Martin Beck Matuštík, '"More than All the Others": Meditation on Responsibility', *Critical Horizons*, VIII/1 (2007), pp. 47–60 (at p. 52); Pynsent, *Questions of Identity*, pp. 11–12.

20 Havel, *Dopisy od Olgy*, p. 342.

21 Letter 122, from 3 April 1982 (unpublished section), AKVH, item 2944.

22 Rocamora, *Acts of Courage*, pp. 200–201.

23 Letter 156, from 27 November 1982, AKVH, item 2976, and letter 158, from 11 December 1982, AKVH, item 2978.

24 Havel's letter to Pavel Kohout, early March 1983, in Václav Havel and Vilém Prečan, *Korespondence (1983–1989)* (Prague, 2011), pp. 651–2.

25 Ibid., p. 6.

26 Ibid., p. 12.

27 Václav Havel and František Janouch, *Korespondence 1978–2001* (Prague, 2007), p. 53, 477.

28 Havel and Prečan, *Korespondence*, p. 25.

29 Ibid., p. 104.

30 Havel and Janouch, *Korespondence*, pp. 83, 87.

31 Václav Bělohradský, 'Krize eschatologie neosobnosti', *Studie*, 66 (1979), pp. 448–73; 67 (1980), pp. 12–27; 68 (1980), pp. 122–44. See also Aviezer Tucker, *The Philosophy and Politics of Czech Dissidence from Patočka to Havel* (Pittsburgh, PA, 2000), pp. 152–3.

32 Bělohradský was not invited, which was indicative of an event that Stoppard considered shambolic; see Ira Nadel, *Tom Stoppard: A Life* (Basingstoke, 2002), pp. 343–4.

33 Havel and Prečan, *Korespondence*, p. 172.

34 Bryce J. Christensen, 'Pitirim A. Sorokin: A Forerunner to Solzhenitsyn', *Modern Age*, XXXVIII/4 (1996), pp. 383–91; Ronald Berman, ed., *Solzhenitsyn at Harvard: The Address, Twelve Early Responses, and Six Later Reflections* (Washington, DC, 1980), p. 19.

35 Herta Schmidová, *Struktury a funkce: Výbor ze studií 1989–2009* (Prague, 2011), p. 314.

36 Constantin Floros, *Alban Berg: Music as Autobiography*, trans. Ernest Bernhardt-Kabisch (Frankfurt, 2014), p. 252.

37 Anna Freimanová, ed., *Síla věcnosti Olgy Havlové* (Prague, 2013), pp. 75–82.

38 Pavel Kosatík, *'Člověk má dělat to, nač má sílu': Život Olgy Havlové* (Prague, 2008), pp. 235–50; Michael Zantovsky, *Havel: A Life* (New York, 2014), p. 245.

39 Havel and Prečan, *Korespondence*, p. 203. It was not written, as Keane claims (*Václav Havel* [London, 1999], p. 315), while Havel was alone and 'guzzling brandy' at Engels Embankment 78.

40 Zdeněk Pokorný, *Václav Havel a ženy* (Plzeň, 1999), pp. 78, 136–46; Keane, *Václav Havel*, pp. 310–14.

41 Pavel Bratinka et al., *Faustování s Havlem* (Prague, 2010), pp. 178–9.
    The Faust history was Jindřich Pokorný, *Kniha o Faustovi* (Prague,
    1982).
42 Putna, *Václav Havel*, pp. 239–41.
43 Josef Šafařík, *Hrady skutečné a povětrné* (Prague, 2008), pp. 44, 203–15.
44 'O člověku "pozdní doby": s Václavem Bělohradským rozmlouvá
    K. Hvížďala', *Kritický sborník*, III (1985), pp. 28–47.
45 Pavel Bratinka and Daniel Kroupa, 'Normální člověk v nenormální
    situaci', in Bratinka, *Faustování s Havlem*, pp. 91–101.
46 Erhard Bahr, 'Václav Havel's Faust Drama *Temptation* (1985): or,
    The Challenge of Influence', *Goethe Yearbook*, VII (1994), pp. 194–206
    (p. 199).
47 Marketa Goetz-Stankiewicz, 'Variations of Temptation – Václav
    Havel's Politics of Language', *Modern Drama*, XXXIII/1 (1990), pp.
    93–105; Joan Erben, 'The Spirit from Below: A Theoretical Approach
    to Václav Havel's *Temptation*', *European Studies Journal*, XV/1 (1998),
    pp. 1–19; Norma J. Engberg, 'The Truncated Passive: How Dr Faustus
    Avoids Laying Blame or Taking Reponsibility', *Journal of the Wooden O
    Symposium*, V (2005), pp. 1–12.
48 Ivan M. Jirous, 'Havlovy hlubiny', in *Čtení o Václavu Havlovi*, ed. Michal
    Špirit (Prague, 2013), pp. 63–9.
49 Václav Havel, *Prase, aneb Václav Havel's Hunt for a Pig* (Prague, 2010).
50 Rocamora, *Acts of Courage*, p. 267.
51 Paulina Bren, *The Greengrocer and his TV: The Culture of Communism
    after the 1968 Prague Spring* (Ithaca, NY, 2010), pp. 140–43; Tomáš
    Koloc, 'Václav Havel v kontextu české a světové kultury', www.blisty.cz,
    12 December 2011.
52 Pokorný, *Kniha o Faustovi*, p. 165.
53 Havel and Prečan, *Korespondence*, p. 440.
54 Kaiser, *Disident*, p. 187.
55 Translated by Paul Wilson as *Disturbing the Peace* (New York, 1990).
56 Havel and Prečan, *Korespondence*, p. 387; Havel and Janouch,
    Korespondence, pp. 175, 182; Erica Blair [John Keane] and A. G. Brain
    [Gerald Turner], 'Doing without Utopias', *Times Literary Supplement*,
    23 January 1987, pp. 81–3.
57 Dagmar Havlová-Ilkovičová, *Podněcování a trest: Téměř další hra
    Václava Havla* (Prague, 2009).

58 Irena Gerová, *Vyhrabávačky* (Prague and Litomyšl, 2009), pp. 37, 58.

59 Havel to Olga, 11 February 1989, AKVH, item 2813.

60 Havel to Olga, 7 May 1989, AKVH, item 2822.

61 Jiří Urban, 'Několik vět', *Paměť a dějiny*, IV/1 (2010), pp. 20–45.

62 Kaiser, *Disident*, p. 212; Suk, *Politika jako absurdní drama*, pp. 290–95; Gerová, *Vyhrabávačky*, pp. 65–73, 120, 133–4.

63 Suk, *Politika jako absurdní drama*, p. 333. On the playful nature of protests across the region, see Padraic Kenney, *A Carnival of Revolution: Central Europe 1989* (Princeton, NJ, 2002).

64 On 1989 as comedy, see James Krapfl, *Revolution with a Human Face: Politics, Culture, and Community in Czechoslovakia, 1989–1992* (Ithaca, NY, 2013), pp. 19–22.

65 Vladimír Hanzel, *Zrychlený tep dějin: Reálné drama o deseti jednáních* (Prague, 1991), pp. 27, 43, 45, 53, 85, 93, 106, 171, 215, 222, 388–9, 395.

66 Ivana Koutská, Vojtěch Ripka and Pavel Žáček, eds, *Občanské fórum, den první* (Prague, 2009), p. 124.

67 Hanzel, *Zrychlený tep dějin*, p. 125; Jiří Suk, ed., *Občanské fórum: Listopad-prosinec 1989. 2. díl – dokumenty* (Prague, 1998), p. 118; Jiří Suk, *Labyrintem revoluce* (Prague, 2003), pp. 66–74.

68 Suk, *Občanské fórum*, pp. 68–9, 76–7.

69 Ibid., p. 179.

70 Ibid., pp. 265–70; Suk, *Politika jako absurdní drama*, pp. 400–402; Zantovsky, *Havel*, pp. 313–16; cf. Keane, *Václav Havel*, pp. 365–73.

71 Suk, *Politika jako absurdní drama*, pp. 385–417; Zantovsky, *Havel*, p. 320.

6 The Presidential Great Work (1990–2003)

1 Jiří Suk, ed., *Občanské fórum: Listopad-prosinec 1989. 2. díl – dokumenty* (Prague, 1998), p. 195.

2 Tomáš G. Masaryk, *Cesta demokracie III: Projevy – články – rozhovory 1924–1928* (Prague, 1994), p. 327.

3 Antonín Klímek, *Boj o Hrad 1. Hrad a pětka* (Prague, 1996), pp. 32–179; Eva Broklová, *Prezident Republiky československé: Instituce a osobnost T. G. Masaryka* (Prague, 2001); Helmut Slapnicka, 'Die Rechtsstellung des Präsidenten der Republik nach der Verfassungsurkunde und in der

politischen Wirklichkeit', in *Die 'Burg'. Einflussreiche politische Kräfte um Masaryk und Beneš*, ed. Karl Bosl (Munich, 1974), vol. II, pp. 9–29.

4   For a group portrait, see Michael Zantovsky, *Havel: A Life* (New York, 2014), pp. 322–9.

5   Letter 153, from 6 November 1982, Archive of the Václav Havel Library, Prague (hereafter, AKVH), item 2973.

6   Daniel Kaiser, *Prezident. Václav Havel 1990–2003* (Prague and Litomyšl, 2014), pp. 26, 74, 111.

7   'Neformální setkání ve vile Amálie', http://old.hrad.cz, accessed 22 July 2015.

8   Petr Volf, *Václav Havel – Bořek Šípek: Hradní práce 1992–2002* (Opava, 2003), pp. 25–31; Zdeněk Lukeš, 'Tenkrát na Hradě', in *Příležitostný portrét Václava Havla*, ed. Anna Freimanová (Prague, 2013), pp. 143–6.

9   Aviezer Tucker argues that Havel did not have to sign the bill: *The Philosophy and Politics of Czech Dissidence from Patočka to Havel* (Pittsburgh, PA, 2000), pp. 199–200.

10 Vlastimil Havlík, Milan Hrubeš and Marek Pecina, 'For Rule of Law, Political Plurality, and a Just Society: Use of the Legislative Veto by President Havel', *East European Politics and Societies*, XXVIII/2 (2014), pp. 440–60; Brigita Chrastilová and Petr Mikeš, *Prezident republiky Václav Havel a jeho vliv na československý a český právní řád* (Prague, 2003), pp. 16–215, 510, 553.

11 Zantovsky, *Havel*, pp. 413–14; Kaiser, *Prezident*, pp. 109–12.

12 The transcript was later published in the Slovak weekly *Domino efekt*, III/15–39 (1994). See also Allison Stanger, 'The Price of Velvet: Constitutional Politics and the Demise of the Czechoslovak Federation', in *Irreconcilable Differences? Explaining Czechoslovakia's Dissolution*, ed. Michael Kraus and Allison Stanger (Lanham, MD, 2000), pp. 137–59.

13 David Danaher, *Reading Václav Havel* (Toronto, 2015), pp. 50–52.

14 On this, and the difficulty of translating *duch* and *duchovnost*, see ibid., pp. 200–213.

15 On Havel's anti-utopianism, see Yves Boisvert, 'Vaclav Havel: Le premier president postmoderne?', *Politique*, 21 (1992), pp. 71–96 (pp. 76–9).

16 Martin C. Putna, *Václav Havel. Duchovní portrét v rámu české kultury 20. století* (Prague, 2011), pp. 285–91.

17 'Vánoční setkání prezidenta republiky Václava Havla s dětmi, Purkrabství Pražského hradu 15. prosince 1995' (AKVH, item 17242).

18 Paul Seaton, 'Václav Havel's *Federalist Papers*: *Summer Meditations* and the Genuine Concept of Politics', *Political Science Reviewer*, XXXII (2002), pp. 183–235.

19 Kaiser, *Prezident*, pp. 174–5; Václav Havel, 'A Call for Sacrifice: The Co-responsibility of the West', *Foreign Affairs*, LXXIII/2 (1994), pp. 2–7.

20 Kaiser, *Prezident*, pp. 247, 269; Zantovsky, *Havel*, pp. 434–7, 491–2.

21 Havel had already expressed concern for the fate of indigenous cultures in a globalizing world in 1969; see Václav Havel, Jaroslav Střítecký and Milan Uhde, 'Trialog o radikalismu', *Host do domu*, XVI/6 (1969), pp. 32–6.

22 John Keane, *Václav Havel* (London, 1999), p. 444.

23 Havel to Kopecký, 27 March 1953 (AKVH, item 1783).

24 Havel's weekly radio address from Lány, 5 January 1997 (AKVH, item 2074); Keane, *Václav Havel*, pp. 481–2.

25 Kaiser, *Prezident*, pp. 205–6; Miroslav Graclík and Václav Nekvapil, *Dagmar Havlová* (Prague, 2013), pp. 191–210.

26 Jiří Suk, *Konstituční, nebo existenciální revoluce? Václav Havel a Federální shromáždění* (Prague, 2014), p. 40; Zantovsky, *Havel*, p. 503.

27 Ladislav Špaček, *Deset let s Václavem Havlem* (Prague, 2012), pp. 94–102; Zantovsky, *Havel*, pp. 460, 466–9.

28 Erik Tabery, *Hledá se prezident: Zákulisí voleb hlavy státu* (Prague, 2008), pp. 85–116.

29 Zantovsky, *Havel*, p. 486; Kaiser, *Prezident*, pp. 240–42.

30 'Celková bilance V. Havla', *STEM Trendy*, 2 (2003), p. 1.

31 Daniel Kunštát, 'Hodnocení působení V. Havla v prezidentském úřadě', Centrum pro výzkum veřejného mínění, an opinion poll available at http://cvvm.soc.cas.cz, 10 January 2003.

32 Kaiser, *Prezident*, pp. 10, 14–15.

33 Keane, *Václav Havel*, p. 488; Kaiser, *Prezident*, pp. 227–8, 274.

34 Marie Homolová, 'Jak bydlí prezidenti', *Mladá fronta Dnes*, 6 August 2005, p. 4.

7 Exiting (2003–11)

1 Josef Šafařík, *Sedm listů Melinovi* (Brno, 1993), p. 215.
2 *Prosím stručně: Rozhovor s Karlem Hvížďalou, poznámky, dokumenty* (Prague, 2006), translated into English by Paul Wilson as *To the Castle and Back* (New York, 2007).
3 From Havel's preface to the English translation (*To the Castle and Back*, p. xi).
4 Šafařík, *Sedm listů Melinovi*, p. 262.
5 Kieran Williams, 'The Company Havel Kept', *Slavonic and East European Review*, XCI/4 (2013), pp. 847–69.
6 Carol Rocamora, *Acts of Courage: Václav Havel's Life in the Theater* (Hanover, NH, 2005), pp. 270–78.
7 All details of the then unnamed new play of 1988–9 come from the notes and draft in the Archive of the Václav Havel Library, Prague (hereafter, AKVH), item 38170.
8 *Literární noviny*, XIII/51–2 (1964), p. 14.
9 Gaston Salvatore, *Stalin: Ein Stück* (Frankfurt, 1987).
10 Josef Topol, *The Voices of Birds and Other Plays*, trans. Věra Bořkovec (Washington, DC, 2007), pp. 231–306.
11 Irena Gerová, *Vyhrabávačky* (Prague and Litomyšl, 2009), p. 67.
12 Milan Fořt, '"Jedna babělost nutně plodí další"', *Lidové noviny*, II/7–8 (1989), p. 5.
13 Tomáš Koloc, 'Václav Havel v kontextu cěské a světové kultury', www.blisty.cz, 12 December 2011.
14 František Rieger (1818–1903) was a leading figure in the early national movement but at the end of his career was seen as too timid by the 'Young Czech' party.
15 Herta Schmidová, *Struktury a funkce: Výbor ze studií 1989–2009* (Prague, 2011), pp. 393–4.
16 Paul Wilson, 'Neměl tak ostré lokty jako jeho oponenti', in *Příležitostný portrét Václava Havla*, ed. Anna Freimanová (Prague, 2013), p. 192.
17 Gerová, *Vyhrabávačky*, p. 73. Havel had reported his intention to finish the play in his letter to Olga on 25 February 1989 (AKVH, item 2814).
18 Gerová, *Vyhrabávačky*, p. 70.
19 Božena Němcová, *Babička: Obrazy venkovského života* (Prague, 1899), p. 77.

20 Schmidová, *Struktury a funkce*, pp. 374–82.

21 Petr Schnur, 'Nesvatí Václavové, dali jste nám zhynout! Politická nepolitika druhé normalizace', in *Kritika depolitizovaného rozumu: Úvahy (nejen) o nové normalizaci*, ed. Pavel Barša (Grimmus, 2010), pp. 163–72.

22 Martin C. Myant, 'Klaus, Havel and the Debate over Civil Society in the Czech Republic', *Journal of Communist Studies and Transition Politics*, XXI/2 (2005), pp. 248–67; James F. Pontuso, 'Transformation Politics: The Debate between Václav Havel and Václav Klaus on the Free Market and Civil Society', *Studies in East European Thought*, LIV/3 (2002), pp. 153–77; John Keane, *Václav Havel* (London, 1999), pp. 438–47, 473.

23 Daniel Kaiser, *Prezident. Václav Havel 1990–2003* (Prague and Litomyšl, 2014), p. 275.

24 'Václav Havel: Život je trvalý zápas o vyjádření', in *České drama dnes: Rozhovory s českými dramatiky*, ed. Petr Christov (Prague, 2012), p. 123.

25 Ibid., p. 122.

26 Jana Patočková, 'Nejen o filmovém Odcházení', in *Čtení o Václavu Havlovi*, ed. Michal Špirit (Prague, 2013), pp. 144–55; Miroslav Graclík and Václav Nekvapil, *Dagmar Havlová* (Prague, 2013), pp. 314–16. For a critic of the play who was more pleased by the film, see Jan Čulík, 'Překvapivě účinná a hluboká omluva od bývalého prezidenta', www.blisty.cz, 2 April 2011.

27 'Václav Havel: Život je trvalý zápas o vyjádření', p. 127.

28 Ibid., pp. 124, 126. Klestilová parodied Stanislav Gross in a 2006 puppet play and Sikora's happenings simulated a cabinet resignation and Václav Klaus's funeral.

29 Ibid., p. 129.

30 The text is in the Havel Library (AKVH, item 8976). It is translated as *Dozens of Cousins* in Václav Havel, *The Vaněk Plays*, trans. Jan Novák (New York, 2012).

31 Havel, normally a stickler for detail, was embellishing: Šafařík died three days later (Jiří Paukert, 'Třináctkrát o Noční můře', in Josef Šafařík, *Noční můra* [Vranov nad Dyjí, 1993], p. 114).

32 Michael Zantovsky, *Havel: A Life* (New York, 2014), pp. 515–17.

33 Jiří Wolker, *Do boje, lásko, leť* (Prague, 1975), p. 90.

34 Vitězslav Nezval, 'Podivuhodný kouzelník', in *Básně I* (Brno, 2011), p. 144. The references in *Leaving* are decrypted in Schmidová,

Struktury a funkce, pp. 394–7. See also Alfred French, 'Nezval's Amazing Magician: A Czech Shamanist Epic', *Slavic Review*, XXXII/2 (1973), pp. 358–69.

Select Bibliography

Translations of Havel's plays

The Garden Party and Other Plays [1963], trans. Vera Blackwell, George
    Theiner and Jan Novák (New York, 1993)
The Memo [1965], trans. Paul Wilson (New York, 2012)
The Increased Difficulty of Concentration [1968], trans. Štěpán Šimek
    (New York, 2012)
The Beggar's Opera [1972], trans. Paul R. Wilson (Ithaca, NY, 2001)
The Vaněk Plays: Four Authors, One Character [1975–8], ed. Marketa
    Goetz-Stankiewicz (Vancouver, 1987)
The Vaněk Plays [1975–8], trans. Jan Novák (New York, 2012)
Selected Plays, 1984–1987, trans. Tom Stoppard, George Theiner and James
    Saunders (London, 1994)
Temptation: A Play in Ten Scenes [1985], trans. Marie Winn (New York, 1989)
The Pig, or Vaclav Havel's Hunt for a Pig [1987], trans. Vladimír Morávek
    (New York, 2012)
Tomorrow! [1988], trans. Barbara Day, in *Czech Plays*, ed. Barbara Day
    (London, 1994), pp. 1–26
Leaving [2007], trans. Paul Wilson (London, 2008)

Translations of Havel's essays and speeches

Letters to Olga: June 1979–September 1982, trans. Paul Wilson (New York,
    1988)
Open Letters: Selected Writings, 1965–1990, trans. Paul Wilson et al.
    (New York, 1991)
Disturbing the Peace: A Conversation with Karel Hvížďala, trans. Paul Wilson
    (New York, 1991)

Summer Meditations, trans. Paul Wilson (New York, 1992)
The Art of the Impossible: Politics as Morality in Practice. Speeches and
    Writings, 1990–1996, trans. Paul Wilson et al. (New York, 1997)
To the Castle and Back, trans. Paul Wilson (New York, 2007)

Biographies

Kaiser, Daniel, *Disident: Václav Havel, 1936–1989* (Prague and Litomyšl,
    2009)
—, *Prezident: Václav Havel 1990–2003* (Prague and Litomyšl, 2014)
Keane, John, *Václav Havel: A Political Tragedy in Six Acts* (London, 1999)
Kriseová, Eda, *Václav Havel*, 2nd edn (Prague, 2014)
—, *Václav Havel: The Authorized Biography*, trans. Caleb Crain
    (New York, 1993)
Putna, Martin C., *Václav Havel. Duchovní portrét v rámu české kultury 20.*
    století (Prague, 2011)
Rocamora, Carol, *Acts of Courage: Václav Havel's Life in the Theater*
    (Hanover, NH, 2005)
Suk, Jiří, *Politika jako absurdní drama. Václav Havel v letech 1975–1989*
    (Prague and Litomyšl, 2013)
Zantovsky, Michael, *Havel: A Life* (New York, 2014)

Secondary literature

Ambros, Veronika, 'Fictional World and Dramatic Text: Václav Havel's
    Descent and Ascent', *Style*, XXV/2 (1991), pp. 310–19
Baer, Josette, 'Imagining Membership: The Conception of Europe in the
    Political Thought of T. G. Masaryk and Václav Havel', *Studies in East*
    European Thought, LII/3 (2000), pp. 203–26
Bahr, Erhard, 'Václav Havel's Faust Drama *Temptation* (1985): or, The
    Challenge of Influence', *Goethe Yearbook*, VII (1994), pp. 194–206
Boisvert, Yves, 'Vaclav Havel: Le premier president postmoderne?',
    Politique, 21 (1992), pp. 71–96
Böker, Uwe, 'John Gays *The Beggar's Opera* und Václav Havels *Zebrácká*
    opera (1975)', in *John Gay's 'The Beggars Opera', 1728–2004: Adaptations*
    and Re-writings, ed. Uwe Böker, Ines Detmers and Anna-Christina
    Giovanopoulos (Amsterdam, 2006), pp. 219–41

Bolton, Jonathan, *Worlds of Dissent: Charter 77, the Plastic People of the Universe, and Czech Culture under Communism* (Cambridge, MA, 2012)

Bratinka, Pavel, et al., *Faustování s Havlem* (Prague, 2010)

Bren, Paulina, *The Greengrocer and His TV: The Culture of Communism after the 1968 Prague Spring* (Ithaca, NY, 2010)

Brooks, D. Christopher, 'The Art of the Political: Havel's Dramatic Literature as Political Theory', *East European Quarterly*, XXXIX/4 (2005), pp. 491–522

Burian, Jarka M., *Modern Czech Theatre: Reflector and Conscience of a Nation* (Iowa City, IA, 2000)

Chrastilová, Brigita, and Petr Mikeš, *Prezident republiky Václav Havel a jeho vliv na československý a český právní řád* (Prague, 2003)

Christov, Petr, ed., *České drama dnes: Rozhovory s českými dramatiky* (Prague, 2012)

Čulík, Jan, 'Václav Havel', in *The Dictionary of Literary Biography*, ed. Steven Serafin (Detroit, MI, 2001), vol. CCXXXII, pp. 110–30

Dalberg, Dirk Mathias, *Der 'Versuch, in der Wahrheit zu leben': Václav Havels Politikbegriff und politische Strategie in den Jahren 1969 bis 1989* (Stuttgart, 2014)

Danaher, David, 'Ideology as Metaphor, Narrative, and Performance in the Writings of Václav Havel', *Slovo a smysl*, XII (2015), pp. 115–27

—, *Reading Václav Havel* (Toronto, 2015)

Ditrych, Ondřej, Vladimír Handl, Nik Hynek and Vít Střítecký, 'Understanding Havel?', *Communist and Post-Communist Studies*, XLVI/3 (2013), pp. 407–17

Drozd, David, 'Dobové kontexty *Sedmi listů Melinovi* Josefa Šafaříka', *Estetika*, XLII/2–3 (2006), pp. 149–87

—, 'Setkání myslitele a dramatika – hry Václava Havla očima Josefa Šafaříka', *RozRazil*, I/8 (2006), pp. 59–69

Erben, Joan, 'The Spirit from Below: A Theoretical Approach to Václav Havel's *Temptation*', *European Studies Journal*, XV/1 (1998), pp. 1–19

Even-Granboulan, Geneviève, *Václav Havel, president philosophe* (La Tour d'Aigues, 2003)

Falk, Barbara, *The Dilemmas of Dissidence in East-central Europe* (Budapest, 2003)

Fawn, Rick, 'Symbolism in the Diplomacy of Czech President Václav Havel', *East European Quarterly*, XXXIII/1 (1999), pp. 1–19

Findlay, Edward F., 'Classical Ethics and Postmodern Critique: Political Philosophy in Václav Havel and Jan Patocka', *Review of Politics*, LXI/3 (1999), pp. 403–38

Fischer, Josef Ludvík, *Krise demokracie* (Prague, 2005)

—, *Listy o druhých a o sobě* (Prague, 2005)

—, *Výbor z díla*, vol. I (Prague, 2007)

Freimanová, Anna, ed., *Přiležitostný portrét Václava Havla* (Prague, 2013)

—, ed., *Síla věcnosti Olgy Havlové* (Prague, 2013)

Garton Ash, Timothy, 'On Olga Havel (1933–1996)', *New York Review of Books*, XLIII/5 (1996), p. 32

—, 'Prague: Intellectuals and Politicians', *New York Review of Books*, XLII/1 (1995), pp. 34–41

Gerová, Irena, *Vyhrabávačky* (Prague and Litomyšl, 2009)

Goetz-Stankiewicz, Marketa, 'Variations of Temptation: Václav Havel's Politics of Language', *Modern Drama*, XXXIII/1 (1990), pp. 93–105

—, and Phyllis Carey, eds, *Critical Essays on Vaclav Havel* (New York, 1999)

Hanzel, Vladimír, *Zrychlený tep dějin: Reálné drama o deseti jednáních* (Prague, 1991)

Havel, Ivan M., *Dopisy od Olgy* (Prague, 2010)

Havel, Václav, and František Janouch, *Korespondence 1978–2001* (Prague, 2007)

—, and Vilém Prečan, *Korespondence (1983–1989)* (Prague, 2011)

Havel, Vácslav (Atom), *Kniha života* (Prague, 2011)

Havel, V. M., *Mé vzpomínky* (Prague, 1993)

Havlík, Vlastimil, Milan Hrubeš and Marek Pecina, 'For Rule of Law, Political Plurality, and a Just Society: Use of the Legislative Veto by President Havel', *East European Politics and Societies*, XXVIII/2 (2014), pp. 440–60

Hejdánek, Ladislav, *Havel je uhlík: Filosof a politická odpovědnost* (Prague, 2009)

Hipp, Markus, 'Identität und Verantwortung im Denken Václav Havels', *Bohemia*, XXXVI/2 (1995), pp. 298–329

Hron, Jan, 'Korespondence Václava Havla', master's thesis, Univerzita Karlova v Praze, Prague (2000)

Ibler, Reinhard, 'Zur Typologie und kulturellen Funktion von Václav Havels *Dopisy Olze* (*Briefe an Olga*)', *Zeitschrift für Slawistik*, LIII/3 (2008), pp. 259–70

Jungmannová, Lenka, ed., *V hlavní roli Ferdinand Vaněk* (Prague, 2006)

—, ed., *Zahradní slavnost: Klíčová událost moderního českého divadla* (Prague, 2015)

—, 'Zrození *Zahradní slavnosti* z Havlových literárních počátků', *Divadelní revue*, XXII/3 (2011), pp. 7–29

Just, Vladimír, *Divadlo v totalitním systému* (Prague, 2010)

—, 'Příspěvek k jazyku experanto aneb Dramatické neosoby Václava Havla', *Divadelní revue*, XV/3 (2004), pp. 3–13

Kosatík, Pavel, '*Člověk má dělat to, nač má sílu': Život Olgy Havlové* (Prague, 2008)

—, '*Ústně více'. Šestatřicátníci* (Brno, 2006)

Krapfl, James, *Revolution with a Human Face: Politics, Culture, and Community in Czechoslovakia, 1989–1992* (Ithaca, NY, 2013)

Kroupa, Daniel, *Dějiny Kampademie* (Prague, 2011)

Kuběna, Jiří, *Paměť básníka* (Brno, 2006)

McDermott, Kevin, *Communist Czechoslovakia, 1945–89: A Political and Social History* (London, 2015)

Markupová, Jana, '"Co je to Já? Ivan Havel? To je jméno, to nejsem já". Biografie Ivana M. Havla', master's thesis, Univerzita Karlova v Praze, Prague (2014)

Matuštík, Martin J., 'Havel and Habermas on Identity and Revolution', *Praxis International*, X/3–4 (1990–1991), pp. 261–77

Matynia, Elzbieta, ed., *An Uncanny Era: Conversations between Václav Havel and Adam Michnik* (New Haven, CT, 2014)

Meche, Jude R., 'Female Victims and the Male Protagonist in Václav Havel's Drama', *Modern Drama*, XL/4 (1997), pp. 468–76

Myant, Martin, 'Klaus, Havel and the Debate Over Civil Society in the Czech Republic', *Journal of Communist Studies and Transition Politics*, XXI/2 (2005), pp. 248–67

Pirro, Robert, 'Vaclav Havel and the Political Uses of Tragedy', *Political Theory*, XXX/2 (2002), pp. 228–58

Pokorný, Zdeněk, *Václav Havel a ženy* (Plzeň, 1999)

Pontuso, James F., 'Transformation Politics: The Debate between Vaclav Havel and Vaclav Klaus on the Free Market and Civil Society', *Studies in East European Thought*, LIV/3 (2002), pp. 153–77

—, *Václav Havel: Civic Responsibility in the Postmodern Age* (Lanham, MD, 2004)

Popescu, Delia, *Political Action in Václav Havel's Thought: The Responsibility of Resistance* (Lanham, MD, 2012)

Procházka, Martin, 'Prisoner's Predicament: Public Privacy in Havel's Letters to Olga', *Representations*, 43 (Summer 1993), pp. 126–54

Putna, Martin C., 'The Spirituality of Václav Havel in its Czech and American Contexts', *East European Politics and Societies*, XXIV/3 (2010), pp. 353–78

—, and Jan Hron, eds, *Rozhovory '36. Stříbrný vítr. Výběr z tvorby Šestatřicátníků* (Prague, 2010)

Pynsent, Robert B., *Questions of Identity: Czech and Slovak Ideas of Nationality and Personality* (Budapest, 1994)

—, 'The Work of Václav Havel', *Slavonic and East European Review*, LXXIII/2 (1995), pp. 269–81

Sabatos, Charles, 'Criticism and Destiny: Kundera and Havel on the Legacy of 1968', *Europe-Asia Studies*, LX/10 (2008), pp. 1827–45

Šafařík, Josef, *Hrady skutečné a povětrné* (Prague, 2008)

—, *Noční můra. Kurs pro utopisty* (Vranov nad Dyjí, 1993)

—, *Sedm listů Melinovi* (Brno, 1993)

Schmidová, Herta, *Struktury a funkce: Výbor ze studií 1989–2009* (Prague, 2011)

Seaton, Paul, 'Václav Havel's *Federalist Papers: Summer Meditations* and the Genuine Concept of Politics', *Political Science Reviewer*, XXXI (2002), pp. 183–235

Shore, Marci, 'The Sacred and the Myth: Havel's Greengrocer and the Transformation of Ideology in Communist Czechoslovakia', *Contagion*, III/1 (1996), pp. 163–82

Špaček, Ladislav, *Deset let s Václavem Havlem* (Prague, 2012)

Špirit, Michal, ed., *Čtení o Václavu Havlovi* (Prague, 2013)

Steiner, Peter, 'Moc obrazu: vizuální poezie Václava Havla', *Estetika*, XLIV/1–4 (2007), pp. 107–24

Suk, Jiří, *Konstituční, nebo existenciální revoluce? Václav Havel a Federální shromáždění* (Prague, 2014)

—, ed., *Občanské fórum: Listopad-prosinec 1989. 2. díl – dokumenty* (Prague, 1998)

Thomas, Alfred, *The Labyrinth of the Word: Truth and Representation in Czech Literature* (Munich, 1995)

Trensky, Paul, *Czech Drama since World War II* (New York, 1978)

Tucker, Avezier, *The Philosophy and Politics of Czech Dissidence from Patočka to Havel* (Pittsburgh, PA, 2000)

Tuckerová, Veronika, 'The Totalitarian Languages of Utopia and Dystopia: Fidelius and Havel', in *In Marx's Shadow: Knowledge, Power, and Intellectuals in Eastern Europe and Russia*, ed. Costica Bradatan and Sergei Oushakine (Lanham, MD, 2010), pp. 95–109

Vodička, Libor, *Vyjádřit hrou: Podobenství a (sebe)stylizace v dramatu Václava Havla* (Prague, 2013)

Volf, Petr, *Václav Havel – Bořek Šípek: Hradní práce 1992–2002* (Opava, 2003)

Wanatowicová, Krystyna, *Miloš Havel: český filmový magnát* (Prague, 2013)

West, Tim, 'Destiny as Alibi: Milan Kundera, Václav Havel and the "Czech Question" after 1968', *Slavonic and East European Review*, LXXXVII/3 (2009), pp. 401–28

Williams, Kieran, 'The Company Havel Kept', *Slavonic and East European Review*, XCI/4 (2013), pp. 847–69

—, 'Václav Havel', in *Mental Maps in the Era of Detente and the End of the Cold War, 1968–91*, ed. Jonathan Wright and Steven Casey (Basingstoke, 2015), pp. 156–73

Wilson, Paul, 'Václav Havel (1936–2011)', *New York Review of Books*, LIX/2 (2012), pp. 4–8

Woods, Michelle, 'Václav Havel and the Expedient Politics of Translation', *NTQ*, XXVI/1 (2010), pp. 3–15

Žáček, Pavel, 'Akce "Tomis III" a ideologická diverze: Václav Havel v dokumentech Státní bezpečnosti, 1965–1968', *Paměť a dějiny*, VI/1 (2012), pp. 70–83

Žák, Jiří, *Hovory s V. H.* (Prague, 2012)

Websites

The Václav Havel Library: www.vaclavhavel-library.org/en
Havel's personal website: www.vaclavhavel.cz
A Havel Bibliography: http://cr.middlebury.edu/pol_sci/havel/biblio.htm
From Havel's 2006 residency at Columbia University: http://havel.columbia.edu

Acknowledgements

Thanks go first to Ben Hayes at Reaktion Books for inviting me to contribute a book on Havel to the Critical Lives series. He was the ideal editor throughout the process – enthusiastic, encouraging and attentive. Maureen Shea, Michael Shea and my wife, Laurie Belin, were my no less ideal test readers: they scoured the whole manuscript quickly but thoroughly, guided by their love of, and expertise in, literature and writing. David Danaher, whose ability to understand and explain Havel's texts is unrivalled, provided eagle-eyed advice on translating Havel's poems. Kimberly Elman Zarecor and Christopher Long shared their insight into Prague architecture.

My debt to Drake University is twofold: to Kris Mogle and the interlibrary loan team at Cowles Library, for their unfailing ability to track down the obscure items I requested, and to the Center for the Humanities, for a generous grant from its materials support fund to cover the cost of licences for photographs used in this book.

Many people at other institutions also helped me obtain documents and photographs: Jan Hron, Pavel Hájek and Martin Vidlák at the Václav Havel Library; Hugh Ferrer at the University of Iowa and Bethany Antos at the Rockefeller Archive Center; Renáta Klvačová at Palacký University in Olomouc, Jaroslava Kacetlová at Masaryk University in Brno, Jana Nováková and Tatiana Rohová at the State Central Archive in Prague, Hana Benkeová at the ArcelorMittal archive in Ostrava and Karel Müller at the Opava regional archive. Finally, I wish to thank several people who kindly provided photographs or facilitated their acquisition and interpretation: Ester Havlová, Bohdan Holomíček, Miloš Hošek, Eva Hrubá, Andrej Krob, Helena Lukas Martemucci, Hana Pilná, Alicia Samuel, Cornelia Schnall, Amanda Short, Michael Shulman and Libor Sojka.

Photo Acknowledgements

The author and publishers wish to express their thanks to the following sources of illustrative material and/or permission to reproduce it:

Archiv ArcelorMittal Ostrava a. s.: p. 98 (archiv číslo 517206040, č. listu NAD 13 – fond Nová huť Klementa Gottwalda, n. p. Ostrava – Kunčice, značka fondu NHKG); Archiv Masarykovy univerzity: p. 39 (fond B 92 Josef Šafařík, karton 21, in. č. 213); Archiv Univerzity Palackého: p. 28 (fond Sbírka fotografií a filmů, k. 1, POU/25); Corbis: p. 179 (© Ivo Lorenc/Sygma/ CORBIS), p. 194 (© STR/epa/Corbis), p. 197 (© DAVID W CERNY/Reuters/ Corbis); ČTK: p. 19 (René Volfík), p. 33 (ČTK), p. 46 (Evžen Beran), p. 60 (Zdeněk Havelka), p. 72 (Venek Švorcík), p. 161 (Karel Mevald), p. 167 (Michal Doležal), p. 180 (Stanislav Peška), p. 198 (Zdeněk Kovár) (© ČTK Photo – 2015); Dagmar Hochová: p. 92 (© Dagmar Hochová – pozůstalost); DPA/Landov: p. 79; Ester Havlová: pp. 18, 149; Bohdan Holomíček: pp. 11, 103, 108, 115, 121, 166 (© Bohdan Holomíček); Jan Kašpar: pp. 138, 147; © Václav Havel – heir c/o DILIA, 1964/66: pp. 69, 80, 91; Knihovna Václava Havla: pp. 21, 22, 23, 30, 31, 56, 64, 148; Jan Lukas: p. 95; Magnum Photos: p. 8 (Gueorgui Pinkhassov), p. 128 (Peter Marlow), pp. 152–3 (Josef Koudelka); Helena Lukas Martemucci: p. 174; Národní archiv České republiky: pp. 133, 157 (SSNV, osobní vězeňský spis, nezpracováno).